RHYTHMS
OF
LEARNING

Creative Tools for Developing Lifelong Skills

CHRIS BREWER
DON G. CAMPBELL

FOREWORD BY
DEE DICKINSON

Zephyr
Press, Inc.®
REACHING THEIR HIGHEST POTENTIAL
Tucson, Arizona

Other books and tapes by Don G. Campbell

Books
Music and Miracles. Quest Books, 1992.
100 Ways to Improve Teaching Using Your Voice and Music. Zephyr Press, 1992.
The Mozart Effect. AVON Books, 1997.
The Roar of Silence. Quest Books, 1989.
Master Teacher, Nadia Boulanger. Pastoral Press, 1984.
Introduction to the Musical Brain. Magnamusic Baton, 1983.
Music: Physician for Times to Come. Quest Books, 1991.

Sound Cassettes and CDs
Healing Yourself with Your Own Voice. Sounds True, 1990.
Essence. Spring Hill Music, 1998.
Music for The Mozart Effect. Spring Hill Music, 1997.
The Mozart Effect. Music for Children. The Children's Group, 1997.
The Mozart Effect. Music for Babies, *from Playtime to Sleepytime.* The Children's Group, 1998.
The Mozart Effect. Music for Newborns. The Children's Group, 1998.

Other books by Chris Brewer

Artists: Exploring Art through the Study of Five Great Lives. Zephyr Press, 1992.
Family Fun in Montana. Falcon Press, 1998.

RHYTHMS OF LEARNING
© 1991 Zephyr Press, Inc., Tucson, AZ
ISBN 0-913705-59-4
Photographers:
    Gerald Askevold: 17, 32, 35, 40, 53, 55, 63*, 84 (a, b), 85 (a-c), 86 (a, c), 87 (a-c), 89, 90, 93, 98, 115, 137 (b, c), 148, 154, 165, 167, 187 (a) 189, 197 (a), 198, 203, 219, 223 (a-d)*, 224, 245, 275 (c), 276, 278, 280,
    Back Cover (a)
    Karen Nichols, Daily Inter Lake: 16, 62, 65, 66, 94, 105, 107, 146*, 161, 162, 163, 201, 204, 226, 240, 251, 275 (b), 284
    Chris Brewer: 29, 85 (d), 86 (b), 102, 134, 137 (a), 187 (b), 190, 192
    Ellen Boyd: 15, 137 (d), 247
    Mark Holston: 158, 194, 197 (b)
    Sal Skog, Daily Inter Lake: 12*, 26*
    Cincinnati Public Schools: 41
    Anne Clark, Daily Inter Lake: 193
    Jeanne Hamilton: 143
    NASA: 275 (a)
    Billie M. Thompson, Sound Listening and Learning Center, Tomatis Center: 21
    * cover photos

Editor: Kathryn Ring
Design & Production: Sheryl Shetler
Cover Design: Michelle Gallardo

Acknowledgments

Thank you:

Dee Coulter, Jean Houston, Robin Van Doren, Elaine DeBeauport, Carla Crutsinger, Paul MacLean, Conrad Toepfer, Herman Epstein, Howard Gardner, Julian Biggers, Grace Nash, Edwin Gordon, Arthur Harvey, Georgi Lozanov, Libyan Labiosa Cassone, Cindy Lambert, Linda Grinde, Win Wenger, Paul Messier, Dee Dickinson, Colin Rose, Barbara Meister Vitale, Gloria Crooks, Alfred A. Tomatis, Billie Thompson, Barbara Marx Hubbard, Barry Louis Polisar, Paul and Gail Dennison, Jacqueline Flowers

Ann Lewin of the National Learning Center in Washington D.C.; Michael Alexander and the Guggenheim School in Chicago; Kalispell Montessori School, the Carden School, and Peterson School in Kalispell, Montana; Kila School in Kila, Montana; The Daily Inter Lake Newspaper and Flathead County Library in Kalispell, Montana

Jeanne Hamilton, Americole Biassini, Carla Hannaford

Gerald Askevold, Sal Skog, Karen Nichols, Ellen Boyd, Anne Clark, Mark Holston

Joey Tanner, Jane Brewster, Kate Ring

Laurie Rugenstein and the staff at the Institute for Music, Health, and Education in Boulder, Colorado; Katie Boyd; and Ken, David, and May Brewer

Dedication

This book is dedicated to the empowerment of the great Learner-Teacher in each of us.

Contents

Chapter IV
Rhythms of Discovery

Foreword

Diversity is one of the most significant characteristics of today's classrooms. Students from different cultural, social, and economic backgrounds and with a great variety of abilities and disabilities are all there together, often with teachers who may not be fully equipped to deal with such a challenge. It is very clear that every teacher today must have on hand a rich repertoire of strategies to meet the needs of these diverse learners.

In recent years, much research has been done to identify learning styles, personality traits, and kinds of intelligence that help students learn through their strengths. As we focus on nurturing these unique characteristics and helping students to utilize them in active and dynamic ways, we make it possible for all students to become successful learners.

The arts are at last becoming recognized as indispensable to this process. Like words and numbers, the arts are symbol systems— languages that people use to communicate and understand ideas. They offer important avenues for the development of self-expression, and they foster the development of higher-order thinking skills.

It has long been recognized that there is a meaningful connection between artistic abilities and academic abilities, notable in the relationship between musical and mathematical/scientific abilities. In a recent worldwide study on the science achievements of fourteen-year-olds, the top three countries include music as an integral part of the curriculum from kindergarten through high school. Hungary, which has been implementing an intensive program in music education since the fifties, ranks first. Japan is second, and the Netherlands is third. (The United States ranks fourteenth out of the seventeen countries in the study.) In "Silicon Valley," California, it has been reported that the top engineers and technical designers are nearly all practicing musicians.

While we do not yet fully understand why or how this relationship between musical and mathematical/scientific ability works, we do know that schools that devote a significant part of every school day to the arts, taught both as separate subjects and integrated throughout the curriculum, are producing the highest academic achievement in the United States today. (Davidson in Augusta, Georgia, is first in the nation, and Ashley River Elementary in Charleston, North Carolina, is second.) Even more important, their students are especially motivated, creative, and independent learners and thinkers who experience learning through mind, body, and spirit.

Until the publication of this book, it has been somewhat easier for many teachers to learn to teach various subjects through the graphic and dramatic arts than it has been to teach through music and dance. Yet these "rhythms of learning," in which the body itself becomes the instrument and the art form, can enhance and accelerate learning for all students. In many cases, music makes it possible to master difficult, abstract concepts faster, more easily, and with greater retention.

Don Campbell and Chris Brewer have combined their musical talents and expertise with their considerable experience as educators to produce this remarkable book. It is filled with rich educational experiences, and backed up with sound theory that can be implemented by teachers in any subject-matter area. Only part of the value of this book lies in the reading. New insights and revelations await those who put *Rhythms of Learning* into practice, as they help their students discover the joy of learning through music and sound and rhythmical activities.

Dee Dickinson
President, New Horizons for Learning

CHAPTER I

PATTERNS OF
LISTENING

The manner in which we listen to the world around us is as individual as our fingerprints. The psychological, emotional, and physiological factors that determine our listening abilities through trust, engagement, and memory of sensory information is so vast, it is immeasurable.

In this chapter on listening, we see the journey to lifelong learning begin as hearing evolves into listening and is then focused with intention. Don Campbell shares his personal journey with music and sound as well as the important research on the ear that has moved listening into a new and vital prominence. Chris Brewer explores the tools of inner speech and inner listening that assist in developing a conscious intent to become engaged in creative, fulfilling lifelong learning. Together they represent the spectrum of attention and awareness that can integrate our patterns of listening with academic knowledge to create a unified intelligence.

Sound Education: The Journey from Hearing to Listening

Don G. Campbell

By the time I was ten years old, I knew I was a musician. There was no thought of becoming a musician; I was somehow already a musician. Music was the world. Everything was vibration, feeling, and movement. Although I could hardly name it with words, I felt the sacred presence of life through sound. Yes, there were the piano, the 78 r.p.m. phonograph, the radio, the organ at church, and my voice. But there was more. Music kept me awake. My body had to move when I heard simple tunes. My lips and tongue had to mimic the rhythms of cat, dog, and people languages. Melodies moved in my head, day and night. Silence was impossible. Quiet was possible from the outer world, so all the internal inventions of sound could be heard. Trees, cars, and even clouds had their rhythms. Words I did not understand had melodies. The world was SOUND.

Now, some thirty years later, after a multidimensional career in music teaching, composing, performing, and book writing, I'm back to that first decade of awareness. The answers to my personal and professional questions lie in remembering, naming, and reawakening that potent and naive power to listen to the world with honest, clear, and "unnamed" awareness.

Ten years ago, prime questions emerged within me about listening, intelligence, and the essential roles of music in education.

- ✧ Why is hearing dynamically different from listening?
- ✧ Why is listening seldom taught in school?
- ✧ Why is music education so intent on performance and note-reading skills when listening skills are taken for granted?

After years of advanced training, I had only a few clues about the nature of listening, perception, and musical skills. The most direct answers to these questions came from professionals outside the music field. Some physical therapists, perceptual development teachers, occupational therapists, and psychologists had keener observations about music and learning than did my colleagues in music. Reading and phonics teachers knew the importance of rhythmic repetition. I sensed these things but could not translate them into practical sequences for optimal results in the music classroom. I knew these primary musical components were not a finished musical product, but they were the basic parts of music that were essential in my quest for defining listening.

By shifting my perceptions of listening, aesthetics became a secondary focus in the teaching of music. My rigid training for perfection in music skills seemed to stand in the way of uninhibited music making. My elitist discrimination between talented and untalented students began to disappear when I became aware that music's basic qualities were available to most students at all times.

14

Music was
in the breath,
the heartbeat,
the walking
movements,
and gestures
of the child.

Music was in the breath, the heartbeat, the walking movements, and gestures of the child. Music, rhythmic patterning, vocal toning, tongue-lip movements, and the awareness of melody in language patterns were everywhere and were primary to life-learning itself. Musicality became redefined - when I remembered my friend, a pianist, who could not sing in tune - when I recalled a flute player who left college as a brilliant performer but could not read music well enough to pass the traditional harmony class - when my uncle was asked to leave the church choir, even though he was an outstanding barbershop singer. Music was an assortment of hundreds of skills, styles, and emotional languages.

Reaching Out to Listen

My nonmusical associates posed fascinating and perplexing questions to me:

- ✧ Are rhythmic skills dependent on the gross motor skills developed in the first three years of life?
- ✧ Are melodic skills dependent on the mother's voice and the sounds heard in the first months of life?
- ✧ Does spoken language depend on elements of musicality heard through the child's auditory perception in the womb?

The ability to listen was key to understanding these diverse and nonaesthetic questions.

To listen in Latin is *ob audire*. It implies "to reach out." Yes, to reach out to the world to make a subtle but conscious effort to connect, to bond, to hold. Listening is an act of extension toward an outer stimulation through any of the senses for the purpose of integration with an inner world. Hearing and listening are two very different actions.

A child's first ten years are a constant dance on this bridge between the inner and outer worlds. A child is virtually into everything the senses can perceive. The adult knows the skill of focus and centering. The child extends and reaches into the world with a natural, rhythmic process of experimentation, at times far quicker than parents or teachers observe. Breathing - movement - listening - babbling - music. Did my art form develop in this order, or did music begin in the womb with the constant and repetitive patterns?

Music is an art in its developed form combining the elementals of beat, pattern, melodic line, and inflection in its fundamental vocabulary. Music is heartbeat and breath in its primal creation. Carl Orff, the German composer and educator, clearly understood how essential this formative awareness was for lifelong learning.

"Elemental music, word and movement, play, everything that awakens and develops the powers of the spirit, this is the 'humus' of the spirit, the humus without which we face the danger of spiritual erosion. When does erosion occur in nature? When the land is wrongly exploited; for instance, when the natural water supply is disturbed through too much cultivation, or when, for utilitarian reasons, forests and hedges fall as victims to drawing-board mentality; in short, when the balance of nature is lost by interference. In the same way I would like to repeat: Man exposes himself to spiritual erosion if he estranges himself from his elemental essentials and thus loses his balance. Just as humus in nature makes growth possible, so elemental music gives to the child powers that cannot otherwise come to fruition."

—Orff 1978

Orff knew little of the biology of music, its neurological functions, or of the emerging validity of integrated arts in education. His keen perception of how movement, play, language development, and music intertwined for lifelong learning was intuitively correct. The ear-brain-body complex does develop through tonal improvisations in speech, movement, and music making.

Carl Orff in Germany, Kodaly in Hungary, Suzuki in Japan, Grace Nash and Edwin Gordon in America, Jacques Emil-Dalcrose and Rudolf Laban in France, G.I. Gurdjieff and Rudolph Steiner in Europe . . . all have asked the dynamic questions of music's role in lifelong learning. Each has an important perspective and valuable observations. No one system has yet to be inclusive enough to focus on so many variables in the growth of the brain, body, and musical aptitude. Yet, the awareness of the connectedness of these components is emerging in education.

Awareness of a forward-thinking educational process has developed out of a sound education curriculum of observation, in which parents and teachers are aware of the physical, tonal, and verbal patterns that weave the necessary ability for a child to communicate and listen to the world. In sound education, the ear is the prime organ for balance, vestibular regulation, language, and hearing.

Students with deficient reading abilities generally score below average on the verbal sections of intelligence tests. When the same test is read aloud, scores show a dynamic range of change. When the same test is read with a rhythmic, natural poetic sense of patterning, again there is a dynamic change in perception. The information is the same, but the mode of the internal-external transfer has changed. Through sound education we recognize that most of our life is spent listening, not reading or writing. When these auditory skills are improved, the language arts can emerge more naturally.

Two of the major studies in listening reflect the amount of time a student and business professional spend in listening. The percentage of listening time increases greatly in the person who works at home and the child under the age of eight. By observing the research of Rankin and Werner, we can easily see the dynamic and essential place of listening in a working day. Within our daily communication activities, listening has gained greater prominence during this century.

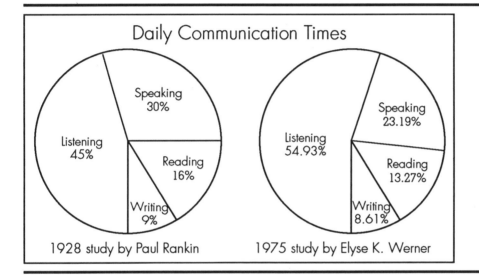

Daily Communication Times

1928 study by Paul Rankin

1975 study by Elyse K. Werner

Listening and the Ear: Research by Tomatis

Listening has been the primary focus of a French physician, psychologist, and educator, Dr. A. A. Tomatis. His critical research of the effects that sound frequencies have on the energy level of the body and the ability to learn language has literally redefined the use of the ear in education and music. The ability of the ear to focus on frequencies determines success in learning, language, and music. An important appendix by Dr. Billie Thompson, Director of the Sound Listening and Learning Center (Tomatis Center) in Phoenix, Arizona, describes and clarifies the work of Dr. Tomatis.

The listening process starts in the womb when the fetus begins to hear by at least four and one-half months. Tomatis believes that the sounds and frequencies in the liquid world of heartbeat, breath, and the mother's voice are sensed primarily through bone conduction and nourish the unborn child. These sounds, heard through the liquid in the middle ear, are very different from the way we hear after birth. The mother's voice to the developing human in utero sounds like a series of S's, Sh's, and Z's, similar to the high chirp of a bird, rhythmically patterned. It is now believed that the ability of a small child to develop listening and speech skills comes from the prenatal patterning of the mother's voice.

We do not hear and listen by air conduction alone. The important, yet subtle, stimulation to the skin and through the bones greatly changes the manner in which we receive information. The information from sight often compensates later for missing auditory stimulation. Without sight, listening sensitivities can become highly developed. Helen Keller's skills of listening through her body were developed beyond the hearing-visual realm. Even people with normal hearing abilities respond to auditory stimulation of the skin and bones.

Tomatis realized that vibratory stimulation of the intrauterine world, beginning in the sixteenth to eighteenth week after conception, creates important neural links for lifelong communication. The eighth cranial nerve pair, which carries auditory information from the ear to the brain, is the first sensory pair to develop. Although it takes another couple of months for the nerves to mature, the early charging of the brain with high frequencies seems to be important in language development.

Listening Deficits

Dr. Tomatis has proven that the voice only represents what the ear can hear, a phenomenon known as the Tomatis Effect. When the perception of midrange and high frequencies is missing in the prenatal and first three years of life, difficulties in listening or learning may arise later. Without any obvious traces in deafness, a deficient ability to hear frequencies below 1000 Hz (vibrations per second, approximately two octaves up from middle C on the piano) can cause great difficulty in understanding and remembering spoken information, especially in male voices. Missing frequencies in the listening curve result in the inability to reproduce those same frequencies with the voice. Defective variations between 1000 Hz and 2000 Hz make it difficult to sing in tune. When there are defects in the hearing range over 2000 Hz, the tonal qualities of the speaking and singing voice can be flat, breathy, and unpleasant.

Generally, our adult hearing range extends just beyond 21,000 Hz, giving us a bright and clear ability to distinguish sounds. Even slight variants in the frequency curve in a higher range can make it very difficult to listen. We hear, but we must strain to listen even though the outer voice is sufficiently loud.

The following chart from the "Overview of the Tomatis Method" by Timothy Gilmor (Gilmor, Maudale, and Thompson 1989) provides examples of listening deficit symptoms.

Identification of a Listening Problem

Receptive Language

At the level of receptive oral language, the following can be considered symptomatic of a listening problem:

✧ A need to have instructions repeated
✧ Distractibility, restlessness, daydreaming, poor attention and concentration in learning situations
✧ A tendency to misinterpret what is being said, which produces odd reactions and impedes communication with others
✧ Difficulty with following and/or participating in conversations in a noisy environment

Body Image

At the level of body awareness or body image, the following can be observed:

✧ Poor balance or coordination
✧ Difficulty coordinating body movement
✧ Clumsiness or awkwardness in body movement
✧ Excessive body movement when speaking or listening (fidgety)
✧ Poor posture: overly tense and rigid (hypertonic) or insufficient tonicity (hypotonic)
✧ Mixed lateral dominance, letter and word reversals, signs of fine motor or gross motor coordination such as poor handwriting
✧ Poor organization and planning skills
✧ The tendency to withdraw or avoid communication in learning situations and/or social situations
✧ A lack of curiosity or interest in learning
✧ Lack of interest in oral communication and, in extreme instances, avoidance or active refusal to use language as the medium through which to communicate with others

Expressive Language

At the level of spoken language, individuals with listening-based communication problems are frequently seen to have very poor audio-vocal control or self-listening. Such symptoms include:

✦ Slow, hesitant, poorly articulated speech
✦ A poorly modulated voice (too soft or too loud)
✦ A poor voice, characterized by a dull, monotonic, and lifeless quality or other impairments of timbre, tone, and fluency
✦ For adults, difficulty in sustaining the interest of a group while making a speech or presentation

Developmental Characteristics

In compiling clinical histories at listening centers using the Tomatis method, the following events have had an unusually high incidence among individuals with listening-based learning and communication problems:

✦ Difficult circumstances surrounding their own birth
✦ Difficult births or early separation from the mother as a result of illness or adoption
✦ Recurring ear infections in the first years of life
✦ The arrival of a younger sibling within two years of birth
✦ Slow or poorly established preference for right or left hand
✦ Delay in language development and, less frequently, in motor development
✦ Difficult adjustment to school life and the recognition of problems by the teacher or by the parent within the first two years of school
✦ Underachievement at school or on the job

Listed above are symptoms commonly observed in individuals who have learning and communication problems. This list is not exhaustive. However, the presence of some or a majority of these symptoms should prompt consideration of the degree to which poor listening ability may be contributing to a child's learning and communication problems.

This way of observing listening abilities does not refer to deafness or great hearing loss as much as "listening loss," an attention deficit. A listening test that includes analysis of both air and bone conduction can provide insights into listening abilities by revealing a frequency response curve. After analyzing a child's listening curve, Dr. Tomatis is able to charge and invite the ear to open and discriminate among a full range of sounds and frequencies. The Tomatis Method can improve the ear's response to missing frequencies and create a healthy, more natural listening curve resulting in enhanced reading, writing, and language abilities.

Dr. Tomatis has developed a device called the Electronic Ear to filter sounds and retrain the ear to listen as a fit ear would. To do this, he stimulates missing frequencies with the use of tapes of the mother's voice filtered to sound as it is heard in the uterus, classical music, and Gregorian chants. The process also involves strengthening the right ear as the lead ear. The right ear has the most efficient neural pathways to the left brain, where the language, reading, and speech centers are located. To allow for proper language development and good audio-vocal control, the right ear would normally be dominant. When we develop a left ear dominance, auditory information must follow an awkward route to the brain's processing centers, resulting in listening difficulties. Left-handedness does not change the need for sonic stimulation to the right ear, just as left-handedness does not change the location of the heart from one side of the body to another.

Dr. Tomatis's approach to the ear, the brain, and language create very important clues to the sound education of children. His method is highly prescriptive and cannot be duplicated by simple stimulation or music filtration processes. Tomatis leads us to pose new questions about auditory abilities that musicians, parents, and teachers have not previously known to ask.

As I become more aware of the great importance of the ear, the brain, and the subtle movements and gestures in the body, I am even more enthusiastic about my career in education with music. The art of being able to observe the child's ability to respond to tone, rhythm, and melody is now fundamental in curriculum development using rhythm, movement, music, and language. Musicians are gifted with the tools and the answers. It is only now that we are beginning to ask the important and correct questions. Art, beauty, and joy are the bridge between that mysterious inner world of learning and the outer sounds that call us to communicate with others.

In this book, the ideas and methods used to empower and accentuate this creative process of sound education are implemented in a model called Phase Forward Education. The following chapters will define how the model uses music, language, and creativity to encourage lifelong learning.

The Art of Listening:
The Journey from Listening to Lifelong Learning

Chris Brewer

As we move toward the enhancement of listening abilities, the boundaries of our human learning potential expand. Attentive listening skills empower lifelong learning by providing tools of communication and understanding in the following ways:

- ✦ The ability to bring language into the inner world and use it for reasoning and reflection
- ✦ The desire and capability to communicate from the inner world to the outer world with confidence

- ✦ The unifying of intelligence through active listening of mind, body, and emotions
- ✦ The satisfaction of becoming engaged in activities that create fulfilling learning experiences
- ✦ The extension of learning throughout life

The journey from listening to lifelong learning begins with the attainment of attentive listening skills and includes the development of inner speech and inner listening. With a strong listening foundation, learning becomes an exciting, lifelong process. Every aspect of life offers an opportunity to listen and learn. The journey never ends.

Inner Speech

Inner speech is the process through which we hear ourselves think and listen internally. To attain skills in reasoning and reflection we must be able to take the spoken word inward and dialogue with it. Inner speech develops slowly from birth onward and by age nine or ten is generally intact. Prior to that time, the tiny voice, which only each of us alone can hear within our heads, does not fully exist. When inner speech is in place, language becomes a tool for the regulation of behavior, reasoning, reading skills, and the attainment of high-level cognitive thought. Without the development of inner speech, we see a child who has little impulse control, who experiences difficulty in reading, and who does not fully attain the power to reason.

Life is a process of organizing patterns. It begins with the patterning of movement. Then as the child learns to use words, the patterns of language and speech become tools for directing behavior and communicating. As words attain greater meaning, language patterns can be carried inward and organized into thinking and reasoning skills.

Young children speak their thoughts aloud because they have not yet developed an inner voice. Until approximately age seven, children must *talk* in order to *think* with words. They must hear themselves say the words out loud in order to respond. The speech of a four- or five-year-old is often a stream-of-consciousness flow of words.

Four-year-old Sharon sits at the table at breakfast. "Mom, did I tell you what Alec did at preschool? He took my doll and wouldn't give it back so I told Mrs. Russell. She's my teacher. Can we go out to eat? I want to wear my red dress." She sings, "Oh, the red dress, the red dress, it is so pretty . . . I just love it." Speaks, "I love you Mom, can I blow you a kiss and a hug?"

Around age seven, the talking has been reduced to a whisper. By nine or ten, the speech has moved inside, and the children now have a tiny internal voice they can use for thinking and making decisions. This is the voice of reasoning.

The development of language as a means of regulating behavior begins in utero as we first experience sounds and become familiar with them. At age two, a massive growth in brain structures occurs that initiates the beginnings of interactive language and the regulation of behavior through words. Two-year-olds explore sounds and their meanings. They may play with "no, no, no," even chanting the words as they continue the behavior initiating the "no." By age four and one-half, the most objectionable behavior is generally regulated by language. When age seven is reached, language has become a mediating force in behavior regulation and can now be used in place of movement to elicit or manage action.

Johnny comes to school and joins the rest of the children in playing on the playground. He sees a group playing kickball and, wanting to play, too, he runs with them and chases the ball. The ball is controlled by the other children and Johnny does not get a chance to kick it. "Let me kick it," he shouts and when it doesn't come to him, he picks up the ball and runs away with it.

Johnny's actions may not be unusual at age five. At age eight or nine, he would have behavior problems. At eight or nine, Johnny is expected to be able to override his impulse for immediate gratification and play fairly. Behavior problems erupt when the child cannot use language to deter movement and regulate behavior. The child with little impulse control may not have developed inner speech and will respond through reaction rather than reasoning. Children whose internal voice is not fully in place need to move in order to think.

In the classroom, children who have not developed an inner voice may have difficulty being attentive when asked to attend to internal thoughts that they cannot hear. Children who are learning to use inner speech may not think of answers quickly when asked and will need time for their inner thoughts to emerge. By allowing children time to listen for the inner voice and dialogue with it, we nurture their reasoning skills.

The development of inner speech is also enhanced when we read to children. Not only does this familiarize them with the sound of the words, but it also provides the realization that language conveys ideas. Some homes are experience based rather than language based, and in these homes, language has a function, but movement may have greater meaning. Reactions may predominate more than reasoning. Reading aloud nurtures the development of language as a reasoning tool and provides an opportunity for sharing and bonding.

Inner speech is an essential aspect of reading. Read through the following paragraph:

> The flying south of birds in the winter is a feature known as migration. It is initiated by an internal rhythm for species preservation that depends on the stimulation of biological clocks. The signals of light and temperature often serve as instigators of the flight.

Now, reread the paragraph one more time and count the number of the letter f's you read.

How many did you find? Four? Six? Eight? The answer is nine, but most people will find only five. The reason for this is that we do not count the f's in the word of because we hear "of" as the phonetic ov when we read. The inner hearing has overridden the visual image in the thought process.

Reading is a complex synthesis of pattern identification and inner speech and entails hearing words internally. When first learning to read, young children who are still developing their inner speech need to read aloud and hear themselves speak the words in order to understand them. For this reason, a classroom of beginning readers will be a noisy place. As the inner voice develops, children may need assistance in blocking outer world sounds, so they can hear their tiny inner voice. Experiments with insulated earphones have increased reading comprehension by allowing the child to hear the inner voice better.

Without inner speech, a child may not be able to create meaning from words or comprehend what he reads. A ten- or eleven-year-old without inner speech cannot go inside and reason. That child will use discrimination in place of reasoning and will look for an answer that uses the exact wording posed in the question. If it is not found, the child will not be able to understand the true meaning of the question and interpret the answer, but instead will claim that the answer is not available.

Inner speech is a tool for regulating movement, and movement, in turn, aids in the development of the inner voice. Inner speech is a function regulated by the frontal lobes of the brain, which are also the center for pattern recognition. Neuro cells that coordinate inner speech have two roles: the regulation of inner speech and the control of high-level motor functions. Movement and rhythm stimulate the frontal lobes and enrich language and motor development. The frontal lobes grow massively between the ages of two and six and do not grow again until around age twenty-two. These early years are especially important times for nurturing the frontal lobes and providing the foundation for pattern recognition.

As young children explore the world through movement they are developing patterns that will provide a model for the organization of speech and thought. When nonverbal sounds are bridged to movement, there is a strengthening of the inner images and gestures related to sound that comes before language. Linking language sounds to movement bonds speech patterns to already developed motor patterns. Once language patterning has occurred, the child can begin to use inner speech for the control of movement behavior and has the tools necessary to develop reasoning skills.

As our inner voice emerges, it builds a bridge between the inner and outer worlds. Reflection and reasoning become lifelong tools of living and learning. Our inner speech allows us to move with intention and conscious thought as our companion on the learning journey.

The Intention toward Attention

It is essential that we empower students with the art of attentive listening, or we risk the possibility that knowledge will become only logical fact. We endanger the development of the skills necessary to turn perception into the conception of ideas. We risk the loss of learning as a lifelong process.

One of Albert Einstein's most famous quotes is "Knowledge is experience; everything else is just information." Einstein was not a particularly good student in school. At age fifteen he left school with poor grades in history, English, and geography and had no diploma. He ultimately graduated from the Federal Polytechnic University in Switzerland, but for Einstein, the most important classroom was the world. There he explored, experienced, and listened, gaining tools for his discovery of new connections and paradigms.

"Knowledge is experience; everything else is just information."
—Albert Einstein

Each year thousands of students leave the traditional classroom. For many, it is the end of their learning process of cognitive knowledge and the beginning of daily survival with little growth in formal education. Many who remain in the traditional classroom learn to listen only well enough to store facts and repeat them at the appropriate time. Biophysicist and brain researcher Herman Epstein from Brandeis University has determined that more than half the population in the United States does *not* reach the Piaget stage of formal reasoning. There are indications that as much as one-third of the population does not even move into concrete thinking. Is it possible that we have created a population of "knowers" but few "thinkers"?

A young child explores the dimensions of water running onto the bare ground. He watches the water attentively as it runs in a single rivulet that overwhelms everything in its path. He sees the water as it pools in low places, in other areas splitting into tiny fingers of movement that slither in interesting shapes down a hill. Within seconds he is engaged with the activity of the water, experiencing its movement in touch, sound, and complementary movement within his own body. He delights in the new textures of flowing water and creamy mud. He babbles his delight in response to the water's own speech. He flows with the water's movement as he explores the rhythms of the water. Swirling his hand through the mud, he begins to create new rhythms, first disrupting the flow and then devising new pathways.

In the seconds this child spent interacting with the water and ground, his encompassing attentiveness to every aspect of the event was spent in listening with ear, body, emotions, and mind. The intention to explore focused the attention to discovery. The process of reaching out to listen entails a desire to participate and an engagement in the activity. The experience becomes a part of the child, and the child becomes a part of it.

Attentive listening moves past the hearing and storage of facts. It extends beyond the normal "hearing" range and triggers actions and reactions from many parts of the mind-body system. The frequencies of attentive listening are vibrations of movement that stimulate the ears and brain, pulse within the body, and create emotional connections. Listening creates a state of unification, a sensory integration that involves the entire mind-body-emotion complex.

For facts to become integrated as knowledge, learning involves the experience of attentive listening. As new information connects with previously stored data, attentive listening creates a neurologic patterning that is imprinted within many circuits of the brain. The information consolidates with data obtained through other senses and learned in different ways, increasing the length and breadth of neurological circuitry. The implications and detail of these patterns will not be easily forgotten.

"Set me a task in which I can put something of myself and it is a task no longer; it is joy, it is art."

—B. Carmen

We listen more attentively when we feel that the relevance of information creates meaning. One of the keys to attentive listening is that it naturally effects changes within the mind-body-emotion complex. These changes may occur quickly or merely be stored and brought out at a later date. They may simply become a part of a greater repertoire of knowing. We listen with more attention when we feel that a change will be effected and that we are in some way responsible for the change.

The intention and focus we hold in learning determines whether we are listening or merely hearing. Students who listen only with the intention of being able to replay information for a test may only hear and register the words. When we listen with the intention of effecting a discovery or utilizing information in a creative process, we listen with insight and engagement.

In teaching the art of listening, we can give students information and provide an opportunity for them to respond creatively. Equally as productive is providing a responsive manner of presentation in which the information is seen, felt, moved, or somehow sensed in as many ways as possible. The student's desire to listen in either case will be naturally extended. The experience of being required to respond to the information entails enhanced, focused listening. The more senses utilized and the deeper the listening involved in the experience, the greater the learning. The creative arts provide safe and easy ways to facilitate the neural stimulation necessary for greater proficiency in listening and learning. The gift of creative intention provides the strength of directed attention.

Inner Listening

Inner listening is a crucial aspect in the creative process of preparation, incubation, illumination, verification, and implementation. Inner listening is the nonverbal process in which incubation and illumination occur. The listening which is done with the body, emotions and subconscious mind generates the Aha! of the creative insight. This illumination, when allowed the time to synthesize information, moves from the unconscious mind to consciousness. The Aha! will reach us if we are using our inner listening powers. Each of us develops our own special way of listening to the inner world. The Aha!'s may come in such ways as reading, playing music, drawing, fishing, doing simple tasks, running, sleeping, taking a bath, or driving or other personal activities.

Great wisdom can be accessed through the inner listening process. Einstein observed that ideas came to him through his body first and then became words. His initial concepts that led to the theory of relativity came to him while working as a postal clerk. When Michelangelo painted the ceiling of the Sistine Chapel, he painted both the major and the minor prophets. The distinction between the two groups can be seen within the art work, for there are divine cherubs at the ears of all of the prophets, but only the major prophets' heads are turned to listen!

The gifts of inner listening are great for they provide us joy and a sense of accomplishment. The excitement of the Aha! discovery creates an appreciation of the creative learning process and a desire to learn more. A deeper sense of understanding of ourselves and the world around us becomes evident. The synthesis that occurs in the incubation process extends a sense of calm and serenity, which reduces stress and creates a feeling of being nurtured. It is a process that carries over to many aspects of our life, bringing with it great rewards.

Attentive inner listening can be practiced in any aspect of learning or life: in an algebraic math problem, in the imagery of a poem, the creation of a painting, the sound of an orchestra, the journey through a historical event, the choreography of a basketball game. All can be approached with engagement and listening with senses, mind, body, and emotions.

To be empowered with the ideas represented in this book, teachers, administrators, and students need to listen attentively to the ideas. By becoming engaged in the activities, the information will be understood by mind, body, and emotions. The journey toward lifelong learning will begin.

Activities for Teachers
Tuning Up Our Teaching

Lifelong learning is dependent on our ability to perceive and listen to the world around us. Becoming aware of patterns of listening is an important step toward understanding the learning process and assisting students in enhancing their listening skills. Developing our own ability to listen attentively increases our ability to perceive listening patterns in students and discover ways to engage them in the learning process.

The activities that follow in this chapter are practical and useful tools for discovering listening patterns. They provide information and insight into how we listen and encourage the use of our senses, mind, body, and emotions for developing listening skills. As we gain a sensitivity to the listening process, we enhance our personal lifelong learning journey and begin to find new ways to travel with students on their learning path.

CORTICAL CHEER

Through the work of Dr. Tomatis has come the discovery that high frequencies have an energizing effect upon the brain. A sound is actually made up of a series of pitches blended together. Variations in sound texture occur because different frequencies are dominant in different sounds. The energizing frequencies are the high parts of a sound that can occur even in a sound that we hear as low in pitch. This poem, which describes the hearing process and the electrical stimulation of the brain from these high frequencies, can be shared with students from grade 5 through adult.

OBJECTIVES
To learn about the process of hearing; to learn about the electrical stimulation of the brain created by sound vibrations

DESCRIPTION
The teacher will read the poem to explore the journey of sound from the air to the brain.

SCHEDULING
5 minutes to read the poem

✦ Read through the Cortical Cheer poem to learn about listening and the brain.

CORTICAL CHEER

It's the sounds, the sounds, that come into your ear
That stimulate your brain and bring you good cheer!
It's the sounds, the sounds, that come into your ear
That stimulate your brain and bring you good cheer!

The sound of the music comes into your ear
And moves into your brain when you hear.
As it wiggles through your ear canals it does a special thing—
It becomes electricity that makes your brain ring!

Take a look at the ear and here's what you will see—
We have three ears that make our hearing come to be.
Their names are very easy and never a riddle
They're simple to recall as the inner, outer, middle.

Sound starts as vibration that moves through the air,
It flows like a sonic wave and finds your ear somewhere.
The outer ear collects the sound and moves it till the eardrum's
    found,
Which makes the sound big - turns it well around!

The sound inside the inner ear meets with many nerves,
Which change the form of energy to gain new verve!
Sound becomes electric impulses that wiggle to your brain.
They travel on nerve tracks just - like - trains.

But different waves do different things when they reach the brain!
High sounds make you happy, but the low sounds cause a strain—
Highs have many nerves to move, the lows just a few,
Highs charge your brain with joy, the lows make you blue!

Our brains get hungry too, you see, and often need to eat
And sounds above three thousand hertz are really quite a treat!
The doctor who first found a brain that needed sound to eat
Prescribed a dose of highs each day. . . and oh it made life sweet!

If you choose to feed your brain you can feed it different ways:
You can make the sounds yourself, by singing through the days,
You can listen to Gregorian chant or Mozart, but get close—
Your brain will thrive when junk food sounds are missing from its
   dose!

It's the sounds, the sounds, that come into your ear
That stimulate your brain and bring you good cheer!
It's the sounds, the sounds, that come into your ear
That stimulate your brain and bring you good cheer!

— Chris Brewer

DOMINANT EARS

❖ When you ask your class a question, be aware of which of your ears is more dominant in listening to the response. Notice as you turn your head if one ear is more receptive than the other. When you are speaking on the telephone, notice which ear you use to listen. Determine which ear you use most often.

❖ The right ear is the informational ear. The left ear is the more affective and tonal ear. Do you process initially in the informational ear or the affective ear?

In rooms that have good acoustics, we may not notice a dominant listening ear, but auditory stimulation can be increased even in rooms with good acoustics. When you find your attention span lessening, try changing your ear position to increase stimulation of the auditory information to the opposite hemisphere of the brain.

It is also important to be very aware of how children listen. You may notice great improvement if you experiment with these techniques to enhance listening:

❖ Move the less auditory children, or those who do not understand auditory information the first time, to a place where their right ear is closer to you and they do not have to turn their head to listen.

OBJECTIVES
To sensitize teachers to patterns of listening; to provide teachers with tools for increasing listening abilities

DESCRIPTION
The teacher will determine his or her ear dominance and also observe personal listening responses as well as those of the students.

SCHEDULING
Throughout the day

39

✧ If students have a dominant left ear, show them how to cup their hand under their chin and let the fingers reach toward the right ear. Speaking into the cupped hand amplifies the vocal sound and stimulates the ear. Reading aloud with this hand megaphone charges and enhances listening potential.

✧ When a beginning reader misreads a word, softly speak the correct word into one ear and then the other. You will assist in both stimulating the reader's hearing mechanisms and setting the correct word in his or her memory systems.

OBJECTIVES
To develop listening and observational abilities that provide insights into the emotional, physical, and mental state of the student; to explore personal rhythms and patterns of communication

DESCRIPTION
The teacher will listen to the verbal, emotional, and physical information given by the students and also observe his or her own patterns of verbal and nonverbal communication.

SCHEDULING
Throughout the activities of the day

THREE WAYS TO LISTEN

There are three different ways we can use to listen. The first way brings in sonic information. The second way listens to the inner voice, thought, and temperament of the moment. The third way responds to the physical body, its posture, health, and well-being.

Rather than listening to a student only one way, begin to pay attention to the following:

✧ Listen to the information given. Is it correct? Is it clear?

✧ What is the emotion within the voice? Is it stressed, natural, or relaxed? Is it rapid, flowing, or disconnected?

✧ What is the posture of the body? Is it stiff? Is it sloppy and bored?

After you have become conscious of how your students speak and give verbal conversation, become conscious of yourself. To compare the rhythm and style of your own voice, you may wish to tape record part of a morning and an afternoon in your class.

When do you find your emotions enhancing the information? When do you find emotions in the way of the information? When is your body at its best to receive information? What is your model for best listening to yourself and creating the power to express yourself as a teacher?

EAR, AIR, BONES, AND SKIN

✧ Begin by vocalizing an *ah* sound.

✧ Place your palms on your jaw line, establishing as much contact as possible with the bone and skin. Notice the vibrations you feel as you vocalize.

✧ Now, continue the *ah* and move it up and down in pitch. With your whole hand on the body surface, explore other parts of your face and head. Be sure to note the vibrations at the top of the head. (If you feel no vibrations, increase the volume of sound; many of us are timid about creating sounds.)

✧ Change vowel sounds and note any differences you may experience.

✧ Now, repeat the process and explore your chest, stomach, back, thighs, and legs for any vibrations you may feel.

Finally, after you have explored sound conduction of bones and skin from the inside world out, note how this exploration has made you feel emotionally. Are there changes in your outlook?

Dr. Tomatis has discovered that high-frequency stimulation of the brain can increase energy levels and create a feeling of calm. Aside from the benefits of discovering sound conduction within the body, this activity may be used to energize you when you feel tired.*

✧ You may want to explore sound conduction with your students as shown in the photograph.

OBJECTIVES
To understand the many ways in which we hear; to experience the energizing effects of sound vibrations

DESCRIPTION
The teacher will explore sound conduction as it occurs through the ear, air, bones, and skin.

SCHEDULING
10 minutes before or after school

* Refer to Don Campbell's book, *The Roar of Silence*, or his sound cassette, "Healing Yourself with Your Own Voice."

41

OBJECTIVES
To understand the
effects of eye position
on listening and
sound production;
to discover a tool for
improving listening
and sound production

DESCRIPTION
The teacher will
explore the changes
that occur in voice
tonality and pitch
when the eyes are in
different positions.

ENVIRONMENT
A quiet, safe room

SCHEDULING
10 minutes before or
after school

LOOKING FOR SOUND

Researchers have discovered that eye position stimulates specific brain functions. The position of the eyes determines much about the way the voice recapitulates what is heard. A lack of eye focus may result in difficulties in reproducing pitches. The tonal voice can be centered through the focus of the eye position. Many people who have not been able to match pitches musically and vocally have been able to do so in a few hours by working with eye focus. To discover how the position of your eyes determines your own voice:

✦ Develop a couple of sentences that describe your day.

✦ Keeping your head stationary and eyes open, repeat the sentences.

✦ Say them again with your eyes closed.

✦ Repeat and continue to change eye positions each time: eyes fixed on one point, looking up to the center of your forehead, and looking down at your chest.

✦ Notice whether your voice changes in any of the different eye positions.

OBJECTIVE
To become sensitive to
the patterns of listening
that occur within the
mind, the body, and
the emotions

DESCRIPTION
The teacher remem-
bers experiences that
occurred during the
day and becomes
aware of how the
experience was per-
ceived with the mind,
body, and emotions.

SCHEDULING
10 to 15 minutes at the
end of a school day

THE LISTENING EXPERIENCE

Review the events of the day and select from them one or more incidents that have special significance to you in some way. Spend a moment or two reliving this experience as you sit or lay quietly with your eyes closed.

When the event is clear, begin to write answers to the questions that follow. (Remember that this exercise is not intended to decide what you should have done but rather to discover your listening abilities.)

✦ What sounds were associated with the event?

✦ What did you hear with your ears?

❖ What can you remember seeing in this event? How did your eyes listen?

❖ Did you listen with your body? What do you remember it experiencing?

❖ What was the emotional tone of the experience? How did you listen to the emotional aspects of the event?

❖ In what other ways did you listen?

You may wish to continue this activity for a week or even a month. Some astonishing realizations about the listening process will be revealed.

Activities for Students

Tuning Up with Students

The patterns of listening that we develop become the bridge between the inner and outer worlds. Moving between these worlds is an essential process that occurs as we organize patterns of movement, speech, and thought. As the student becomes more attentive in both worlds, he or she can develop greater insight to the patterns and connections between them. Communication and lifelong learning can emerge with a natural sense of wonder and enjoyment.

These activities explore different ways of reaching out to listen. Some of the activities strengthen the development of inner speech. Others increase listening and awareness skills and deepen the students' appreciation of learning to prepare them for being attentive in future activities. The activities in this book that integrate art with sound or movement have been developed at the Creativity Center by Jeanne Hamilton and Chris Brewer.

TURNING ON YOUR EARS

OBJECTIVE
To stimulate the ears
and related nerves
and muscles for
increased listening
abilities

DESCRIPTION
Students will perform
two movements.

GRADE LEVEL
Kindergarten through
adult

SCHEDULING
2 or 3 minutes

Paul and Gail Dennison of the Educational Kinesiology Foundation have developed simple and enjoyable movements that assist the integration of senses and brain functions to enhance learning. These activities, from their Edu-Kinesthetics Brain Gym program, are based on over fifty years of statistical research in developmental optometry and sensory motor training that relate the effects of movement to learning. The activities can be done quickly and easily. Once students are shown the techniques, they often request the opportunity to do them.

—THE OWL

The owl movement activates the brain and assists listening by crossing the auditory midline. Auditory attention, recognition, perception, discrimination, and comprehension are improved. The stimulation of the activity aids inner speech and both short- and long-term memory.

The owl specifically releases shoulder stress related to reading or hand-eye coordination. In the activity, the lengthening of the neck and shoulder muscles restores the range of motion and circulation of blood and energy to the brain necessary for improved focus and attention. Use it before reading or language arts activities and following intensely focused sessions of reading, writing, math calculations, or computer tasks.

✧ Ask students to cross their arm over their chest and place their hand on their shoulder between the neck and arm. They should squeeze the muscles firmly.

✧ Next students turn their head toward the same shoulder as if looking over it.

✧ Students breathe deeply and pull their shoulders back.

✧ With their hand still in place, students turn their head slowly to look over the other shoulder. The chin remains level and eyes track smoothly as the head moves. Students breathe deeply and again pull the shoulders back.

✧ Have students repeat the process and then drop their chin to their chest, breathing deeply, and letting the muscles relax.

✧ Students repeat the process with the other hand on the opposite shoulder.

✧ You might want to ask students to alternate their listening by focusing the ear which is over their shoulder.

✧ For younger children, make the owl's "whoooo" sound on exhalation.

—THE THINKING CAP

This activity stimulates the outer ears and the reticular formation of the brain, which is responsible for tuning out distracting, irrelevant sounds. The activity integrates the speech and language systems and makes the words and meaning of language more accessible to students. Short-term memory, inner hearing, balance, and the screening of sound sensations are activated by the thinking cap. Listening comprehension, speaking, singing, inner hearing, spelling, mental arithmetic, and concentration for computer work can all be enhanced through the use of this movement.

✧ With head upright and chin at a comfortable level, students gently pull their ears back and "unroll" them. With thumbs and index fingers, students massage the whole outer part of the ear. The unrolling starts at the top of the ear and moves to the bottom, with a slight tug on the ear lobe.

✧ Repeat two or three times.

✧ Observe students for changes in breathing and energy levels. Does the resonance of their voice change? Are they more attentive? Are their jaw and facial muscles more relaxed?

SOUNDSCAPES

OBJECTIVES
To attune students to the attentive listening process; to provide students with the experience of listening to the sounds around them; to understand that ambient sounds create a "sound-scape" or aural landscape

DESCRIPTION
Students become aware of the sounds around them and the "soundscapes" of their day.

GRADE LEVEL
Kindergarten through adult

SCHEDULING
5 minutes

We are surrounded by sounds! We awaken to familiar sounds, listen to music we enjoy, endure unwanted sound (noise) over which we have no control. Familiar, routine sounds orchestrate the structure of our day while new sounds bring exciting accents and rhythms to our inner world. This symphony of sounds blends tones to create a sound landscape or *soundscape*, a term coined by music educator R. Murray Schafer to define our auditory environment.

Every person has unique soundscapes. For some, a morning soundscape might include the local disc jockey on the early shift signaling the time to rise, while the pattering of the water in the shower calls attention to the onset of the day, and the teapot whistle and microwave beep herald a greeting to the stomach. For others, a morning soundscape might be the insistent nagging, "If you don't get up, you're gonna' be late!" while the bacon sizzles, and the kids fight over first place in the bathroom.

When we stop to listen and become aware of our sound environment, we develop the skill of attentive listening, an important tool in living and learning. The following activity assists in this process:

   ✧ Ask students to become aware of the sounds around them.

   ✧ Provide a three-minute quiet period to allow students to listen to the sounds around them. Discuss the sounds heard.

   ✧ Have students think back to the sounds they heard earlier in the day. Share these sounds.

   ✧ Explain that the sounds in our daily routines create our own unique sound landscape or soundscape. Discuss soundscapes that occur regularly within the day. What other soundscapes do we have?

TONING THE VOICE

This invigorating and entertaining activity stimulates the brain and tones the voice. Because it stimulates the mind, the activity is especially appropriate to use before assigning tasks that require concentrated effort. More oxygen is provided to the brain through the increase of breath, and the amplification of the frequencies at close range stimulates the electrical charge of the brain.

✧ Stand in a circle at close proximity to one another (you may want to link elbows), and have everyone release three or four loud sighs on the vowel sound *ah*.

✧ Pick a tone in the middle of your students' range and have them sustain this pitch with the *ah*.

✧ Switch to the vowel sound *eeeee* in a high pitch, continue with this sound for one minute, and breathe where necessary.

✧ Using the vowel sound *ooooo*, sing a low pitch, and sustain it for one minute.

✧ Next, ask students to begin to move freely in pitch. They may also begin to choose different vowels. Continue for at least two minutes or longer.

✧ Experiment with eyes closed, eyes opened, and fixed gaze versions of this activity. Do the students' sounds have a different quality?

✧ Have students match your pitch while changing eye positions. Do they maintain pitches closer to the ones you select in any of the eye positions? What differences do you note?

OBJECTIVES
To explore the range of the voice; to discover effects of sound on the mind, body, and emotions; to stimulate the brain with oxygen and electrical charge

DESCRIPTION
Students will stand in a circle and experiment with making extended vowel sounds at various pitches.

GRADE LEVEL
Kindergarten through adult

SCHEDULING
5 minutes

INNER HEARING

OBJECTIVES
To develop inner hearing and inner speech; to assist in the memorization of songs or poems; to have fun

DESCRIPTION
Students will sing a familiar song or read a poem and leave silent spaces for specified words.

GRADE LEVEL
Kindergarten through adult

SCHEDULING
A minimum of 3 minutes

This technique, used in Education Through Music methods, offers a wonderful way to develop inner speech. The implications for reading and comprehension skill development are phenomenal. Use the technique with any song or poem although songs with repetitive words or phrases work best as in "Row, Row, Row Your Boat."

✦ Sing through the song two times. Then explain that sometimes we hear and say words out loud so that everyone can hear them, and sometimes we say and hear things only in our mind. These inner sounds are called "inner hearing."

✦ Suggest that one of the words in the song "Row, Row, Row Your Boat" be selected to put into our inner hearing. Select or have a student select a specific word, for example: the word *merrily*.

✦ Now sing the entire song again - this time, however, *merrily* will be sung inside the head only. All other words will be heard and sung outside:

> *Row, row, row your boat*
> *Gently down the stream*
>
> _____ , _____ , _____ , _____
> *Life is but a dream.*

✦ There will be silence during the time when merrily would be sung, as each singer hears it inside his or her head but does not sing it out loud.

✦ The song can (and probably will) be sung a number of times again using different words for the inner hearing.

You might also use this method to help students memorize a song. They will gladly sing it over and over without becoming bored. By using different words for inner hearing, the singers become more aware of where words fit into the song. The technique is extremely beneficial for the development of inner speech. Inner hearing also develops the skill of sensing rests and silence in music.

DIRECTIONAL LISTENING

In this activity, designed to increase student listening capabilities, your sensitivity to the best learning modes of individual students may also be increased.

Select a subject in which you will need to give specific assignments for work tasks each day of an entire week. Explain to your students at the beginning of the week that you will be giving them directions for that subject in five different ways. You will repeat the directions more than once if necessary, but you will not give directions in more than one way on any particular day.

✦ On the first day, give your instructions verbally.

✦ The second day, write your instructions on the board.

✦ The third day, sing or rap the directions. This can be done by creating a short rap such as:

> *What you need to do*
> *is read page two,*
> *then start to write*
> *and see the light*
> *in questions*
> *one through ten.*

A rhyme is not necessary, for if the assignment is spoken in a singsong manner with a regular pulse, you will attain a rap effect. As an alternative to rapping, you may want to pick a familiar tune and sing the assignment to the melody or make up your own melody.

✦ Your directions on the fourth day will be drawn on the board with symbols and colored chalk. For numbers, you may want to draw the number of objects: for example, five apples to depict the number 5, or two trees and six flowers for 26. Parentheses within double or triple digit numbers will keep you from having to draw 135 giraffes.

✦ On the fifth day, mime the directions. For numbers, make the shape with your body or hold up fingers.

OBJECTIVES
To stimulate new patterns of listening; to provide insight into students' learning modes

DESCRIPTION
The teacher will give the regular class-room or homework assignments differ-ently each day: verbally, in writing, in rap or song, with symbols, and in mime.

GRADE LEVEL
1 through adult

MATERIALS
Colored chalk and chalkboard

SCHEDULING
5 minutes while giving classroom and homework assignments

✧ At the end of the week, discuss the different methods used, and ask students which they preferred. Did they find their attention increased when directions were given in different modes? Did their listening abilities increase at other times? What did you find about their attention and listening abilities?

As you observe, you will discover your students' preferred and weak modes of perception. You may want to keep a record of their responses. Addressing different learning styles in the presentation of directions can be important for students. Additionally, writing directions on the board in symbol or pictorial form may provide easier access for those children whose sense of imagery is strong.

You may wish to repeat this series for giving instructions periodically. For variety, give the students an opportunity to create the directions.

"RITHEM"

OBJECTIVE
To experience rhythm and sound in language; to learn to spell rhythm

DESCRIPTION
Students will use pulse and sound to explore rhythm by spelling the word "rhythm."

GRADE LEVEL
1 through adult

SCHEDULING
5 minutes

Rithem, rhythem, rith . . . m. No matter how often we use the word, it is a challenge to spell. The *American College Dictionary* defines rhythm in a musical context as "the pattern of regular or irregular pulses caused in music by the occurrence of strong and weak melodic and harmonic beats." For a child, it may be understood as the beat and pulse of movement in music, body, or thought.

Even when it is defined, it is difficult to explain without a demonstration. One of the easiest ways to experience rhythm in a classroom is to give students a heart test.

✧ Ask them to find their pulse in their wrist, neck, or chest.

✧ Ask them to make a sound with their pulse. A healthy rhythm will have a constant flow, a standard beat. Demonstrate a healthy beat with "tha-thump, tha-thump, tha-thump, tha-thump."

❖ Next, play active music and ask children to clap or tap a steady beat with the music.

❖ When a class can easily experience the beat, pulse, and basic rhythm of a piece of music, use the following exercise to learn how to spell the word "rhythm."

Chant the letters and clap in 4/4 time:

Now divide the class into two groups, and ask the second group to jump on imaginary motorcycles as they rev up the engine and growl:

Then start a third group. This time each letter is a whole note getting four beats. The "R" begins in the low register of the voice and swoops up for four beats, the "H" glides down for four beats. Continue the spelling as you alternate swooping up and the gliding down. For younger children, movement of the hands or body engages attention.

Blend the three parts like a round under the enchanting spell of rhythm.

PATTERNS OF LISTENING

OBJECTIVE
To become sensitive
to the patterns of
listening that occur
within the mind, the
body, and the
emotions

OBJECTIVE
To become sensitive
to the patterns of
listening that occur
within the mind, the
body, and the
emotions

DESCRIPTION
Students remember
an experience that
occurred during the
day and become
aware of how the
experience was
perceived with their
mind, body, and
emotions.

GRADE LEVEL
4 through 9

MATERIALS
For each student:
writing paper and
a pencil

SCHEDULING
10 to 15 minutes at
the end of a school
day

✧ Ask students to review the events of their day individually and select an incident that had special significance to them in some way. Have students spend a moment or two reliving the experience as they sit quietly with their eyes closed.

✧ When the event is clear, ask students to write answers to the following questions:

> What sounds were associated with the event? What did you hear with your ears? What can you remember as you see this event?

> How did your eyes listen? Did you listen with your body? How did it feel? Was it relaxed, tense, tired, energized?

> What was the emotional feeling of the experience? How did you listen to the emotional aspects of the event? In what other ways did you listen?

You may wish to continue this activity for a week or even a month. Some astonishing realizations about the listening process will be revealed.

CHAPTER II

CREATIVE TEACHING:
PHASE FORWARD
EDUCATION

Rhythmic Awareness

We *are* rhythm in our physical movements, our emotional inflections, and every utterance we make. Each thought has a rhythm, be it constant and clear or irregular and scattered. Rhythm enables us to communicate, learn, and teach. This does not at all imply that a knowledge of musical rhythms is needed. It implies a need for more awareness of our personal rhythms and an attentiveness to the rhythms surrounding us. This is the inner music of life.

Every age has a different physical, emotional, and intellectual rhythm, and the pulse within a class depends on the success of the teacher to entrain to the rhythms and learning patterns of the students. The rate and speed of the school day, the teacher's personal tempo, and the pace of the school day in relationship to home life can either create an integrated life experience, or it can be so out of synchronicity with the children that their learning seems quite disconnected.

The success of many teachers is not based solely upon their knowledge and methods. A teacher's effectiveness develops from a verbal, emotional pacing: a rhythmic empowerment of delivery and instruction that becomes a subtle and critical tool for improving personal teaching methods and styles. This creates a way for the child to integrate information with his or her individual pace of learning. Within these essential communication and human relations skills, teachers have had little developmental assistance.

Our tradition implies that as long as we teach in ways that speak success for the outer world through knowledge and achievement, we can credit ourselves as successful. However, it is the strength of a solid inner-world development plus a healthy inner- outer-world communication that leads children to an emotional sense of safety and well-being, fundamental for both academic and physical success throughout their lives. In the past, we have left the inner-world development to parents and churches. Presently, we are all responsible for preparing each other for a healthy inner- and outer-world experience without any invasion on each other's belief systems.

This book does not provide the teacher with another "recipe" method for specific classes. Its aim is to produce an awareness of our own rhythms and styles as teachers and parents. When we are more aware of what allows us to be effective as teachers, we can then translate our personal success to students as we motivate them towards pleasurable, creative learning. Dare we make a commitment to the perceptions in ourselves so that we can truly feel a sense of connectedness and cohesion with our students?

Education is more than developing the mental or intellectual ability to recapitulate information. In learning, there is a physical education that builds the body and releases academic stress imposed on us as learners and workers in this society. An emotional education also exists that may be secondary to our traditions but is very important in the development of our motivation and enthusiasm toward building a creative and healthy socio-academic structure.

The physical body is the very core of learning. Its explorations begin the learning process. As young children, we organize movement into patterns that later become a vehicle for developing patterns of thought. In sleep, play, music making, movement, and concentration, the body's inner and outer rhythms coordinate the mind's perception of consciousness. The body becomes a blueprint, manifesting mental and physical rhythms into a physical signal that illustrates a person's state. These messages can be read and used as a tool for effective teaching and learning.

Rhythmic awareness in education is ancient. A famous story in Plato's *Symposium* tells about a banquet in which great discussions and interesting commentaries are taking place. In the midst of the musical background and charmed discussions, a drunkard, Alcibiades, comes into the room and completely disrupts the atmosphere. By introducing other rhythms into the room, he creates havoc with the activities of Socrates and the guests.

Is this any different from the school drills, announcements, the traffic noise, or the emotional needs of a hyperactive child in an elementary classroom? Notice how many times a day you feel distracted by the intrusion of an unexpected rhythm. After a few years of teaching, we realize that part of the rhythm of each day is its interruption. Many times an interruption cannot be helped, but when we allow ourselves to become distracted, the distraction is amplified through the students.

Socrates tried a variety of ways to bring Alcibiades into the rhythm of the group. He had little success because of the very different rhythms of response. Yet without Socrates' awareness of his own rhythm and wise empowerment of responsiveness, the banquet would have been totally disrupted. Here is a model that we can begin to cultivate, for if we can emulate Socrates' awareness, we can then begin to orchestrate the rhythms of the day and create a high potential learning environment.

Empowering ourselves in ways that transform the learning styles of our students into optimal motivation, ease, and memory is the first step in a project called Phase Forward Education.

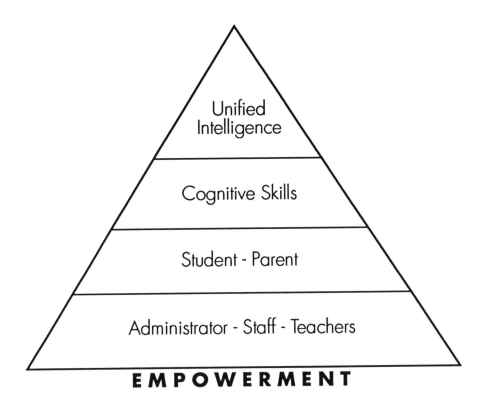

EMPOWERMENT

Phase Forward Education

In order to create learning models that can accommodate a variety of teaching personalities, as well as social, cultural, and ethnic backgrounds, a reframing of lifelong learning has been necessary. At the Institute for Music, Health, and Education in Boulder, Colorado, and the Creativity Center in Kalispell, Montana, the authors have explored how to establish a viewpoint of education that is based on an organic, natural growth of mind and body skills.

The Phase Forward Education model was created to develop powerful, exciting, and creative education for students, teachers, and administrators. The model depicts a discovery of the creative potential that enhances learning. The process begins with an empowerment of teachers, administrators, and staff and then moves forward to students and methods. Through this process, a unified sense of intelligence is created. Each of the four levels in the model has specific goals to meet the needs of all who are engaged in the learning process.

```
┌─────────────────────────────────────┐
│     Administrator - Staff - Teachers  │
└─────────────────────────────────────┘
```

E M P O W E R M E N T

Level I

✦ To empower teachers, administrators, and staff with the knowledge that their potential has powerful uses to release stress, boredom, and nonuseful repetition

✦ To establish a variety of human resources from the talents that exist within the faculty

✦ To allow the staff and faculty to see each other in creative forms of communication that enhance interest, enthusiasm, and the facility to improve their work

✦ To create ways for the administrative staff and faculty to bond while eliciting more concern for each student, no matter what the course of study

The activities within this book are guidelines to help teachers develop a recognition of the rhythms that strengthen their teaching abilities, so that they can discover teaching techniques that build their creative potential. It is essential that teachers stay empowered.

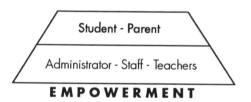

E M P O W E R M E N T

Level II

✦ To develop learning techniques that honor the valuable talents, intelligences, and learning styles of each student

✦ To recognize learning approaches that enhance a student's interest in school and learning

- ✦ To understand some of the basic functions of the brain and the psychology of learning that allow students to safely progress on their own learning timetable, without always having to conform to a class standard
- ✦ To develop ways to encourage parents to communicate more effectively with their children about education and the development of healthy study patterns

Many of the activities at the end of the chapters present creative, rhythmic, and musical ways to help students and adults to explore their own natural potential.

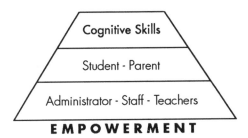

Level III

- ✦ To use the methods and curriculum suggested by the school system, administration, and teachers as a structure for the development of creative thought and intelligence
- ✦ To create a learning environment that provides a sense of safety and excitement for learning and encourages positive experiences that build cognitive, emotional, spiritual, and physical skills

When teachers and parents have explored their own creative potential, it becomes easier to enhance the creative impulse within students. Accelerated memory techniques, forms of imagery, and creative expression become tools that increase the speed, enjoyment, and retention of cognitive education. The activities in this book are successful examples of activities that foster creativity within cognitive skills. With these as models, teachers can create their own most appropriate and comfortable activities.

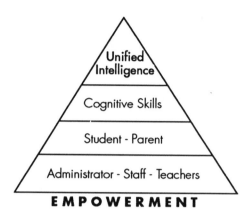

Unified Intelligence

Cognitive Skills

Student - Parent

Administrator - Staff - Teachers

EMPOWERMENT

Level IV

✦ To unify intelligence, knowledge, and experience in ways that create a continuity between education, home, and creative entertainment or sports

✦ To see each part of the learning and educational experience as a part of a lifelong investment

✦ To celebrate the integrated use of mind and body for a healthy, creative, and spirited life

✦ To create a sense of global connectedness with the earth and the respective rhythms of learning in all children

Relevant brain and learning research is expanding at a phenomenal rate, and teachers must have easy access to this information. In the Phase Forward Education project, the vital left-brain philosophy is integrated with the joyous creativity of the right brain and limbic brain, blending theoretical, academic information with practical activities. Through the stimulating ideas in the texts at the beginning of each chapter and the accompanying activities for personal development, teachers will find ways to improve their own inner model of self-discovery and translate this information to learning activities for a wide range of ages.

The activities and information in this book are included to help you integrate your personal strengths with the methods used in a classroom and assist you in building a unified sense of intelligence. As each class, whether math, reading, history, or science begins to integrate music and vocal patterning, your potential unfolds new forms of awareness.

Barry Louis Polisar's song about school provides an interesting thought on what can happen when empowerment does not occur for administrators, teachers, students, and methods.

I Don't Wanna Go to School

"I don't wanna go to school,"
Tom said to his mommy.
"You know you have to go to school,"
Mom said back to Tommy.

"No one likes me there, " said Tom.
He hid beneath the covers.
"I'd rather stay in bed, " he said.
"Grow up," said Tommy's mother.

"Only little boys and girls
Ever act like you do.
Now sit up and dry your eyes,
Get dressed and tie your shoes."

Tom ducked his head beneath the sheets
And kicked his feet about.
His mother heard him whimpering
And told him not to pout.

"I can't face another day.
The children are not nice."
She wiped his cheek and told him to
Follow her advice.

"But people laugh at me at school,"
Tom told his mom again.
"The teachers will not talk to me,
I don't have any friends."

"Now, Tom, get up,"
Said Tommy's mom.
She hoped he was convincible.
"You've got to go to school," she said,
"Because you are the principal."

—Barry Louis Polisar

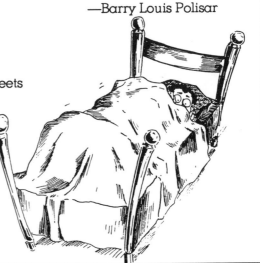

Taken from *Noises Under the Rug* by Rainbow Morning Music 1985. Reprinted with permission.

A New Look at Intelligence

The evolution of a unified, creative intelligence requires that we first examine our understanding of intelligence. The word intelligence comes from the Latin *inter leger*, meaning to choose between, and implies more than memorization and repetition of specific facts. Intelligence requires that we first *perceive* our choices in order to *conceive* of an appropriate action. We must see and learn in order to act and create. Every aspect of living involves either taking in information or acting in some way from what we know.

The simple equation: LEARNING + CREATING = LIVING defines the basic rhythm of life. Within this context, our ability to listen and respond, to intuit and observe, to feel and act, are dynamic aspects of intellectual development. The ability to perceive or grasp life through recognition of the surrounding rhythms enables us to conceive, to originate, imagine, or to give form to: to create the rhythms in our life and in our classroom.

Howard Gardner, co-director of the Harvard Project Zero, has determined there to be many modes of intelligence (Gardner 1983). He notes eight separate categories: music, logic-mathematics, linguistic, intrapersonal, interpersonal, spatial (visual), spiritual/intuitive, and bodily-kinesthetic.

These intelligences are individually unique in their development. A student who flourishes in one intelligence is no less intelligent than a student who has great skills in another. Individuals develop intelligences to a different degree but optimally cultivate them all. The educational system can nurture growth in many intelligences by providing for the development of a broad range of thinking and feeling skills.

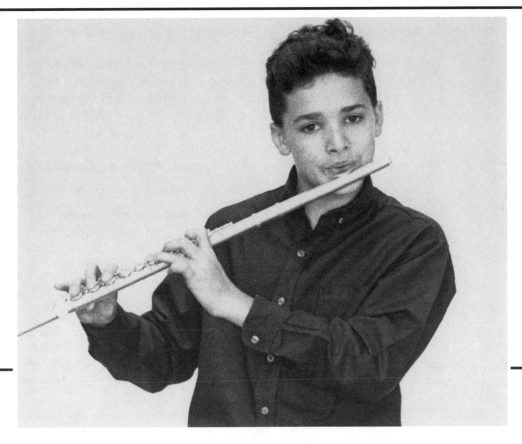

Creative Intelligence

The blending of perception and knowledge (learning) with the creative process of thought (creating) evolves thinking into creative intelligence. This high-level thinking process reaches beyond formal reasoning into a "fifth" Piagetian stage, a problem-finding stage that has historically brought critical advances into human paradigms. Today, it offers bright promises for the future in our fast-changing world.

Students expand their creative intelligence through the development of logic and creative thought processes combined with a sensitivity to the rhythms of mind, body, and emotions. These necessary skills move perceptions and ideas into creative, intelligent actions. Logical thought processes have been taught in our educational system through the development of formal reasoning skills. However, many people in our society do not feel creative. Art, music, movement, and drama have been labeled as extra activities in which the talented participate rather than models that help to develop an important thinking skill.

Creativity is often viewed as an artistic product: an object of visual art, a musical composition, a dance, or a literary work. But there is creativity in a tantalizing salad, a satisfying relationship, a new marketing idea, or any part of living. They are the result of the creative process, a problem-solving technique that can apply to any area of thought. This important process is currently being recognized in business, the health fields, and education, and is composed of the following critical steps:

Preparation:	gathering information and exploration
Incubation:	a period of processing in the mind and body
The Aha!:	an exciting point of insight
Verification:	insuring the integrity of the insight
Implementation:	putting the information and insights into a usable framework

When the creative process is used in education as a learning rhythm, the process connects the inner and outer worlds. In the first step of creativity, inner exploration accentuates the wonder of learning and leads the learner on. Students and teachers develop inner strength in their knowledge as they gather information in this preparation phase. The incubation step provides time for the mind, body, and emotions to make vital connections in the inner world, and the resulting Aha! experience manifests with a sense of excitement and inner fulfillment. These inner experiences are bridged to the outer world as insights are verified and as ideas are implemented in the final steps of the creative process.

The creative thought process becomes a rhythmic pattern that brings fresh insights and new ideas to every area of life. The perspective of problem-solving expands when a subject can be viewed in both logical and creative ways. The tension of a critically challenging field can be minimized when blended with one that is natural and integrates previously developed sensory patterns. Creative pursuits become more fruitful when the process of logical organization can be used to complete activities. The integration of the creative and logical thought processes is an important key to the development of intelligence.

Often, as the educational process develops in the middle school and secondary years from operational to concrete and formal thought, there is a tendency for less integration between subjects, learning modes, and the needs of mind, body, and emotion. It is true that math and history, music and art all have diverse cognitive needs, and different processes are necessary to achieve success in each. But when integration is maintained between these subjects, many aspects of education are enhanced and accelerated.

Logic skills have been highly developed in our teaching techniques. The development of creative intelligence begins by exploring creative arts and using them as a model for creative thinking skills. Learning to use the reasoning powers of intuition and attaining the ability to see patterns of connections in a creative manner cultivate the process of creative thought as a learning and thinking tool. The Phase Forward Education model reflects this manner of teaching and learning. This new model provides an opportunity for creativity to manifest and for the rhythm of the creative process to become a tool of lifelong learning, blending with knowledge and logic to emerge as creative intelligence.

"To cease to think creatively is but little different from ceasing to live."
—Benjamin Franklin

Activities for Teachers
Tuning Up Our Teaching

One of the first steps in tuning up our teaching is to become attuned to the rhythms within ourselves. This involves a process of inner listening in which we become aware of the rhythms of our mind, body, and emotions. In this discovery, we discern rhythms with varied emotional contexts, diverse tempos, and distinct physical and mental characteristics. The rhythmic awareness of patterns and habits provides insights into our teaching. With this knowledge, we can develop a rhythmic teaching repertoire to call upon as our needs and desires dictate.

Rhythm can initiate a pace and sense of consistency through physical, emotional, and cognitive patterning. As we create personal patterns that reflect joy in teaching, we instill a joyous rhythm in our students. By emulating rhythms that reflect varied emotional attitudes, we not only accentuate teaching but also model the potential range of inner rhythms. Combining the appropriate skills to manifest a rhythm of creativity blends the rhythms of our inner and outer worlds.

The following activities enhance sensitivity to our own rhythms and that of the students.

TWENTY-FIVE THINGS TO IMAGINE

Thoughts are things. They are signals that put the body into the necessary rhythm for the task at hand. By providing ourselves with joyous, stimulating thoughts we can creatively initiate an inner rhythm of joy.

These "Twenty-five Things to Imagine" that create joyous rhythms will empower you with more energy and excitement than two cups of coffee ever did.

Close your eyes and imagine one or two of the following experiences:

- ✤ clouds of circus ponies riding in a bright, blue sky
- ✤ jumping into the warm blue ocean from a sandy beach
- ✤ dancing with your shadow on the sidewalk on a sunny spring day
- ✤ smelling freshly baked bread coming from your kitchen
- ✤ looking at your planet Earth from outer space
- ✤ stroking the soft, fuzzy fur of a young kitten
- ✤ listening to the tinkling of wind chimes
- ✤ biting into a crisp, juicy apple
- ✤ watching the dawning of a smile of understanding on a student's face
- ✤ smelling the perfumed air in a garden of velvety red roses
- ✤ riding a bicycle downhill on a long, winding road lined with trees
- ✤ singing the "Hallelujah" chorus with a choir of two hundred
- ✤ reading the last page of an inspiring book
- ✤ sipping a refreshing drink of ice-cold water on a hot summer day
- ✤ watching red and yellow leaves as they float down from the trees gently to your feet
- ✤ enjoying the smell of the green grass, freshly mown
- ✤ receiving a certificate of merit for outstanding teaching performance from your principal
- ✤ feeling the warmth of a crackling fire on a cold day
- ✤ hearing the sound of your voice as it slides up and down with you on a roller coaster

- seeing the splendor of the ancient Egyptian pyramids rising in front of you
- conducting an orchestra performing Beethoven's Fifth Symphony
- holding a small child's hand in yours
- greeting a close friend for the first time in ten years
- turning in circles with your arms out to your side till you dizzily fall to the ground
- laughing with a friend until your side hurts

Breathe deeply and allow your positive imagination (your inner "image nation") to revitalize you during a stressful or exhausting time. Start with this list and each month replace some of the items with your own joyous imaginings.

RAPPIN' RHYTHMS

Raps are an entertaining and highly effective way of sharing information. There are different ways to create a rhythmic flow in a rap. Everyone develops a comfortable, individual style. Once you get the feel for your own style, it will become natural to read with a rhythmic flow. Experiment with reading raps in different ways, and you will soon discover a style that suits you best.

Hints for rap reading:

- Begin by feeling a steady pulse. Clap a regular beat for a minute to set the pulse and then begin to read the words while you clap.

- In raps, the rhythm of the words dictates the flow of the sound. Experiment with stressing different words or syllables within each line. You can leave slight pauses and hold one word longer than another to create a pleasant rhythmic flow. You will find that a sing-song rhythm helps to develop the flow and creates an enchanting experience.

OBJECTIVE
To explore rap techniques

DESCRIPTION
The teacher will read a rap in different ways to develop his or her own style of rapping.

SCHEDULING
10 to 20 minutes

✧ Repetition helps to set the rhythm, get students involved, and stress important points within the rap. Any of the lines or entire verses of raps can be repeated to enhance the activity. Between verses you can repeat the word *do, uh,* or even *hm* in a rap rhythm to help set the pulse and provide more time for the students to entrain to the activity.

Here is an example of a rap that can be used as a warm-up for content-oriented raps such as the Rhythmic Spelling rap in the student activities section of this chapter. The capitalized words or syllables are stressed, held longer than the others, and are read on the clap of the pulse.

✧ In this reading, some words are read before the first pulse (clap) of each line. For example: "It's" is read before you clap and say TIME in the first line and "But we'll" is read before DO in the second line.

WARM-UP RAP

It's TIME to RAP and it's REALLY a SNAP—
But we'll DO it BEST if we're NOT at REST!
So get those FINgers SNAPpin', those TOES a-TAPpin'
We've GOT to be MOVin', we've GOT to be GROOVin'.

We've GOT to JIVE just to PROVE we're aLIVE
Get those HANDS a-CLAPpin'— those KNEES a-
    SLAPpin'
MOVE those HIPS like THEY were big SHIPS
We've GOT to be MOVin', we've GOT to be GROOVin'.

It's TIME to RAP and it's REALLY a SNAP
We've GOT the RHYME, we've GOT the TIME
We're REALLY movin', we're REALLY groovin'
So HERE we GO — ON with the SHOW!

✦ In the following version a number of changes have been made in the rhythmic flow. The emphasis in line two is changed to different words ("WE'LL" and "WE'RE" instead of "do" and "not"). Words or syllables have been stretched through a whole pulse, such as "FIIIIN" (of fingers) and "TOOOOOES." Extra beats have been added to create emphasis and a new flow. The ° symbol is used here to indicate that a beat occurs in silence. "FIIIIN ° gers" in this case is now rapped over two beats, and there is a beat of silence after "SNAPpin," "TOOOOOES," and "TAPpin." "So," in line three, is in parentheses in this version to suggest that you experiment with the feel of the flow when it is eliminated.

> It's TIME to RAP and it's REALLY a SNAP—
> But WE'LL do it BEST if WE'RE not at REST!
> (So) get those FIIIIN ° - gers SNAPpin' ° those
>   TOOOOOES ° a-TAPpin' °
> We've GOT to be MOVin', We've GOT to be
>   GROOVin'.

✦ Actions can accentuate the rhythm and flow of the rap. Feel free to conduct, point, clap, or otherwise move your body, especially your hands. In the first verse, it helps to clap, snap, slap, tap, sway your hips, and otherwise move when you rap with your students to encourage them to do the same and get involved in the rhythm.

✦ You will find that impromptu changes in the text sometimes occur during a rap reading. Often these changes enhance your rapping style. You may even be brave enough to make up impromptu raps that enhance a special situation. Don't worry about rhyming if you do this; the rhythmic pulse will carry the words and students love these impromptu raps.

TOOLS OF EXPRESSION: DRAWING

OBJECTIVES
To explore art
materials for draw-
ing; to learn which
materials are most
appropriate for
various uses; to feel
comfortable with the
materials used for art
in classroom learning
experiences

DESCRIPTION
The teacher will
explore different
kinds of paper and
drawing mediums.

MATERIALS
Paper of different
weights and textures,
crayons, markers,
pencils, and oil
pastels, a cassette
tape from each of the
three categories
listed on page 218,
and a cassette
player. (If you do not
have any of these
selections, find
similar selections
from your own
personal music
library that fit into
each of the three
categories: swinging
rhythms, strong
accents, and little or
no accents.)

SCHEDULING
20 to 30 minutes

Drawing can become an important learning tool in the classroom. With appropriate drawing materials, the art activities will be successful with your students, and your comfort level with using art as a learning technique will be raised. If you have the opportunity to assist in ordering art supplies for the school year, this activity will give you suggestions for the most appropriate materials. If you do not have the opportunity to assist in ordering supplies, use this activity to help you find appropriate materials from your available supplies.

Paper

Variations in texture, weight, and size of paper can make a difference in the success of learning experiences that use art. Texture of paper varies; some are rough, others are relatively smooth, and still others are nearly slick. Optimally, your school will have some of each available. Paper weights vary as well. Newsprint is generally very light, and some paper sold as drawing paper may be almost as heavy as construction paper. Markers will bleed through some of the very light papers. Very heavy papers are usually more expensive and should be used only when needed.

Some of the activities in this book are more effective when students use large arm movements. Often students limit themselves to very small drawings. A larger sheet of paper may encourage students to fill the space with more images.

The following list of paper suggestions provides a variety of appropriate materials to choose from:

> Light paper: newsprint, layout paper (very slick)
> Medium weight paper: copier paper, white drawing paper
> Heavier weight: card stock, construction paper (heavily
>   textured), mat board
> Butcher paper: This paper, available in large rolls from meat
>   suppliers, comes in a variety of weights. It can be cut to
>   very large sizes that might be difficult to obtain otherwise.

Drawing Tools

Pencils, crayons, markers, and oil pastels all have their own unique properties for drawing. The standard number 2 pencils make fine detail lines, crayons are colorful and easily accessible, markers can add bright color and an ease of flow, oil pastels blend together but are the messiest of these tools. Since each tool has its own applications, a supply of all of these tools in the classroom will provide the most options. Markers with wide, cone-shaped tips make a variety of line thicknesses depending on whether you draw with the point or the side of the marker. Ebony black drawing pencils, which are larger and softer than the standard number 2 leads, can be held sideways to make thick lines and smeared to create a greater array of effects. The paper around oil pastels and crayons should be peeled off and the crayons or pastels broken into smaller pieces, so students can use them sideways if they choose. You may want to experiment with other mediums such as chalk pastels, charcoal, or graphite.

✧ Find paper in different sizes and textures from among your school supplies.

✧ Get a number 2 lead pencil, a drawing pencil, markers, crayons, and oil pastels, as well as any other drawing tools available from your school supplies.

✧ Now you are ready to explore combinations of drawing tools and papers. As you do the following activity, be aware of how easily the drawing tools move across the paper as you draw. Explore different ways to use each tool: making fine lines, wide lines, small dots, smearing the medium. Notice which types of paper feel best to you as you experiment.

✧ Select one of the papers and a drawing tool. Play the first musical selection on page 218 and begin to draw shapes and lines, allowing the musical rhythm to dictate the flow of the lines. Your drawing will not be a picture of an object but lines that reflect the movement of the music.

✧ Change paper and explore drawing to the movement of the music using the new paper. Continue changing paper until you have explored all of the different papers with this tool.

✧ Now, change drawing tools and play music from a different category. Explore the feel and flow of this drawing tool with the new music. Use this tool with different papers. Continue to change papers as you explore the rhythms of the music.

✧ Play the last musical selection and continue to explore tools and papers until you have used all the different tools and papers in a variety of combinations.

✧ Look at your artwork and notice which combination of tools and paper worked best for you. Did you have some favorite combinations? Were some combinations not suitable? Compare your findings to the following list of tools and suggested mediums below:

> Drawing pencils: drawing paper, newsprint, card stock, butcher paper, copier paper
> Crayons: drawing paper, newsprint, card stock, butcher paper, copier paper
> Markers: layout paper, card stock, butcher paper, copier paper (smoother textured papers)
> Oil pastels: butcher paper, mat board, construction paper, other shiny surfaced papers

TOOLS OF EXPRESSION: CLAY

Clay can be used in the classroom to provide an outlet for tension for both students and teachers and make learning more relaxed and effective. Simply work the clay with the hands or use it as an instructional tool as in the Clay Creations student activity.

Contrary to many teacher's fears, working clay in your hands does not distract the mind from focusing on learning activities. For many people, this use of clay may enhance attention. Kinesthetic students who are asked to keep still in the classroom may have a very difficult time not moving. Providing these students with clay to work in their hands often fulfills their need for movement and increases their ability to follow classroom activities.

We recommend a polyform type of clay because it is nongreasy, does not dry out, and will keep well for an entire school year. (The clay may become crumbly if you attempt to save it for the next year.) Polyform clay can be purchased in bulk from local art supply shops, from school catalogues, or directly from clay production factories. Beeswax may be used for these activities as well, and may be preferable for children under the age of eight.

If you feel the need to explore clay on your own before using it in class:

❖ Purchase a small amount of polyform clay for yourself.

❖ Work it in your hands as you read, watch television, or talk to a friend or member of your family. Notice how the clay feels in your hands. Do you find it distracting? How do you feel after you have worked it for awhile?

❖ Keep your clay close at hand at home for a week. Use it often and observe the effects it has for you.

Most people are surprised by the benefits of clay. Based on your experience, you may want to purchase some for your class. Even if you have not personally found it effective, notice which student in your class is particularly oriented to kinesthetic learning. Give your clay to this student for a week. Observe his or her use of clay and any changes in attention patterns. Does the clay provide a positive benefit?

OBJECTIVES
To discover the uses for clay in the classroom; to explore the effects that clay has as an outlet for stress; to experience the benefits clay can provide for increasing student attention

DESCRIPTION
The teacher will explore the feel of polyform clay and observe student use of clay in the classroom.

MATERIALS
Polyform clay

SCHEDULING
10 minutes for exploration by the teacher; observations of students throughout the day

You may want to purchase clay for all students in the classroom and observe their reactions and the benefits they receive from using the clay.

✦ Purchase enough clay so that each student will have a piece of clay about the size of a racquetball. Place each piece in a plastic sandwich bag.

✦ Give students a bag of clay to keep in their desk. Allow students to take the clay out and work it in their hands at different times of day. Lecture sessions, reading time, and free time are especially appropriate times to use the clay. You will find that some students just work it in their hands while others make specific shapes. You may want to allow students to select the times they wish to use the clay, especially the kinesthetic students.

✦ Polyform clay can be baked and painted as well. For a special end-of-the-year project after students have created objects from the clay, bake them at 200 degrees for 20 minutes, and paint the objects with acrylic paint. These art-works make a nice souvenir of the students' year in your class.

DYNAMIC EMPOWERMENT

✦ Select a charged piece of music that you like such as "Flashdance," "What a Wonderful Day," "That's What Friends Are For," or a theme from a favorite movie.

✦ Sit, dance, conduct, or envision the music in your own way, optimizing your energy, attention, and joy of teaching.

OBJECTIVES
To empower the teacher by rhythmically entraining mind and body; to provide an opportunity for the release of stressful body tension; to explore creative movement

DESCRIPTION
The teacher will listen to an energizing piece of music and respond to its movement.

ENVIRONMENT
A spacious room

MATERIALS
Energizing music and a cassette player

SCHEDULING
5 to 10 minutes before or after school

Activities for Students
Tuning Up with Students

A student's rhythmic sense can be developed by providing insightful opportunities to explore his or her own rhythms through sight, sound, touch, and movement. Taking the time to work and play with these rhythms strengthens and honors the importance of the inner-outer world communication skills. Tuning in to the inner world of the emotions and expressing their rhythms can be a positive method of reducing stress and energizing the class. Experiences in which both students and teachers are becoming rhythmically entrained will give teachers a chance to observe differences in how they and their students respond to the same rhythms.

The following activities allow students to begin to explore the inner rhythms and provide excellent opportunities for teachers to develop insights to the student's inner world and outer behavior.

MOVING ART

OBJECTIVES
To stimulate imagery; to develop the ability to move mental imagery into body movement and visual pictures; to encourage self-expression in movement and drawing

DESCRIPTION
The class will be divided into two groups; one to move and the other to illustrate movements.

GRADE LEVEL
Kindergarten through 4

ENVIRONMENT
An open space with freedom for movement

MATERIALS
For each student: a large sheet of unlined paper, colored markers, or pencils

SCHEDULING
20 minutes

✧ Divide your class into two groups: the artists who are given pencils or markers and paper and the dancers who are given a movement idea from the list below. (The artists are not told what the movement idea is.)

Movement List

a leaf falling from a tree
a rabbit hopping
popcorn popping
a snake slithering
a bird flying
a spinning top
a robot that moves abruptly

✧ Choose a movement idea from the list and ask the dancers to imagine being that object. After a moment of imaging, they may begin to move in a way that expresses the idea.

✧ Ask the artists to move their pencils or markers in the same way the dancers are moving their bodies. Artists make marks on their paper that reflect the dancers motions. Allow three minutes for the drawing.

✧ Let the dancers sit while the artists show their pictures. Ask the artists to guess the movement idea.

✧ Reverse the groups and ask the artists to move while the dancers draw to a new movement idea.

78

BODY MUSIC

✦ After you ask your students to stand in a circle, clap a short rhythmic pattern which they can maintain.

✦ Have them clap it repeatedly with you until the rhythm is consistent.

✦ Now, change the location and style of your clapping in the following ways and have them imitate you.

Do the rhythm:

        on the thighs
        on the head
        stomping the feet
        with the cluck of the tongue
        snapping the fingers
        blinking the eyes

OBJECTIVE
To feel rhythm and pulse throughout the body

DESCRIPTION
The teacher claps a simple rhythm pattern and students repeat it, exploring different ways and places on the body to make the sound.

GRADE LEVEL
Kindergarten through 8

SCHEDULING
5 minutes

Combine one or more of the actions so that different movements are included in each repetition. Some suggestions are:

✦ alternate between the thighs and stomach
✦ feet first, then clap
✦ alternate between clap and snapping fingers
✦ eyes blink, then tongue clucks
✦ stomp the feet, then cluck the tongue
✦ tap the head, then the thighs

Pair students and have them devise their own rhythm patterns and play them with both their own and their partner's bodies.

RHYTHMIC SPELLING

The following rap is an example of how to transform the arduous task of learning to spell into an exciting and highly successful activity. A few examples are provided, but almost any spelling words can be used in rhyme. You may use this technique for longer spelling words that are harder to rhyme by putting the spelling word at the beginning of the line with an easy-to-rhyme word at the end. This type of rap also works well for word definitions and memorization of historical dates.

✦ Students stand in a circle during the rap to enhance rhythmic movement, the sense of play, and group cohesion. The rap is most successful if you feel free to repeat sections and phrases over. Students don't mind hearing the repetitions, which improve memory. Add cues for repetition and student participation such as "What do you do? You spell it, too."

✦ For visual reinforcement, hold up a 5" x 7" card for each word with a picture and/or the spelling of the word on the front as you rap. A rhyme can be written on the back of each card. This will help you remember the words and assist in maintaining the pace and flow of the rap.

✦ Use the warm-up rap from the Rappin' Rhythms activity in this chapter to instill the rap rhythm and get students into the flow of rapping. The following two verses can be added to the beginning and end of the warm-up rap to introduce spelling:

Add to the beginning:

> It's TIME to SPELL and we can DO it WELL—
> But we can DO it BETter if we FIND the right LETter!
> But we've GOT to be MOVin', we've GOT to be GROOVin'
> We've GOT to JIVE just to PROVE we're aLIVE!

Add to the end:

> It's TIME to SPELL and we can DO it WELL
> But we can DO it BETter if we HAVE the right LETter
> So HERE we GO with WORDS you KNOW!
> We can LEARN to SPELL and DO it WELL.

✦ When students are warmed up, begin your spelling rap. Here is an example of the technique.

Spelling Rap

> HERE'S the CAT from the CAT in the HAT—
> C- a- T spells CAT, like THAT!
> I said C- a- T spells CAT, like THAT!
>
> So WHAT do you DO? You SPELL it TOO!
> C- a- T spells CAT, like THAT
> C- a- T spells CAT, like THAT!
>
> If you WANT to spell EAT it will BE a TREAT
> for E- a- T is EAT, how SWEET!
> E -a- T is EAT, how SWEET!
>
> SPELL it NOW - you TELL me HOW!
> E- a- T is EAT, how SWEET!
> E -a- T is EAT, how SWEET!
>
> We've HAD our SPELL and DONE it WELL
> But we DID it BETter when we KNEW the right LETter.
> Now it's TIME to GO but I'm SURE you KNOW
> We'll SPELL aGAIN . . . I'll TELL you WHEN!

✦ After students understand the game, have them create their own rap with assigned spelling words to share during a spelling rap session. This creative method will also help your students develop their rhythm and rhyming powers.

CLAY CREATIONS

To enhance learning by kinesthetically teaching subject material with clay; to provide a creative, refocusing break following a curriculum lesson; to blend creative expression and cognitive lessons for the development of a creative intelligence; to add fun and interest to learning

DESCRIPTION
Students will actively develop knowledge gained in curriculum lessons by making clay objects that relate to the subject material.

GRADE LEVEL
1 through adult

MATERIALS
For each student: clay or beeswax

SCHEDULING
5 to 20 minutes following a lesson or lecture

Cognitive subject material can be made more interesting and relevant when students have the opportunity to work with ideas in a creative manner. Clay can provide a multitude of opportunities for students to explore cognitive ideas in their own personal way, creating greater meaning and higher memory retention.

The following example is appropriate for any grade level studying cell structure:

❖ Have students soften their clay in their hands while you define the components of a cell.

❖ When you have provided students with the information for the lesson, divide the class into groups of two or three and have each group build a clay cell with all the appropriate components. Allow 5 minutes for the cell construction.

❖ Have the groups share their cell creations and point out the components within their cells.

This technique has unlimited applications. Listed below are just a few ideas of different subject areas for clay use. You will find many uses on your own.

Use clay:

❖ In science to make or build:
   clay ecosystems
   the parts of a flower
   neurons (then have the students connect them)
   a volcano

❖ In history to make:
        a scene from a historical time period
        various forms of transportation, showing changes
           through time
        a world of the future

❖ In mathematics to:
        make various geometric shapes
        learn numbers by making a specific number of objects
        build equations

❖ In music to make:
        whole, half, quarter, and eighth notes or rests
        an object that depicts the feeling reflected in a
           specific piece of music

❖ In health to make:
        an example of each of the four basic food groups

When you become sensitive to the rhythms and needs of your class, you will find that clay becomes an invaluable tool for providing an educational refocusing break that increases student appreciation of material and builds creative intelligence.

TWELVE DAYS OF CHRISTMAS

OBJECTIVES
To energize the class by stimulating the mind and body; to add a new dimension to a holiday favorite

DESCRIPTION
As students sing "The Twelve Days of Christmas," they will add appropriate movements to the song.

GRADE LEVEL
Kindergarten through adult

SCHEDULING
15 minutes the first time, 10 minutes the following times

This athletic version of the traditional "Twelve Days of Christmas" is guaranteed to wear out excited children, be a welcome change at the yearly holiday program, and take inches off the waists of cookie eaters and holiday gourmets.

✦ Ask students to stand and follow your movements while singing the song. On each day, hold up the appropriate number of fingers (you'll figure out 11 and 12 somehow), and cross the palms over the heart for "true love."

*"On the first day of Christmas
my true love gave to me
a partridge in a pear tree."*
Place your left hand over your head with a vertical palm on the word "partridge," then a right hand in the same position for "pear tree."

*"On the second day of Christmas my
true love gave to me
two turtle doves . . ."*
This day brings two turtle doves with their feathered flippers out at their sides. As you continue, always repeat the previous gifts at the end of each verse.

84

*"On the third day of
Christmas my true love
gave to me
three French hens . . ."*
The third day causes those three French hens to put their hands on their hips, elbows out, and do a little roly-poly tremelo with the hips and elbows in counterpoint.

*"On the fourth day of
Christmas my true love
gave to me
four calling birds . . ."*
The fourth day requires a little more coordination. With the wrists together, place your hands underneath your chin and bend your knees while leaning forward at a 13 1/2-degree angle. Now you can call for help to get out of this position.

*"On the fifth day of
Christmas my true love
gave to me
five gold rings . . ."*
The fifth day is one of repose. As you can see in the photo, the five golden rings are just a big circle made with the hands above the head.

*"On the sixth day of
Christmas my true love
gave to me
six geese a-laying . . ."*
There is no graceful way to do this. When you demonstrate, just get into your best egg-laying position and hope you don't lay anything other than imaginary eggs.

*"On the seventh day of Christmas
my true love gave to me
seven swans a-swimming . . ."*
Seven swans a-swimming takes thought, practice, and aesthetic devotion. Kneel and face the South Pole with the right hand under the chin. Meanwhile the left hand points to the North Pole behind the back and makes a duck tail. Now this may sound complicated, but remember, we are available for weekend workshops to teach this fine motion.

*"On the eighth
day of
Christmas my true
love gave to me
eight maids
a-milking . . ."*
This movement is made simply by squatting again and pulling down with the hands. Don't be so udder-ly embarrassed.

*"On the ninth day of Christmas
my true love gave to me
nine pipers piping . . ."*
Here we use the most musical of postures by assuming the stance of the effortless flautist.

*"On the tenth day of Christmas my
true love gave to me
ten drummers drumming . . ."*
By this time you have worn off 97 1/4
calories and the 10 drummers drumming just march for a moment and beat
an imaginary drum.

*"On the eleventh day of Christmas my
true love sent to me
eleven lords a-leaping . . ."*
Now things get really exciting as 25 bodies attempt lordly leaping and end up in
rather unsophisticated crashes. But never
fear, you only have to do this two times.

*"On the twelfth day of Christmas
my true love gave to me
twelve ladies dancing . . ."*
This is the most poetic of all the motions. Simply put the fingertips of the
right hand on the top of the yuletide
head, and make a wonderful full
turn in a fashionable clockwise direction.

You'll be surprised how often students ask to repeat the song. It can
take the place of your regular aerobics class and does make a nice
ending to holiday programs. Even parents in the audience are will-
ing to do the movements if the auditorium lights stay off.

CONDUCTING CREATIVITY

OBJECTIVES
To empower students by rhythmically entraining the mind and body; to provide an opportunity for the release of stressful body tensions; to experience free, creative expression

DESCRIPTION
Students will listen to an energizing piece of music and, with eyes closed, move to the sounds.

GRADE LEVEL
Kindergarten through adult

ENVIRONMENT
An open room with space to move

MATERIALS
An energizing musical selection and a cassette player

SCHEDULING
5 minutes in the morning or during an energy lull

Music has great ability to refresh and invigorate, especially when we physically move with it. Music even moves our internal body though we may not be aware of it. (Orchestra conductors have been known to lose weight during a performance and have one of the longest life expectancies. No doubt, music has much to do with this!)

Use this activity to create a sense of vitality and confidence in your students.

✧ Select a charged piece of music that your students like such as "Flashdance," Hooked on Rock Classics, a piece of break-dance music, or any of the music from the "Motion Pictures" activity, Group 2, on page 218.

✧ With eyes closed, have students stand and conduct the music using their hands first, then arms, legs, knee, foot, toe, nose, ear, head, elbows, and mouth. (Feel free to explore the rhythm with other body parts.)

✧ Have students imagine moving rhythmically with their kidneys, pancreas, liver, or other internal organs.

✧ End with whole-body conducting.

CHAPTER III

OBSERVING
INNER RHYTHMS

All fundamental responses to life are rhythmic, from the seemingly unobservable rhythms of inner language and thoughts, to the gestures of hand and body, to the movements of the eyes during listening. Language and vocal responses to outer stimulation have noticeable rhythms of tone, pulse, and mood. Every life-supporting organ in the body has a rhythm. Even the speed of thought in the brain can be measured in pulsing electrical charges known as brain waves.

Rhythmos is Latin for rhythm and is translated as "a particular way of flowing." Plato defined its meaning as "the order in the movement." From the milliseconds of muscular actions to daily sleep-wake cycles and century-long human life cycles, rhythms pulse through time, creating order in the movement of life.

It is important that professional educators explore new research and ideas to increase the possibility of becoming better teachers, learners, and parents. However, the pace of keeping up with the immense volume of important educational research may be counterproductive. More realistically, we can slow down and pay attention to our own rhythms, without judging or criticizing them. Learning to notice how they harmonize (entrain) with others and when they do not entrain but cause disharmony is an important part of creatively finding new ways to invite communication, trust, and better listening. We can also look carefully at the rhythms affecting our students and classroom flow. Developing a sensitivity to these rhythms allows us to intentionally create synchronous learning experiences.

Inner Patterns

Changes occur in the mind, body, and emotions from one moment to the next. The science of chronobiology, the study of biological rhythms, finds that while we cannot predict what will change, it is possible to predict that a change will recur regularly.

Chronobiology has uncovered rhythms with cycles of different lengths. The ultradian rhythms repeat several times during a day, while the circadian rhythms are roughly a day, and infradian rhythms are cycles with periods longer than a day. Rhythms of sleep, hunger, emotional highs and lows, daydreaming patterns, and others recur consistently within one or more of these cycles.

"I close my eyes when I want to see."
—Paul Gamarin

The chart, Rhythms of Life, displays some of the recurring rhythms within each cycle length. There are many others that affect our daily lives, and most natural systems are subject to multiple rhythm patterns of different lengths. For example, brain-wave patterns cycle in seconds, 90-minute, and daily time lengths. The synchrony between different rhythms is not a unified performance of a single rhythm but a complexity of many rhythms blended to create a richly diverse syncopation.

Rhythms of Life

Ultradian Rhythms (several times during the day)

Multiseconds:
Muscular action
Cell division

Seconds:
EEG (brain-wave rhythms)
Heartbeat
Respiration

Minutes:
Blood pressure

90-Minute Cycle:
Basic Rest-Activity Cycle (BRAC)
Urination
Hunger and oral stimulation
needs
Brain hemisphere dominance

Circadian Rhythms (about a day)

Skin and body temperature
Activity-rest patterns
Sleep-wake cycle
Hormone balance
Sense of taste, smell, and hearing
Brain chemistry
Short- and long-term memory
Muscle strength
Time estimation
Mental performance

Infradian Rhythms (longer than a day)

Weekly:
Blood pressure
Duration of the common cold

Monthly:
Sexual cycles
Moods
Pain tolerance
Fertility

Annual:
Disease susceptibility and
immunity
Birth and death rates
Depression

Centennial:
Human life cycles

Rhythm and pulse begin from the moment of conception and develop as we grow and change. In the infant, patterns of movement and rest, attention and inattention flow generally within a 45- to 60-minute cycle. This lengthens later in childhood to a 90-minute interval. The rhythm of neural brain development changes after the teen years. The daily patterns that repeat every 25.8 hours at age 20 will be shorter at age 60. Every age brings with it special patterns that have unique developmental characteristics.

Inner rhythms begin to be affected by the rhythms of the outer world even before birth. As we grow, our experiences with outer rhythms mold our development. The rhythms of our childhood emerge from a blend of sensory interactions with the environment, the expressions of our inner world, and the knowledge attained in our cognitive development as shown in The Rhythms of Childhood.

The Rhythms of Childhood

The Intellect
Memory Development through:
    listening patterns
    speaking patterns
    movement patterns
    logical, critical patterns (math)
    communication with peers
    communication with elders
    musical patterns
    inner thought patterns
    emotional patterns

The Senses
Rhythmic Reception of:
    tone
    touch
    smell
    sight
    taste
Rhythmic Response through:
    hearing and listening
    moving and feeling
    looking and seeing

Integrated Arts
Rhythmic Participation through:
    singing
    music making
    visual arts
    sculptural play
    storytelling
    poetry
    story listening
    humor
    dancing
    improvised movement

The Environment
Rhythmic Reception and Response through:
    home
    family
    environment
    nature
    pets
    friends
    religion
    economics
    television

The ability to counterpoint and blend personal rhythms with the rhythms of school, work, and social life is crucial for achieving happiness and success. When life lacks a rhythmic cohesion, the result is imbalance. This dysrhythmia can take acute forms such as autism or simple symptoms noticed in speech, kinesthetic skills, or eye movement.

Outer rhythms can stabilize rhythmic imbalance through entrainment, the process of two rhythms developing the same pulse through proximity to one another. Each of us must find techniques that help us to unify personal rhythms. Sound, art, movement, exercise, meditation, nature, and hobbies are all powerful forces altering human response.

One of the most effective entrainment tools is the human voice. As early as infancy and before birth, the impact of the human voice is great. Infants respond rhythmically in their body movements of limbs and head to the sounds spoken to them. They shift in posture and eye position when songs are sung to them or when a different language or voice is heard. When a voice is full, rich, and creatively engaging, a baby responds with great attention. When a voice does not inflect with some emotional engagement or sonic richness, the baby becomes inattentive within a few minutes. Dr. William S. Condon of the Boston University School of Medicine has observed that both listeners and speakers of all ages respond to language syllables with subtle yet predictable external body movements. Human rhythms are affected on many levels by the voice.

In the classroom, the tonality of the human voice has great potential to entrain student rhythms. The voice can soothe, irritate, excite, create boredom, or entrain attention. A change in voice tonality perks interest. The emotional texture of the teacher's voice can raise or lower a student's self-esteem. A child's irregular voice can be strengthened in a very noninvasive way by first matching the voice, pulse, and speed, then slowly bringing the entraining voice into smoothness and regularity, eliciting an imitative flow.

"What lies behind us and what lies before us are little matters compared with what lies within us."
—Unknown

Each person develops his or her own personal repertoire of pace and tempos. We may develop a fast-paced flow or a slow, relaxed pace. Our tempo changes throughout the day and from one day to the next, depending on our activities. Music has the power to entrain us to different tempos; fast-paced music increases our sense of liveliness and excitement while slow music may relax our pace.

Within the span of a lifetime, our approach to life and our pace changes. Different styles and tempos in music will speak to us at different times. While fast-paced music and rock beats may provide an entrainment and sense of satisfaction in youth, this music most often creates a sense of dysrhythmia for an adult. Conversely, slow, relaxing music is sometimes an ineffective tool for young people.

We are all intuitively aware of how music affects us. An exploration of various styles and tempos of music provides insight into the vast range of effects available. Music has great potential as a tool to help create specific moods and states of mind. An intentional use of music can allow us to develop effective and productive rhythms for work, home life, school, and entertainment.

The sounds and rhythms within music are also effective entrainment tools. Musical tones can soothe emotional imbalances and provide an avenue for personal expression. Learning can be enhanced by using musical rhythm to impose an internal pattern to which information can be integrated. Sound and rhythm can initiate brain wave patterns that encourage learning. A vocal or movement pattern repeated with music entrains quickly and easily. Think of aerobic exercises. How difficult it would be to keep the rhythmic pace of movement without the power of the music.

No one method will pattern and work for every child, teacher, or parent. Teaching and learning methods that incorporate an awareness of physiological, neurological, psychological, and emotional patterns are highly successful. These methods nurture rhythmic sensitivity and create a sense of safety. They encourage the learner to be challenged and adopt new patterns of attention and learning.

Learning Rhythms

Each person develops unique patterns for resting, thinking, learning, and creating. The synchronicity of these patterns regulate every child's and adult's sense of well-being and health. These patterns vary between individuals, but an awareness of generalized patterns can assist in the recognition of the flow within ourselves and those we teach. Rhythms of attention, memory, brain growth, and energy level fluctuations are especially important to teaching and learning.

Rhythms of Attention

The ability to focus and become attentively engaged comes in part from a biological cycle of activity and rest, which is present at many levels. Patterns of activity and rest are found in milliseconds of brain-wave focus, within individual monthly patterns of attention, and in the focus of each generation to the growth and development of society. All affect our learning ability and enthusiasm.

Infradian Attention Rhythms

The seasonal fluctuations of daylight and darkness influence emotions and the desire to participate in activities. A prevalence of darkness can cause a condition known as SAD, seasonal-affective-disorder, resulting in moodiness, depression, and varied attention for learning. People living in the extreme northern and southern hemispheres can sense a natural desire to be less active during the colder, darker months and feel a burst of energy in springtime.

Monthly rhythms also affect our attentiveness. Among them are the hormonal cycles that develop in the teen years. In these years, the dramatic fluctuations and lack of emotional stability may strongly affect learning processes. Even as adults, monthly hormonal flow affects our ability to focus and be attentive.

The infradian rhythms that span the length of a generation have impact on attention patterns. In an era when order and logic are emphasized, cultural priorities differ from an era when creative expression and individual freedom predominates. The paradigms of a society determine the attention it gives to methods of teaching and learning. Whether the survival skills that are taught will include finding food and water or obtaining a graduate degree and management training depends on the progress and values of the society.

These and other infradian attention rhythms guide our attitudes and approach to daily living in many ways. An understanding of the psychological and emotional impact of these cycles is as important to living as an appreciation of other cycles commonly taught in schools: weather, history, plant, and reproduction cycles. The emotional impact of extended periods of rain or darkness, the effect of specific foods on our concentration and energy levels, the influence of hormonal fluctuations on our mind and emotions, even the relevance of cultural paradigms to personal attitudes and habits are important aspects of living that need to be a part of the educational curriculum.

The Rhythms of the Day

Within the flow of a day, we experience physical, emotional, and mental patterns which become a part of our relationship to the world. Some of us greet the morning with a smile and great energy. Others come slowly to attentiveness, savoring the departure from sleep and entry into awareness. As we move through the day, our ability to focus evolves into a recurring pattern. Our awareness of the events around us affects our ability to work and play. In the classroom, we can see differences in student rhythms even as the first bell rings. While some students move slowly through their morning routine, others may be well ahead or even off to other activities. Some children desire and need afternoon rest while others do not.

There is a daily rhythmic flow of high and low peaks of attention and energy. Since high energy levels are strongly associated with a rise in body temperature, we can determine our own peak activation time by looking at our daily temperature cycles. Intuitively, we recognize attention patterns within ourselves and others. When not forced to follow a rigid work or school schedule, we move into the pattern most natural to us.

As seen in the Rhythms of the Day chart, most people reach the highest peak of energy around noon. However, there is variation in the flow of energy during the rest of the day. The morning-active people have high energy in the morning hours, while afternoon- or evening-active people have lower energy in the morning but higher alertness in the afternoon and evening. They may keep going long after morning people have retired for the day.

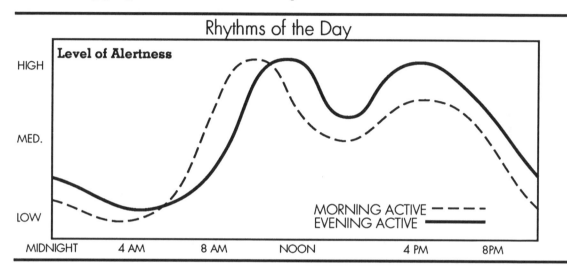

Rhythms of the Day

Level of Alertness

HIGH

MED.

LOW

MORNING ACTIVE – – – –
EVENING ACTIVE ————

MIDNIGHT   4 AM   8 AM   NOON   4 PM   8PM

There is a sudden drop in alertness from approximately 1:00 to 2:00 p.m. Although this dip has often been blamed on the noontime meal, this letdown happens even when lunch is rescheduled, specific foods eliminated, and other changes made. All of us know the frustration of trying to keep the attention of a class at this time. While proper nutrition, catnapping, stimulating music, and other energy-increasing measures will help to increase alertness, the early afternoon hour remains a time of low energy. During this energy lull, simple repetitive tasks not requiring complex thought are best. Organizational tasks, easy and entertaining movement-oriented and manipulative tasks, simple paperwork, or responsive computer work will be especially successful during this slump.

Energy levels of afternoon- and evening-active people rise in the afternoon and early evening. This is the time when they shine while the morning people feel less active. We all gradually decline in energy during the later evening, although morning people decline more quickly. For everyone, the low energy point is between 3:00 and 6:00 a.m.

99

Individual daily rhythms have varying cycle lengths. One person may have a repeating pattern every 24.2 hours while another may have a 25.8-hour cycle. We use time cues, called *zeitgebers* by chronobiologists, to reset our body clocks and comfortably agree on a schedule within society.

Among the strongest of these cues is sunlight, although natural electromagnetic fields and even bird songs act as daily time cues. Personal habits and cultural patterns create other regulating cues. When we get up at a regular time, eat meals at distinct intervals, work specific hours, and have our morning cup of coffee at a certain time, we are using cues to keep in synchrony.

Within the classroom regular patterns of activities serve as time cues. Classroom breaks and recess, lunch schedules, morning organizational times, afternoon stories, and other classroom routines become cues by which students and teachers reset their daily clocks. Experimenting with different types of routines may provide students and teachers with strong reinforcement of these important time cues. Teachers who have used music cues to change or initiate specific activities recognize the fulfillment of basic regulatory needs and a sense of comfort from these cues.

School Day Harmony

Within these patterns of attention and energy lie important keys to understanding student rhythms and developing the ability to blend them into an optimal learning situation. The traditional school day is most effective for students with morning-alertness patterns. Their energy between 8:00 a.m. and noon rises faster than afternoon- or evening-active people, who often don't begin to get warmed up until after 10:00 a.m.! Evening-active students are forced to perform peak mental performance activities when they may be least capable. Some of their highest daily energy levels may occur from 3:00 to 10:00 p.m., when school has ended for the day.

Because of this, afternoon- and evening-active people tend to be less successful or at least look less successful in their learning. Julian L. Biggers, an educational psychology professor from Texas Tech University, discovered that students with afternoon- and evening-active patterns generally had lower grade point averages than those with morning-active rhythms. Fortunately, they also tend to be flexible in their ability to adjust to different rhythms, but the overall performance of afternoon- and evening-active students does appear to be affected because the school's learning tasks are not synchronized with their natural rhythms.

There are many individual differences in rhythms, especially between morning-, afternoon-, and evening-active people. In general, morning-active people do well with cognitive, complex work in the morning but should avoid it in the afternoon. The afternoon- and evening-active students should wait till late morning for this type of work and continue in the afternoon.

Optimally, students should be free to determine their own best patterns for information input and evaluation. In reality, tests are scheduled for them, learning activities happen at set times, and students must adapt as best they can to the moment at hand. A student who appears to have concentration problems may be struggling to blend personal rhythms with differing classroom rhythms.

It is beneficial for teachers to explore the potential variations in daily schedules. Montessori-structured systems allow many opportunities for students' individual rhythms to be nurtured. Even within a traditional public-school classroom, we can allow groups of individuals with specific needs and rhythms to use their time efficiently and effectively. One teacher discovered that the best time for learning math for many of his students was 2:00 p.m., but others' prime time was between 9:30 and 10:00 a.m. This discovery led him to schedule two sessions for the presentation of math. While one group learned math concepts, others worked on math drills, depending on personal rhythm patterns. When the students' natural rhythms were nurtured, they were able to maximize their learning potential.

Teachers are also affected by personal rhythm patterns and can be more effective when they have a sense of their own rhythms. In elementary grades, teachers may intuitively set a pattern of activity that enhances their own. Thus their teaching tasks are in synchrony with their abilities. Secondary teachers have less flexibility and may be required to teach difficult subjects during low performance times or relatively easy courses during their peaks, ignoring their individual rhythmic cycles. Scheduling with sensitivity for these low and high performance times can enhance learning and teaching.

101

The 90-Minute Cycles

Even within one class period, concentration may vary. Although a teacher or speaker may be interesting and engaging, students may still have to resist the temptation to daydream or rest. This drifting attention is the result of 90-minute cycles of attention flow.

Within a 90-minute time period, activity and rest cycles flow in a rhythmic pattern that is reminiscent of our sleep patterns. This Basic Rest-Activity Cycle, or BRAC, functions whether we are awake or asleep. During sleep, it moves us through deep sleep to the active rapid eye movement (REM) stage and back again to deep sleep. In daytime, we undergo subtle changes in brain-wave patterns, eye movement, daydream susceptibility, sleepiness, and muscle tone that follow this same cycle.

This pattern may create a tendency toward fatigue every 90 minutes. In the morning hours, the length of the sleepiness period is shorter than it is in the afternoon, which accounts for our ability to nap more easily in the afternoon. A student may be earnestly interested in classroom activities but may not be able to control these innate rhythmic tendencies.

Rhythms of attention and focus may fluctuate within even shorter time periods: in approximately 4-, 7-, 15-, 30-, and 45-minute cycles. These and our 90-minute cycles peak at different times but combine to create a symphony of rhythms that becomes our state of consciousness.

The Learning State Rhythms

One of the goals of this book is to assist teachers and students in understanding how to reach and use different learning states. Lifelong learning is enhanced when students can direct their own focus and attention. Thought processes then become learning tools. Our sensitivity as teachers to the many aspects that regulate attention will help guide students toward an awareness of how to motivate their own attention and develop strong learning skills.

Creative intelligence depends upon different learning states. There are times when an active state is necessary and other times when we benefit from different states, such as relaxed alertness. As shown in the Brain Wave Rhythms chart, the electrical activity of the brain, or the rate of neuron firing, creates rhythmic brain-wave pulses that produce these characteristic states.

Brain Wave Rhythms

Brain Wave State	Wave Frequency in Cycles Per Second (CPS)	Characteristics
Delta	slow neuron firing 0.5 to 3 CPS	deep, dreamless sleep
Theta	4 to 7 CPS	unconscious sleep state deep meditation, reverie deep creative dreaming* deep creative thought*
Alpha	8 to 12 CPS	relaxation daydreaming connection to subconscious creative imagination inspiration high suggestibility information synthesis fact assimilation integrated learning state
Beta	13 to 40 CPS	logical thought processing analysis alert, active

*currently being researched

Slow neuron firing creates brain-wave pulses that are found in deep, dreamless sleep: the delta cycles. The theta pulse is faster than the delta and is generally accepted as an unconscious sleep state but can be associated with deep meditation and reverie and is being researched in connection with deep creative dreaming and thought. Alpha brain waves are faster than the theta and are produced when we relax, daydream, and use our imagination. We often experience this highly suggestive state of consciousness moments before falling asleep and just as we are waking. Accelerated learning techniques have shown this state especially important in learning. The fastest brain rhythm, known as the beta state, occurs when neuron firing and thoughts are highly active. This state of the conscious mind is predominant when we are busy talking, moving, and being active.

When the left- and right-brain hemispheres are producing similar brain-
wave patterns, a rhythmic synchron-
ization occurs. This hemispheric integration develops a coordination of
rhythms that sets the stage for accelerated listening and learning. Music,
movement, and art are especially
valuable as integrating tools in syn-
chronization.

The state of relaxed alertness is an important integrated learning state. It is
characterized by alpha and high theta
waves coordinated with relaxed body
rhythms. Accelerated learning and
listening techniques emphasize this
state. It can create optimal conditions
for learning facts, synthesizing information, enhancing memory, and
inspiring creativity. This coordination
of mind-body rhythms can be orchestrated within any classroom and with
most subjects. To obtain it, music is
used to entrain the mind and body into
relaxation and provide a stimulus that
keeps the subconscious mind alert and
receptive to new information.

The incubation stage of the creative thought process is especially
important to orchestrate. Many people develop methods of "incubat-
ing" problems and find that their Ahas! come when they have allowed time and space for their bodies and minds to unconsciously
reflect upon the situation. Running, walking, simple chores, shower
time, driving or bus time are common incubation times. The mind
often moves into the alpha state during these times, which enhances
the consolidation of information. The quiet, reflective time that leads
to the Ahas! of creative thought may not be always available to
children in their home. We can strengthen the process of creative
thought by providing time for reflection at school and allowing
students the opportunity to recognize the incubation stage as an
important part of learning.

Memory Rhythms

The ability to remember well is an essential tool for lifelong learning. Failure to cultivate memory abilities in an educational system that depends on memory can hinder the learning process. Memory can be nurtured through presentation methods and in the structure of daily classroom activities. By teaching in rhythm with the memory process, we can assure students the opportunity for success and develop positive learning skills.

Memory patterning within the brain begins with sensory memory, a one- or two-second memory of the sensation attached to a stimulus. If the event is accorded importance, it may then enter into short-term memory, a working memory that lasts for about 15 seconds. It will be encoded into the more advanced long-term memory system based again on our value of its importance. Determining the importance of an event begins with the enthusiasm of parents and teachers and is manifested in students through their excitement and joy in learning.

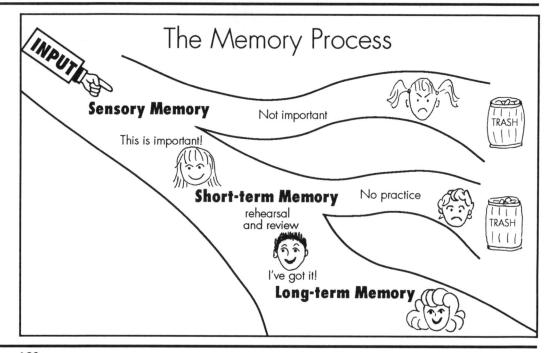

Patterns of Memory

We can use rhythm as a tool to develop memory. While short-term memories can be stored as images, they are often stored by sound, especially in the recall of words and letters. In general, short-term memory has the ability to hold about seven bits of information. When related groups of information are bonded together, they may be remembered as one bit of information, and the volume of material that can be stored increases. Information spoken in a rhythmic pattern will easily hold information together as a unit.

Rhythm and memory have effects upon our ability to comprehend, speak, and read. Much of the early learning of language is dependent upon the rhythmic presentation of words. For a learner beginning to use language, the rhythms in patterns of speech create meaning. A phrase repeated in a rhythmic pattern becomes stored in this manner within memory. We recall the phrase as a rhythmic pattern and remember it as a unit. Poor readers have been found to have difficulty with the ability to hold an auditory rhythmic pattern in memory.

The gift of a rhythmic sense to young children enhances their future reading abilities. Songs, raps, chants, and games assist in developing rhythm. Among the techniques that build upon these skills are the works of Edwin Gordon, Grace Nash, and Mary Helen Richards. When we use a rhythmic flow of intonation and space within our teaching voice, we can expect to see listening and comprehension abilities increase.

Many aspects of memory are assisted by repetition. Frequent reviews and repetition are important in long-term memory consolidation. A pattern for optimal use of review time, compiled by Colin Rose, founder of Accelerated Learning Systems in England, suggests appropriate rhythms of review to assist in long-range memory development:

✧ Initial learning session 45 minutes
(sufficient repetition to transfer
information from short-term memory
to long-term memory)
✧ 10 minutes after initial session   5-minute review
✧ one day later   3-minute review
✧ one week later   3-minute review
✧ one month later   3-minute review
✧ six months later   3-minute review

Reinforcement of information through repetition that uses rhythm and creatively engaging activities enhances motivation to remember and stimulates various areas of the brain.

Daily Memory Rhythms

Within the flow of a day there is a circadian rhythm for memory. Short-term memory processes are at their best in the morning, while information presented for long-term processing is remembered better in the afternoon. Between approximately 9:00 and 11:00 a.m. the brain is 15 percent more efficient than any other time of day for short-term memory processing. This is possibly related to greater subvocal rehearsal, the inner repetition of information. Information at this time may be remembered more easily verbatim. Therefore, tasks that depend on working memory or rote learning should be included in the morning schedule. Because the speed and accuracy of problem solving improves when the working memory load is increased, math calculations should also be scheduled. Spelling or music theory are other examples of subject matter that benefit from this heightened short-term memory ability.

Semantic or "elaborative" processing, based on understanding the *meaning* of information, is generally lower in the morning but increases throughout the day and is at its highest in the afternoon. Because this type of processing allows new information to be more readily integrated with previously stored information, the presentation of information for long-term memory is strongly reinforced. Afternoons are a good time for literature, history, and other subjects that rely on reading comprehension and content memory. This is also a good time to introduce material for transfer from short-term memory to long-term storage. Retrieval of information from long-term memory does not appear to be dependent on time of day.

There is no one recipe that will work for everyone or will even be consistent from day to day. Research is being conducted to discover more about daily rhythms, but the following Daily Flow chart suggests some general guidelines for a rhythmic order of lesson plans within a day:

Daily Flow

9:00 a.m. to Noon
- ✦ Optimum time for short-term memory processing
- ✦ Rote learning (remembering verbatim)
  - spelling
  - math calculations
  - music theory
- ✦ Complex, abstract tasks (logical reasoning)
  - problem solving
  - test reviews
  - report writing

Noon to 2:00 p.m.
- ✦ Simple repetitive tasks (low alertness and energy)
  - movement-oriented learning activities
  - manipulative work
  - simple paperwork
  - easy, responsive computer work
  - naps
  - music appreciation
  - singing
  - art projects

2:00 to 5:00 p.m.
- ✦ Optimal time for long-term memory processing (Comprehension and understanding of the meaning of information is at its highest daily level)
  - literature
  - social studies
  - history
  - studying
- ✦ High manual dexterity
  - musical instrument practice
  - sports activities
  - typing

Rhythms of Presentation

The rhythms of attention and memory give meaning to our habits of changing instruction patterns regularly to perk up minds that might be drifting into daydream or sleepiness modes. Regular breaks of free time, movement, change of teaching pace, new music, or position changes assist students and teachers through their 90-minute cycles. Accelerated learning techniques incorporate changes in activities, voice tonality, and music cues to match the 4-, 7-, 15-, 30-, and 45-minute cycles. These changes can be incorporated into a rhythmic flow within classroom presentations to create exciting and successful learning.

Although it is not possible to put learning and teaching methods into exact time frames, it is helpful to develop a rhythmic outline for lesson plans. After experimenting with a few lesson plans, a pattern of flow will evolve that can serve as a model for many subjects. In accelerated learning methods a contrast of pulse in the drills, lectures, and active and passive activities is beneficial to memory development and fact retrieval. Classroom attention span can be increased when there are a number of contrasting activities incorporating a variety of teaching materials and methods.

An optimal rhythm of learning will rotate between a focused time for information input and a contrasting time with new focus. The contrast can be a review of material, change in voice pattern, learning games, movement activities, art exercises, a personal story, a short imagery, the use of music, or other activity to either stimulate the classroom mood or relax the intensity of focus.

One of the most successful schools now using this rhythmic patterning of subject focus is Brainworks, a private tutorial school in Carrolton, a suburb of Dallas, Texas. The director, Carla Crutsinger, has instinctively developed an outstanding system that integrates accelerated learning techniques, SOI (Structure of Intellect), I.Q. testing, perceptual development skills, music, and biofeedback, plus a wide array of methods. In the Brainworks' methods every activity is directed in a

15-minute module that includes a minute to set up and a minute or two to ask questions. In an hour and a half tutorial session each student has completed six distinct activities that integrate the kinesthetic, visual, auditory, and verbal modes. The rate of learning and success is high. The use of one-on-one tutors from the local high school gifted program has created a brilliant system of interpersonal skills, creativity, and cognitive skills in a very concise rhythmic pattern.

A similar pattern for a rhythmic teaching plan, incorporating optimal attention span lengths for each age group and including general estimations for the length of focused and refocused activities is shown in the Rhythmic Teaching Plan chart.

Rhythmic Teaching Plan

Age	Concrete Informational Focused Time	Contrasting Creative Refocusing Time
4 - 5	5 - 7 minutes	1 minute
6 - 7	7 - 8 minutes	2 minutes
8 - 9	7 - 10 minutes	2 minutes
10 -11	13 - 15 minutes	2 minutes
12 - 13	15 - 17 minutes	2 minutes
14 - 18	21 - 22 minutes	2 minutes
Adult	21, 30, or 45 minutes	2 , 3, or 5 minutes

The rhythmic power of contrast within a teaching period can be experienced in lesson plans that utilize this flow. The timing of the activities may need to be decreased or expanded according to the individual class and the time of day. Within the day there will be a need for incubation times, extended creative projects, and other activities to assist with the development of learning skills.

We know that repetition of the same pattern of teaching for extended times becomes boring and ineffective. During the operational phases of development and the early stages of concrete learning, repetition and rote learning are without a doubt the best model for integrating information into ownership. Multiplication tables, alphabets, spelling out loud, and poetry are memorized in the early years through patterns. That is also true for the concert pianist, the Olympic athlete, and others who are learning to perfect repetitive skills. When there is little enthusiasm during these repetitive times, however, there is very little improvement. The improvement rate is far higher when the mind is engaged in positive visualization and creative ways of repeating the event anew each day.

The methods used in rhythmic teaching enhance many aspects of learning. The changes in the cadence and intonation of our voices alter listening and concentration abilities. Rhythmic repetition of information allows for rehearsal of information leading to increased memory abilities. The cycles within our presentation create a rhythmic entrainment. The preparation of the mind-body system creates a state of alert relaxation, and periodic changes of pace in instruction methods maintain an optimal level of attention. Our use of time cues during the day can help us maintain a synchronous flow with others. All of these techniques of rhythmic teaching blend together to create the dance of educational synchrony.

Educational Synchrony

The rhythms of our changing world are altering quickly. Our ability to adapt to new patterns is dependent upon how creative and flexible we are within our basic concrete and formal patterns. Today, Piaget would have to name a creative phase of development that takes into account the rapidity of repatterning our ability to respond, adapt, and creatively integrate new information and environments.

This flexibility of actions and abilities can be seen in our sociological history. Our great-grandmothers who could not read, write, or drive might be considered stupid in the late-twentieth-century society. They had little formal education, but their abilities in the operational and concrete worlds were outstanding. Psychological, spiritual, and physical skills were developed to remarkable levels. Needless to say, many of us would not know how to live a month without electricity, running water, a convenience store, a television, or a car. Although we have the intuitive resources to develop these skills if needed, our society has not trained us to do so.

By going faster or by quickly moving into outer stimulative modes we will not suddenly attain the adaptability necessary for better teaching and learning. Rather, by being able to observe and control the inner rhythm of each day, balancing the fast, stimulated times with slow, contemplative times, we can be successful. The flow of instructional rhythms in the classroom creates the time, space, and resonance for creative, fulfilling learning.

We now realize the importance of exercise, relaxation, balanced diets, water intake, daily doses of sunlight, and other techniques for balancing our rhythms within the daily pace. Educating children to be aware of these needs keeps them from patterning their lives around "lack." Children and adults who are in physical and emotional balance learn far better than those whose primary energy is expended in physiological and emotional imbalance and stress. Life and learning skills can be taught within a regular school day.

We now
realize the
importance of
. . . physical
and emotional
balance . . .

The Phase Forward Educational model provides a strong, resource-
ful environment while developing the empowerment of the student
through the empowerment of the teacher, administrator, and methods.
The tools of rhythmic teaching nurture the rhythms of childhood and
create a balance that is essential for unified intelligence and lifelong
learning.

The art of thinking and learning is a luxury. We live on a planet
where many people do not know how to read and write. Our global
family is still living in a dozen centuries of human realities and
rhythms. As we come closer to understanding that the physical body,
the emotional heart, and the conscious brain all have intelligences,
we realize that the greatest harmony in body and mind will come
through an acceptance and harmonization of these many rhythms
into resonance and balance.

Activities for Teachers

Tuning Up Our Teaching

When we develop a sense for our personal rhythms, we begin to recognize the source of our teaching potential. These rhythms develop into important patterns of flow. A familiarity with cycles of high and low energy and attention provides a guideline for arranging schedules and activities to accentuate and nurture our rhythms. We can isolate various rhythmic tempos within our teaching and use these intentionally to set the pace and mood of the learning environment.

Rhythmic awareness can be extended to a recognition of student learning states and classroom dynamics. Developing a rhythmic sensitivity to students allows us to match and entrain to their rhythms and direct our teaching tempo to move students toward a positive learning state.

As we develop the creative process in education, we provide a model for using both the active phase of consciousness and the relaxed alertness state. The activities in this book will assist students and teachers in discovering the different rhythms of consciousness and provide opportunities to use them in a variety of ways.

OBJECTIVE
To assist teachers in determining their daily rhythm of energy and attention

DESCRIPTION
The teacher will observe his or her physical, mental, and emotional energy and attention levels throughout the teaching day.

SCHEDULING
Throughout the activities of the day

116

FINDING YOUR TEACHING RHYTHM

The success of our teaching depends to a great degree on our ability to be in harmony with our personal rhythms. We may discover surprising patterns when we take the time to observe the rhythms of our day.

 ✧ Observe the rhythms of your day by completing your Rhythm Chart for 5 days or more. (For your convenience, you may wish to photocopy the chart.)

 ✧ Review the chart and look for patterns within your day. Where are your emotional, physical, and teaching

Rhythm Chart

Teaching Hours	7 a.m. to 8 a.m.	8 a.m. to 9 a.m.	9 a.m. to 10 a.m.	10 a.m. to 11 a.m.	11 a.m. to Noon	Noon to 1 p.m.	1 p.m. to 2 p.m.	2 p.m. to 3 p.m.	3 p.m. to 4 p.m.
Best teaching hour									
Next best teaching hour									
Average teaching hours									
Challenging teaching hours									
Difficult teaching hours									
Good physical hours									
Average physical hours									
Poor physical hours									
Best emotional hours									
Shifting emotional hours									
Poor emotional hours									

highs? Where are the lows? Can you determine a predictable pattern for your daily rhythms? To what degree are these patterns of flow related to your own personal rhythms and how are they related to your students' rhythms?

✧ Experiment with changing the daily lesson plan to boost your low periods and maximize your daily highs. Notice if students' rhythms change as your personal rhythms are nurtured. If not, observe students' rhythms carefully to determine if they need your help to create a better personal rhythmic flow.

THE RHYTHMS OF YOUR CLASS

OBJECTIVES
To observe and experiment with the rhythms of presentation; to create optimal learning experiences by exploring changes in class structure and pulse

DESCRIPTION
The teacher will observe and explore the rhythms of flow within class periods.

SCHEDULING
Throughout the day

An optimal learning experience for each class period or lesson plan requires that you focus attention on the effectiveness of your presentation and the rhythms of each class.

✧ Begin by noticing which parts of your lesson presentation or class periods have a slump. Notice what part is most challenging. Is this due to your own energy or the rhythm of the students' energy?

✧ If the class is particularly difficult or boring, or perhaps has a slow time following lunch, begin to make changes in your presentation. Experiment with pacing your voice differently. Change the location that you speak from in the room. Explore changes in the pacing of the class. Utilize the focus and refocus time suggestions from the Rhythmic Teaching Plan chart on page 112 to enhance the presentation flow.

✧ Change your lesson plans from day to day. Notice how the sense of time changes when your teaching pulse flows from creativity and empowerment. "Automatic" teaching and listening disengage empowerment.

✦ Keep a journal of your discoveries or add comments to your lesson plan at the end of each day. Review these for insights.

✦ Have your students do the Rhythms of the Day activity, page 124. You can use this information to provide ideas for altering your teaching plan to better accommodate students' rhythms.

RHYTHMSCAPES

The technique of reflecting auditory, emotional, mental, or physiologic rhythms through visual expression in "scapes" has been developed extensively by Chris Brewer and Jeanne Hamilton of the Creativity Center. Rhythmscapes helps you to develop a sensitivity to your personal pacing by increasing awareness of your rhythms as they change and flow throughout the day. Do this activity to heighten rhythmic awareness and initiate the process of intentional use of specific rhythms:

✦ Begin by making four circles on a large sheet of drawing paper. (Tracing around the end of a paper cup works well.) These will be used to make your rhythmscapes.

✦ Close your eyes and remember back to early morning before you arrived at school. What was your rhythm like? Was it jagged, smooth, energetic, tired? What color or colors would best illustrate your mood?

✦ Open your eyes and, using colored markers or crayons, fill in your first rhythmscape circle with the lines, shapes, and colors of your morning memories.

✦ Repeat the process in the remaining three circles with the following rhythms:
　　　Midmorning rhythmscape
　　　Afternoon rhythmscape
　　　Evening rhythmscape

OBJECTIVES
To allow the emotional midbrain responses to daily activities and rhythms to be seen in a visual format; to sensitize teachers to their personal rhythms

DESCRIPTION
The teacher will recall his or her rhythms from different times of day and use line, shape, and color to create a visual image of their daily flow.

ENVIRONMENT
A quiet place

MATERIALS
A large sheet of paper, crayons or colored markers, and a paper cup to trace around

SCHEDULING
20 minutes

◇ Spend a moment reviewing your drawings and answer the following questions:

How do the lines, colors, and shapes differ from one rhythmscape to another? What do your rhythmscapes tell you about your daily pace? When are your stressful times? When are your relaxed times? Do the rhythms of one place carry into another?

Are you affected by outside influences? What control do you have over these influences? Would changing them improve your daily rhythms?

Which of your rhythms have an effect upon your teaching? Do your students respond to your rhythms? What rhythms empower you and your students? Which rhythms do not? How can you alter your rhythms to improve your day?

◇ Date and keep your rhythmscapes.

◇ Repeat this activity periodically and compare previous circles with new ones to see where changes have occurred.

120

CHANGING TEMPOS

In the preceding rhythmscape activity you increased your awareness of your daily personal pace. You now have a clearer sense of how your rhythms flow through the day and of the patterns of energy your work and home life require. Your personal rhythms may or may not match the flow of your work day and home life. Music can be used as a tool to help you bridge between your personal rhythms and the demands of your day.

✧ Review your day and note when your work and home routines require you to be active and energized compared to when you may slow down and relax. You may want to use your rhythmscape drawings to provide insights.

✧ Now review your personal tempo and pace through the day. Your Rhythm Chart (page 117) will help you to understand your daily rhythmic flow.

✧ Decide when your personal energy levels do not match the optimal levels needed in your work or home life. When do you need an energy lift? When are your rhythms energetic? When would a more relaxed state be beneficial to you and those around you? Note the times of day these discrepancies appear.

✧ Review your activities during the time when you need a change of energy. Music can often be used as a background sound to alter your energy levels without any effort on your part. Be careful in using music to alter your tempo if you do not want to change the tempo of those around you in the same manner.

✧ Experiment with using music as a tool. At times when you need more energy, play music from the active styles list or a favorite tape from your personal library that provides you with a sense of energy and excitement. When you would like to slow your pace, experiment with listening to music from the passive or relaxation lists. Check your personal library for musical selections that provide you with a sense of calm and relaxation.

OBJECTIVES
To identify times during the day when your pace should be changed; to use music to comfortably change your pace

DESCRIPTION
The teacher will review the day to identify times when the use of music could assist in speeding up or slowing down his or her tempo.

MATERIALS
Musical selections from the passive or relaxing styles and the active styles lists on pages 254 and 255, musical selections from your personal music library, and a cassette player or Walkman®

SCHEDULING
20 minutes

◆ After you have experimented with using music for two or three weeks, you may want to do the rhythmscapes activity again and see if there are differences in your personal flow. How do you feel now during these points of changing energy? Has the music assisted you in altering your rhythmic flow?

HOW TO HAVE QUIET WITHOUT REALLY ASKING

OBJECTIVE
To find effective tools for focusing student attention

DESCRIPTION
The teacher will explore different methods of gaining student attention.

SCHEDULING
At any time during the daily activities

In a busy classroom when students frequently want to share ideas with each other or participate in socializing activities, the teacher's need for quiet is often disrupted. We sometimes find ourselves demanding attention or repeating a request for students to listen over and over. The following techniques can be used to acquire student attention without making demands or repeating requests for quiet:

◆ Soundbreaks. Find short snatches of music that are particularly interesting, exciting, or different. Play one for five seconds when you want the attention of the class. You may find two or three favorites that will come to be a sound cue for attention. (For more information on this technique, see Eric Jensen in the resource list in the appendix.)

◆ Say the words "quiet, quiet, please" in a singsong, rap style (qui-et, qui-et, plee—eese). Start loudly and in three or four repetitions, bring the dynamic level down to a whisper. You may find the class will join you.

◆ Change the tone of your voice to a loud stage whisper as you speak. When students' attention is focused, resume in your regular voice.

◆ Raise your hand and stand in silence as a cue for quiet. Explain to the students that when they see your hand raised, it is a cue for them to be quiet and raise their hands as well. When all is silent, continue speaking.

Activities for Students

Tuning Up with Students

As we provide students with rhythmic sensitivity, we can begin to encourage effective lifelong learning skills that contribute to harmonious and synchronous learning. We are moving from an educational priority of learning facts to a priority of establishing creative intelligence. For students, this means accepting responsibility for developing thinking and learning skills. Personal awareness of rhythms allows students to wisely orchestrate optimal learning patterns. Learning about inner and outer rhythm patterns also assists in life skills development and adds relevance to the school curriculum.

In the following activities, students will become aware of their patterns of energy and attention flow and begin to understand personal rhythms as learning tools.

RHYTHMS OF THE DAY

OBJECTIVES
To attune students to
their attention and
energy rhythms; to
initiate an awareness
of responsibility for the
development of
personal learning
skills

DESCRIPTION
Students will become
sensitive to their daily
patterns of attention
and energy levels as
they chart them for a
week and then look
for recurring patterns.

GRADE LEVEL
3 through adult

MATERIALS
For each student: five
copies of the attention
cycle chart and, if
needed, the tempera-
ture cycle chart

SCHEDULING
2 to 3 minutes each
hour while completing
the chart; 15 to 30
minutes to explore
and discuss recurring
patterns

Developing children's sensitivity to their own internal rhythms should begin early in life. By allowing time in the classroom for students to determine their natural attention and energy patterns, students will be taking the first steps toward rhythmic education and learning to use personal rhythms effectively.

In this activity, particularly relevant to student science projects, students will love the opportunity to study their own chronobiology scientifically and obtain information useful throughout their lives. Teachers gain valuable insight into each child's inner world and individual patterns of attention.

—WEEK 1

✧ To help students become attuned to how they feel at different times during the day, ask the following questions periodically:

   *"When are you tired? . . . When does your energy feel
   high? . . . When does it feel low? . . . How often do you
   find yourself daydreaming? . . . When are you particularly excited about learning?"*

✧ To help students identify their energy and attention patterns more clearly, you may want to have them also do the
   Soundscape Circles activity from this chapter.

—WEEK 2

✧ Have students keep an hourly record of their attention levels on charts each day. At the end of the week, look for a
   pattern of attention flow within each student's day. Discuss
   these with the students and compare similarities and differences between classmates. You may want to keep a record
   of these patterns for future reference.

✧ If no pattern emerges, you might use a more elaborate sys-
   tem of checking body temperatures to determine a pattern
   of attention. Temperature coincides very closely to attentiveness patterns. By charting temperature readings every
   other hour during school for three or four days, a representation of attention rhythms can be approximated.

Attention Cycle

Attention Level	8 am	9 am	10 am	11 am	Noon	1 pm	2 pm	3 pm
Active								
Alert								
Attentive								
Daydreaming								
Sleepy								

Temperature Cycle

Temperature	8 am	9 am	10 am	11 am	Noon	1 pm	2 pm	3 pm
99.6								
99								
98.6								
98								
97.6								
97								

OBJECTIVES
To explore different brain-wave states; to assist students in developing their own optimal learning state for studying; to provide insight into the use of music as a studying tool

DESCRIPTION
Students will be guided with imagery into a positive learning state and then explore the effect of different background sounds on their ability to concentrate.

GRADE LEVEL
5 through adult

ENVIRONMENT
A quiet room

MATERIALS
For each student: study materials. For the teacher: a cassette tape from the suggestions of Baroque classical music from the passive styles list on page 254, a tape for relaxation from the list on page 255, a cassette player, and a radio

SCHEDULING
5 to 30 minutes on five or more days

An optimal learning state for one person may require an acceleration of pace but for another person a slowing down. Effective studying techniques may require a combination: perhaps slow, relaxing music to settle a busy mind and body, followed by a somewhat faster but evenly rhythmic selection that maintains a state of concentration. The most satisfactory combination is individually unique and dynamic.

Empowering students with the tools for accelerated studying gives each student the opportunity to make intelligent learning choices and provides important learning skills. Students can make use of music as a personal studying tool.

Reinforcing the joy of learning with suggestions for success can be a necessary step toward effective lifelong learning. The following imagery can be used before studying and will attune students to their positive learning experiences while initiating a relaxed alertness state. Follow the introductory procedure with your students on several occasions until you sense that they have mastered the technique of establishing a state of relaxed alertness:

❖ First, ask students to close their eyes and listen as you play music from the list of musical selections for relaxation.

❖ After two minutes, read the following imagery to your students while the relaxation music continues.

"Begin by preparing your body and mind for absorbing information. With your eyes closed, slow your breathing to a regular, relaxed pace and focus only on your breath for one minute. (Allow time for the breathing before continuing.) Now let your mind drift back in time to an incident in which you experienced a great Aha! related to learning something new. It might have been about a school subject, a sport, a musical activity, or any event in which there was joy in learning. The event might have occurred today or years ago.

Spend a moment reliving this experience in its entirety. Remember the emotions you experienced. How did your body feel?. . . What did you think about?. . . Did you share the experience with someone else?. . . What did you say to them?. . . How did they look when you shared the event?. . . How did you look as you recreated the event?. . . Fully experience the event. (Allow time for students to imagine the learning event.) *Hold this memory within your mind, your body, and your emotional sense as you open your eyes and return to the present time."* (Allow the music to continue for a moment or two until students are focused again in the classroom.)

—PACE AND MUSIC

✧ After your students can readily achieve the state of relaxed alertness, conduct the following study experiment on three separate days, using the following musical paces.

   Variation 1
   ✧ Plan a study session for your students using your class subject material or have them bring study materials for this activity.

   ✧ Play imagery music from the selections for relaxation list and read the imagery to your students.

   ✧ Turn off the music about a minute after the end of the imagery.

   ✧ Have students open their eyes and begin studying in silence immediately.

   ✧ After 15 minutes of studying, ask the following questions:

"How does it feel to be learning new information?. . . How does your body feel?. . . What are the emotions you are experiencing?. . . Does the learning feel easy?"

✦ Share the feelings of the experience in group or dyad discussions, or ask students to write or draw their feelings and experiences.

Variation 2
✦ Plan a study session for your students using your class subject material or have them bring study materials for this activity.

✦ Play the imagery music as you read the imagery. Turn off the music about a minute after the end of the imagery.

✦ Now play Baroque classical music from the selections for passive styles list at low volume and have students begin to study.

✦ After students have studied 15 minutes, ask them how they felt in this learning situation. Use the questions from variation 1 and also ask:

"Does the music assist in maintaining a study rhythm?. . . How is this study session different from the previous variation?"

✦ Share the feelings of the experience in group or dyad discussions, or ask your class to write or draw their feelings and experiences.

Variation 3

✧ Plan a study session for your students using your class subject material or have them bring study materials for this activity.

✧ Play imagery music as you read the imagery. Turn off the music about a minute after the end of the imagery.

✧ Turn on the radio at a moderate volume to a popular music station and ask students to begin studying.

✧ At the end of 15 minutes of study time, again ask the questions concerning the student's learning state. Also ask:

> *"Do the radio sounds assist in maintaining a positive learning state?. . . How is this study session different from the first and second?"*

✧ Share the feelings of the experience in group or dyad discussions, or have the students write or draw their feelings and experiences.

✧ When you have reviewed the writings, drawings, or discussions of all three study experiences, ask the following questions:

> *"In which situation did you feel the most positive about your learning state?. . . Was studying easier in any of the studying situations? . . . In which situation was it easiest to maintain a focus on your studying?. . . In which state did your body feel the most relaxed?"*

✧ Suggest that students continue the experiment at home with different styles of music. Ask them to share results with their classmates.

SOUNDSCAPE CIRCLES

OBJECTIVES
To allow the emotional midbrain responses to students morning activities and rhythms to be seen in a visual format; to sensitize students to their personal rhythms

DESCRIPTION
Students will close their eyes and remember how they felt in the morning before school. Using line, shape, and color, they will create a visual image of their mental, physical, and emotional rhythms during their morning.

GRADE LEVEL
3 through adult

MATERIALS
For each student: large sheets of plain paper, colored markers, a paper cup to trace around. For the teacher: colored chalk and chalkboard

SCHEDULING
20 minutes

This activity encourages students to listen with their eyes and give form to sounds. The emotional rhythms of the day can often be seen in a student's visual expression of an aural landscape. Attentive listening skills increase as students integrate sounds through the visual and kinesthetic senses used in drawing soundscape circles.

✦ Explain that we all have an aural landscape, called a soundscape, made up of the sounds which surround us.

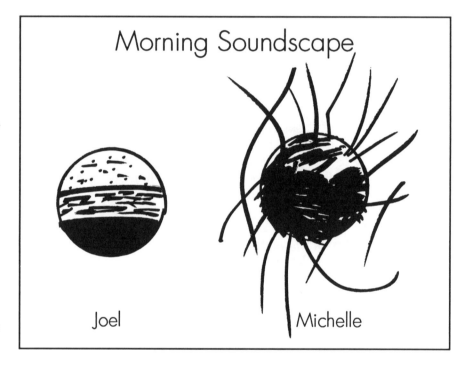

Morning Soundscape

Joel Michelle

✦ On the chalkboard draw and label a soundscape similar to Joel and Michelle's. Ask students to describe the type of morning the circles depict. Point out that Michelle's bold lines indicate a louder, sharper sound while Joel's more flowing, smooth lines represent a peaceful morning soundscape. Share the following descriptions of the two students' mornings:

"Joel described his morning soundscape as a gradual awakening with a slow increase of sound while Michelle described her awakening soundscape as abrupt and involving considerable stress and outside stimulation."

—MORNING SOUNDSCAPES

✦ Give each student paper, markers, and the cup to use for tracing a circle.

✦ Ask students to close their eyes and remember their morning with special attention to the sounds that first greeted them. Share the remembered sounds in group discussion.

✦ Now ask your students to create their own morning soundscape circle with lines and color (no words or symbols). Allow five minutes to complete the circle.

✦ Ask students to share an explanation of their soundscape drawings with the group or, if the class is large, with another student.

✦ Display the morning soundscape circles on a bulletin board.

Do the lines and colors reflect the rhythms the students described?

SOUNDSCAPE DIARY

OBJECTIVES
To provide students with an awareness of the range of rhythms and tempos within life; to give students a feeling for their personal patterns and overall tempo; to teach students a tool of inner expression; to provide a refocusing activity

DESCRIPTION
Students will create a soundscape diary by keeping a collection of various sound-scape drawings in a notebook.

GRADE LEVEL
3 through adult

MATERIALS
For each student: several sheets of unlined paper and a folder or binder, or a notebook of unlined paper; colored markers; and a paper cup to trace around

SCHEDULING
10 minutes for each soundscape

Often, patterns in our life are not obvious until we look at them in a new light. A collection of soundscape drawings provides the chance to see routines and habits with a different perspective.

✤ Give each student markers, paper, and a paper cup to trace around.

✤ Select a soundscape topic from the following list and have students spend a minute imaging the sounds they might have heard in their experiences with that soundscape.

     a morning soundscape
     a breakfast soundscape
     a getting to school soundscape
     a school morning soundscape
     a circus soundscape
     a soundscape from a friend's house
     a soundscape in the woods
     a city soundscape
     a rainy day soundscape
     a Saturday soundscape
     a radio soundscape
     a going to sleep soundscape

✤ Allow students three minutes to create a soundscape circle of the sounds they remembered.

✤ Share the soundscapes. Ask students the following questions:

"Do the colors describe the feeling of the events?. . . Can you see the sounds in the lines that are drawn in the circle?. . . How do our feelings differ from each other?. . . How are they the same?"

✤ Repeat the process each day with a new topic. (This is a nice refocusing break.) Invite students to keep their soundscapes together in a diary folder or notebook.

You might want to add your own soundscape ideas or have students think of their own.

A TIMELESS WALK

The experience of slowing down and allowing ourselves to be in a state of timelessness is a rare occurrence. Some children may not have had the experience. Teaching children the benefits of being able to create a slow tempo is part of the process of allowing time and space for incubation and consolidation of thoughts.

✧ Students and teacher sit on the floor.

✧ Ask each student to locate a point with their eyes that is about ten to fifteen feet away.

✧ Now, tell students that they are entering a time warp in which all time and movement are slowed down. They must get up and physically move toward the spot they located and then return to their place in the circle.

✧ Demonstrate and lead the timeless walk so the children will understand the technique. Because they are in a time warp, it may take as long as 10 minutes to move to their spot and return to the circle. Their movements will look and feel as if they are in a movie played in slow motion.

✧ During the walk, play gentle, slow music to aid in keeping the movements slow and flowing.

✧ When students have returned to their places, ask them:

> "What did it feel like to be in a time warp?. . . How did it feel to slow down that much?. . . Did your breathing patterns also slow down?. . . Did you feel as if 10 minutes had passed?. . . What effect did the music have?. . . Were you more aware of the music during your walk than at times when you are sitting and quietly listening to music?. . . How do you feel now?"

✧ Suggest that slow music might help students to relax or slow down at other times when they need to be quiet and relaxed. Note the level of concentration they reached during their walk. Explain that this state of mind is also beneficial during study and learning times.

OBJECTIVES
To experience a sense of slowness in time; to expand the student's repertoire of mind states by creating a mind focus similar to that of incubation; to slow down and relax the classroom tempo

DESCRIPTION
The teacher and students will move very slowly as if in a time warp.

GRADE LEVEL
2 through adult

ENVIRONMENT
An open space with freedom for movement

MATERIALS
A selection of music from the passive styles or relaxation lists on pages 254 and 255, and a cassette player

SCHEDULING
15 to 20 minutes

133

BRAVO THE CONDUCTOR

OBJECTIVES
To develop a sense of the energy levels of loud and soft sounds; to stimulate the imagination; to energize a class

DESCRIPTION
The teacher will model various body postures and gestures while students respond with a loud or soft sound to reflect the movement.

GRADE LEVEL
Kindergarten through 5

SCHEDULING
5 to 15 minutes

❖ Assume the following body postures and ask the students to guess whether these postures would best be accompanied by a loud or soft sound:

> Make your body as small as you can.
> Wildly wave your hands.
> Put one index finger to your lips in the *shhh* position.
> Reach as high above your head as you can.
> Close your eyes and be very still.
> Jump into the air.

❖ Have students vocalize your body postures using a continuous *aaaaa* sound. Conduct their volume by changing from one position to another. Students will want to take turns conducting the class through loud and soft sounds by using these body positions. See what kinds of new positions they can invent to elicit dynamic changes from the other students.

❖ Reverse the process and make *aaaaa* sounds at different dynamic levels while students make body postures to reflect the sound level. Have students take turns making the sounds while the class responds appropriately.

134

UNDER THE SPELL OF RHYTHM

Rote and repetition are creative words when they hold empowerment and energy. Every muscle in the body, each word that is uttered, and the kaleidoscopic emotional responses of a child are created by repetitive patterns. The use of rhythm enhances memory when bonded to a student's visual, linguistic, or kinesthetic patterns. Repetitious patterning can be essential in very primary learning but may also be used to ease the acquisition of more sophisticated cognitive skills.

For example, here is a suggestion for spelling, using the word "rhinoceros."

—STEP 1

✧ Say the word "rhinoceros."

✧ Now, tap a steady pulse. You may want to have students tap it with you.

✧ As you read through the following rhythmic patterns for pronouncing "rhinoceros," keep the pulse throughout (beats are shown below the spelling words in groups of four). Do each pronunciation two times and have students repeat them with you.

```
Rhi------noc----er--os
1 2      3 4   1 2 3 4

Rhi--noc-------er--os
1    2 3 4     1 2 3 4

Rhi-noc-er-----os
  1   2   3   4 1 2 3 4

Rhi---------nocer-os
1 2 3        4    1 2 3 4
```

There are dozens of patterns for every word of four or more syllables. Your students may think of others.

OBJECTIVE
To use rhythm and intonation creatively as a tool to enhance spelling

DESCRIPTION
The teacher will experiment with different ways to read and spell words.

GRADE LEVEL
1 through 6

SCHEDULING
During regularly scheduled spelling sessions

—STEP 2

❖ Spell the word rhinoceros with each letter as a beat. Each hyphen in these examples prolongs the letter by a beat.

R h i - noc- e-ros

Rh - - i n - - o c - - e r - - o s

R - h i n o - - c e r o - s

R - - h - - i n o - - - c e r o s

—STEP 3

❖ Now adjust the pitch of the spelling so that each time you spell the word it has a different melody.

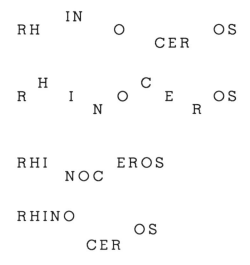

—STEP 4

❖ Combine both methods of spelling "rhinoceros" and let the letters melodically sound in rhythm.

❖ Addition and multiplication tables can be learned with similar forms of repetition.

❖ The alphabet can be sung, tapped, jump-roped, and danced in a dozen ways to enhance memory.

CHAPTER IV

RHYTHMS OF DISCOVERY

Within the fundamental goal of education in our country is the promise to nurture the thinking potential of every person. This promise optimally creates a joyful, fulfilling life with inner rewards for the individual, significant contributions to the progress of society, and an attitude of harmony and justice toward people throughout the world. Our trust that education will improve life and society manifests in the way that the learning process is nurtured, a gift from one generation to the next.

In the 1990s we are exploring the inner dimensions of ourselves for personal understanding. The educational paradigm is rapidly changing to recognize the importance of the rhythms of the inner, feeling world. As we reach into the inner realms, we find that answers come to us when we make room for the enlightening process of discovery.

The human brain is the organ through which we learn and create. As the connecting link between logical thought, feelings, and the sensations of the body, the brain orchestrates the many rhythms discussed in this book. The growth and development of the brain follows rhythmic patterns that are stepping-stones in cognitive development. The nurturing of each step facilitates the ability to perceive and create from knowledge and develop a creative intelligence. The patterns of brain growth indicate a timetable that can be used as a tool for teachers to gain insights into the most appropriate and meaningful framework for presenting information and developing skills.

To enter the world of the child is to move back in time when the very structure of the brain is different. Abilities and skills are developing in complexity. As we remember the feeling of a newly discovered ability, we experience again the dramatic Ahas! of the learning process. The magic of the discovery is followed by a desire to explore the new discovery in as many ways as possible. In the same manner that a toddler will taste, smell, throw, look at, hit, stroke, and listen to a new object, a 10-year-old whose sense of discovery is intact will want to do the same with a new concept. As we move through the brain's connecting and growing journey, we can re-experience the impact each new skill provides.

When neurologically ready, learners can entrain with information and become eagerly engaged in the various dimensions of their learning discoveries. Frustration, self-doubt, superficial understanding, awkward skill developments, and learning "turnoff" may emerge if learning demands are placed upon students before the necessary brain structures are in place. Taken as a guideline for what will eventually occur rather than as a set of rules, a neurologic timetable can provide insight into when and how learning potential unfolds for the learner. A sensitivity to neurologic rhythms can assist teachers in participating in learning as a co-discovery and give them freedom to experiment with a variety of pacing and learning enhancement tools. New paradigms for building curriculum and establishing educational goals emerge as education envisions the individuality of the learning process.

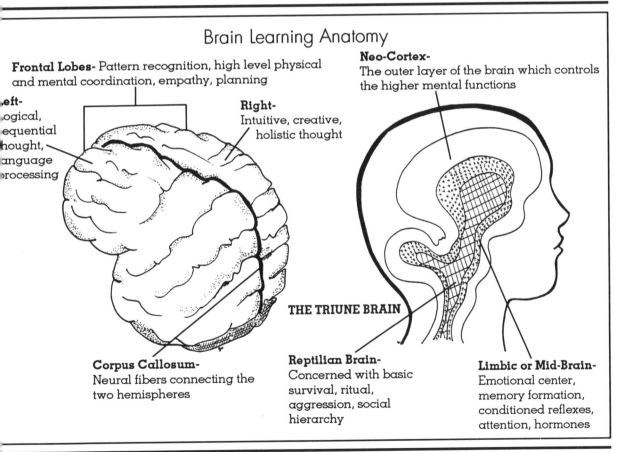

Brain Learning Anatomy

Frontal Lobes- Pattern recognition, high level physical and mental coordination, empathy, planning

Neo-Cortex- The outer layer of the brain which controls the higher mental functions

Left- Logical, sequential thought, language processing

Right- Intuitive, creative, holistic thought

THE TRIUNE BRAIN

Corpus Callosum- Neural fibers connecting the two hemispheres

Reptilian Brain- Concerned with basic survival, ritual, aggression, social hierarchy

Limbic or Mid-Brain- Emotional center, memory formation, conditioned reflexes, attention, hormones

The Rhythmic Brain

In the past, human cognitive development has been perceived as emerging along an ever-increasing continuum of complexity. Jean Piaget, a Swiss zoologist and child psychologist, carefully observed and recorded children's behavior and the development of logical thought processes. From this, he recognized that the development of thought occurs in a series of stair-step stages, increasing in complexity from stage to stage, each stage built upon the previous one. We can compare these stages to neurologic growth patterns and see a correlation that provides a basis for a pattern of alternating brain growth and rest cycles rather than a straight-line continuum of development.

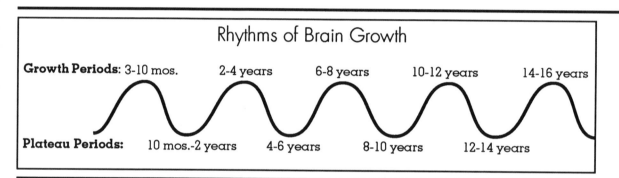

Rhythms of Brain Growth

Growth Periods: 3-10 mos.   2-4 years   6-8 years   10-12 years   14-16 years

Plateau Periods: 10 mos.-2 years   4-6 years   8-10 years   12-14 years

Periods of neurologic brain growth occur during intensive spurts indicated by increases in skull size and brain weight. Biophysicist Herman Epstein discovered this process of brain growth and named it "phrenoblysis." *Phreno* is Greek for "skull or mind" and *blysis* means "welling up." Brain growth in about 90 percent of humans occurs along a similar time line. During the growth cycles, different areas of the brain connect and grow, bringing new levels of potential ability. Each growth spurt is followed by a plateau period of virtually no growth in the brain.

For some teachers, specific information on the way in which the brain comes to new levels of understanding may be helpful. For others, the learning implications of brain growth alone will provide new insights for rhythmic teaching. Most important is the development of a sense of the brain's rhythmic role in orchestrating new information into thought and feeling.

The Growing Brain

Brain growth spurts result from increased neuron networking, the development of blood vessels to bring more oxygen to the brain, the refinement of body to brain connections through spinal cord motor fibers, the growth of supportive glial cells, and the important production of myelin.

Development begins with the formation of neurons, cells that transmit electrical signals throughout the brain. There are an estimated 100 billion neurons in the brain, each composed of a cell body, message-receiving dendrites, and message-sending axons. A quadrillion different connections are possible between brain neurons, forming the structures that permit the development of cognitive skills. As brain structures develop and new skills are learned, an increase in neuron networking occurs.

Myelination is the process of building insulation around neuron axons to provide quick and efficient transmission of electrical messages within the brain. Of particular importance is the myelination of the corpus callosum, the fibers that connect the left and right hemispheres of the brain. Corpus callosum fibers bridge specific cells from one hemisphere to specific cells in the other. When these connections become myelinated, communication between the two sides is greatly improved and new skills and abilities become available. Corpus callosum myelination begins at the back of the brain shortly after birth and progresses to the front of the brain. By age ten or eleven the process is complete.

The formation of neural connections between centers of the brain regulating specific mind and body functions contributes to brain growth spurts and provides new integrating abilities. The primary and secondary sensory areas regulate vision, hearing, speech processing, speech comprehension, and sensorimotor abilities. Other associative areas located throughout the brain integrate information between these centers, add an emotional perspective, and incorporate memory patterns. The frontal lobes rank at the highest level of function and are responsible for planning, establishing goals, integrating high-level brain functions, making judgments, and developing global emotions, such as empathy and altruism. When these various brain centers link, new abilities become available to the child.

The extension of spinal cord motor fibers upward and into new regions of the brain is an evolving process, and each new connection brings greater coordination and refinement of movements with expanded potential for planned actions.

The Rhythms of Brain Growth

Jean Piaget outlined four stages in the process of attaining logical thinking skills. A fifth stage of development is now generally accepted. Although Piaget knew nothing of neurologic brain growth spurts, there is a correlation between his developmental stages and the rhythm of neurologic brain growth. Each of Piaget's cognitive stages correlates roughly to one complete growth cycle beginning with a brain growth spurt and followed by a plateau period of slow, little, or no growth. The newly defined fifth stage also follows this pattern. The unfolding of the thought process can be seen in a new light when we recognize the neurologic basis of cognitive development. These connections are outlined in the Rhythms of Discovery chart beginning on page 150.

The learning implications of the plateau periods have not yet been fully confirmed in research, but in Phase Forward Education they are viewed as incubation times in preparation for the next cognitive advance. During the incubation period, ideas are consolidated and refined and growth occurs in other aspects of the mind and body.

The neurologic activity that occurs during the growth spurts correlated with the development of cognitive thought provides insights into learning behavior. Dr. Dee Joy Coulter, an instructor in cognitive studies at the Naropa Institute in Boulder, Colorado, has done extensive work toward understanding the behavior and development that evolve from neurologic changes. The following information about brain developments and learning implications draws heavily on her work of integrating scientific research with her more than 20 years of behavioral observations.

The Discovery Cycle

As children's brain growth and experiences move them through the learning process, their discoveries acquire greater depth and meaning. The Discovery Cycle illustrates the series of discovery modes that lead us through the various levels of cognitive thought in childhood. Each cognitive stage focuses on a particular level of discovery, explores it fully, and optimally anchors it into the learning process. This process is still valid in adulthood when new ideas are explored. We begin the discovery cycle when we become aware of something new in our surroundings, which creates a sense of discovery and excitement. As we explore further, we learn to move, verbalize, and think about this new discovery. We develop the process of analyzing and thinking of it in abstract terms. Finally, we are able to fully appreciate the interconnections between our discovery and previous knowledge.

The Discovery Cycle

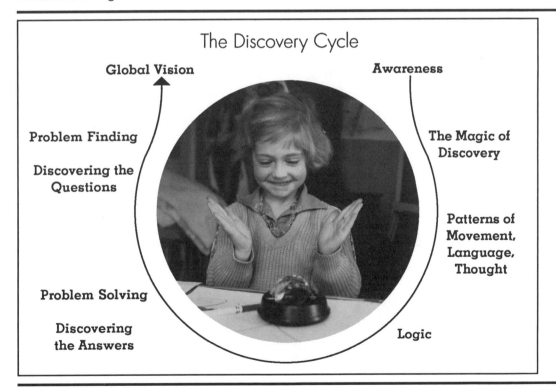

Global Vision

Awareness

Problem Finding

Discovering the Questions

The Magic of Discovery

Patterns of Movement, Language, Thought

Problem Solving

Discovering the Answers

Logic

At the adult level, the awareness of an idea may come concurrently with the recognition of higher levels of discovery, as previous experience in shaping the tools of movement, language, thought, logic, problem solving, and problem finding has anchored the process. Even younger children explore higher levels of discovery, but they do not have the insight and wisdom that will be present after future cognitive advances.

"Reason can answer questions, but imagination has to ask them."
—Ralph W. Gerard

As we journey through the brain's growth patterns and the development of cognitive thought, the discovery cycle unfolds the learning process. This is our opportunity as teachers, parents, and administrators to experience the fresh awakening that occurs at each level and gain new perspectives of our role as facilitator of learning.

In reality, the brain's growth timetable varies considerably in the ages at which changes occur. Ages used here are generalized and may vary as much as a year or more for different learners.

The Beginnings of Discovery: Awareness

Conception to 2 Years
Growth Spurt: 3 to 15 months
Period of Slow, Balanced Growth: 15 months to 2 years
Piaget Development Stage (Sensorimotor): Birth to 2 years

Brain Developments

In these first months of life, within the womb and outside of the womb, the brain develops rapidly. By six months, the infant has developed a lifetime supply of nerve cells. From conception to three months prior to birth the motor fibers in the spine have reached the thalamus, the main crossroads of the brain. These fibers continue to develop, permitting movement within the womb as well as general sensations of touch and even pain.

The auditory system is growing from five months before birth and the fetus can hear environmental tones and body sounds. The hearing system is completed by four months after birth and is one of the most highly developed senses in this early stage. The visual area also grows rapidly, completing its growth spurt by five months, when the connecting fibers between the right and left hemispheres have completed their myelination in the visual area. The infant now has the capacity for adult visual perception in short time spans.

Lastly, the frontal lobes grow in these early months of life beginning around birth and continuing for six months. The lobes grow in spurts until age six and then again beginning at age twenty-two. The motor areas have linked to the frontal lobes between one and four months of age and the infant can then experience success in reaching and grasping explorations of the outer world. From ten months to two years there is a slow, balanced brain growth with no spurts in any particular area.

Learning Potential

From conception to age two, discovery occurs as the fetus and infant gather their first outer- and inner-world experiences. Everything is new and mysterious. This is an essential time for bonding and creating a sense of safety and comfort in the child's inner world. Exposure to touch, melodic sounds, rhythmic movement such as rocking, and an array of sensory stimulators is important.

In the Piagetian sensorimotor developmental stage, sensory and motor patterning is developed as the infant learns simple motor tasks and becomes interactive with the surroundings. The infant learns to anticipate events and develops a sense for the rhythms and activities of the day. During this time, the infant explores patterns of arm and leg movement, eye tracking, visual and tactile stimulation, reaching and grasping, and auditory patterning.

The Magic of Discovery: Developing Patterns of Movement and Language

2 to 6 years
Growth Spurt: 2 to 4 years
Plateau Period: 4 to 6 years
Piaget Developmental Stage: Preoperational (ages 2 to 7)

Brain Developments

Now the brain enters a rhythm of growth in the areas necessary for language acquisition and sensorimotor coordination. Language development stems from growth in the auditory speech sounds system and the frontal lobes. The child's use of interactive language expands as myelination occurs between the speech production and speech comprehension areas of the brain.

The corpus callosum myelinates at the sensorimotor cortex, allowing improved coordination of movement between the left and right sides of the body. The visual and auditory areas begin to link directly to the motor regions, and the child can begin to coordinate actions with what is seen and heard. When the spinal cord motor connections reach the frontal lobes around age four, the child can plan more complicated, smoother movements than before and imitate movements more accurately. The growth of the frontal lobes between birth and age six is extremely important to the development of thinking skills.

Learning Potential

The inner and outer worlds have begun to take shape at age two and the child eagerly explores these worlds, led on by the magic and excitement of discovery. Between two and six discoveries are especially focused on experiences of patterning movement, speech, and world perceptions. During this time, children develop the intention to regulate their own behavior. It is the era of exploring personal will through body and muscles.

Piaget called the period from age two to seven preoperational, referring to the child's active level of interaction with the environment but lack of adult logic thought processes. Others have called this the age of the "magical child" because of children's ability to verbalize and act out their fantasy-logic. Because they cannot fit their reality into abstract logic, their deductions of what their perceptions mean and how they relate to life often appear humorous to the adult. Logical, sequential thought will not develop until further myelination occurs in the corpus callosum.

While the child's world does not match the adult perception of reality, it does contain an important, creative quality of recognizing patterns and connections. Nurturing this natural ability to see the whole picture becomes especially important to the development of problem-finding skills and creative intelligence later in life.

The frontal lobes are the center for pattern recognition, and their growth during this time is critical. The frontal lobes attend to the simultaneous processing of information and variables. In a sense, they become like an orchestra conductor who hears the end result of the individual parts, who can detect and bring out the important patterns and can instill compassion into the structure of the music. In these ways, the frontal lobes are extremely important in life's symphony. The frontal lobes are also the center for empathy and altruism, and if these traits are cultivated by parents and teachers at this time, the expression of these qualities emerges around age thirteen or fourteen.

Learning from two to six is thoroughly linked to movement. The young child cannot even stop incoming information from being expressed as outward-moving activities because neurologic linkages are simple, direct connections between the body and brain centers: auditory to body, visual to body. In order for actual learning to occur childrens' bodies must participate in physical experiences. Sensorimotor, visceral, experiential learning will accomplish this for the child during this cycle. Direct manipulation of objects and body movement is nearly impossible to stop at this age.

"Play teaches children to master the world."
—Jean Piaget

Almost any type of movement-oriented learning will match the neurologic capabilities of this age. Combining simple rhythms with information in raps, songs, marching, visceral phonics, or eurythmy makes the words move on and in their bodies and increases memory. Suggestions for activities include teaching math through marching or dancing numbers and geometric shape patterns. Phonics or the alphabet may be learned through bonding speech sounds to movements. Care must be taken to keep rhythm patterns simple, as complex rhythm patterns draw upon the right temporal lobe, which is not fully myelinated until the child has passed through the upcoming growth spurt. Rhythmic activities are especially important in stimulating activity within the frontal lobes.

Before the next growth spurt, the magical child may have a potent rote memory system, and he or she may appear to know concepts of phonics, math, and music notation (rhythm and pitch). Such apparent mastery is only a process of memorization and does not imply understanding of the concepts. We often feel that children at this age have a poor memory, but this may be because we have given them information to remember with their ears or eyes. At this stage, their bodies are the main pathway for memory and learning, and when they do not move with information, they have great difficulty remembering it. Children between two and six will more easily understand information when it is given as patterns rather than sequences. Cognitive understanding of concepts will not occur to any great degree until after the next brain growth spurt.

149

Rhythms of Discovery*

Brain Growth Cycles	Brain Developments
Growth Spurt: 2 to 4 years	Auditory speech sounds system begins a growth spurt.
	Frontal lobes grow and link with spinal cord motor connections.
	Connection between the speech comprehension and speech production area myelinates.
Plateau: 4 to 6 years	Corpus callosum myelinates past the sensorimotor cortex (around 4 years).
	Visual to auditory and visual to motor regions begin to link.
	Spinal cord motor connections reach frontal lobes.
Growth Spurt: 6 to 8 years	Spinal pathways become more elaborate, which initiates a multiregion brain growth spurt.
	Connections between visual, speech, and motor areas improve.
	Growth spurt occurs in skull size.
Plateau: 8 to 10 years	Corpus callosum myelination begins in frontal lobes (around 8).

*Ages are approximate and brain growth may vary in individual children. Adapted with permission from Chronological Chart of Neurological Growth by Dee Joy Coulter (*The Science Teacher* 1982)

Learning Developments	Recommendations for Teaching Strategies
Increase in language skills begins around age 2.	Speech patterning activities
	Activities that teach through movement: sensorimotor, visceral, or experiential learning
	Rhythmic learning activities using raps, teaching shapes or math through marching or dancing numbers or geometric shape patterns, visceral phonics (at 5 or 6)
Sensorimotor coordination improves.	
Coordination between sensory input and actions takes place at a more conscious level.	
Greater skill in imitating movements is attained.	
More complex movements can be planned with greater ease.	
Inner speech development begins to guide thinking.	Inner speech activities
Connections are made directly between auditory, visual, speech and motor regions.	Reading aloud (especially between 6 and 8)
Code work begins to be truly understood (around 7 or 8).	Code work: phonics, math, music notation (beginning around 7 or 8)
	Categorizing, record keeping, fact collecting, data gathering
	Middle of growth spurt, best time to start mathematics and reading
Concrete reasoning skills improve and logical thought processes develop (around 8).	Experiential activities
Hemispheric thought processes and specialization of skills become more distinct (around 9 or 10).	Art and music activities that build skills while retaining creativity
	Vocabulary building

(cont.)

Rhythms of Discovery (cont.)

Brain Growth Cycles	Brain Developments
	Auditory speech sounds system begins new growth spurt (around 9 or 10).
Growth spurt: 10 to 12 years	Corpus callosum myelination completes around age 11.
Plateau: 12 to 14 years	Brain growth occurs in areas of the brain that make high-level cognitive connections.
Growth spurt: 14 to 16 years	Growth spurt in brain and skull size occurs.
Plateau: 16 to 19 years	Major fibers in rear associative network finish myelinating.

Learning Developments	Recommendations for Teaching Strategies
Increase in auditory discrimination, vocalizing abilities, and language processing skills (around 9).	Introduction of foreign language vocabulary (around 9 or 10)
	Exploration with the voice and instruments that emphasizes sound discrimination, the ability to blend and harmonize, and dramatic activities
	Reinforcement of behavior rules, grammar, protocol
Logical thought processes become available to the student and abstract thought develops.	Activities that reinforce personal expression and creativity through experiential learning
Problem-solving abilities develop.	Activities that nurture social consciousness, living skills, and global awareness
	Practical life experiences such as community service projects, human problems, and daily needs, (especially valuable between 12 and 14)
	Activities that allow freedom to express personal ideas and emotions
	Group bonding exercises
	Exercises that shift students' focus from self-consciousness to involvement: masks, costumes, hats, lighting effects, guided imagery
Abstract reasoning improves.	Self-directed work such as research projects
Problem-finding skills begin to develop (around age 15).	Student participation in presentation of material
Ability to identify issues and ideas independently increases.	Creative thinking activities that develop problem-finding skills
Critical self-evaluation skills develop.	Activities to encourage group dynamics and communication skills
	Focused attention to specific personal talents and skills in sports, arts, or cognitive areas

The Discovery of Logic

6 to 10 years
Growth Spurt: 6 to 8 years
Plateau Period: 8 to 10 years
Piaget Developmental Stage: Concrete Operational (ages 7 to 11)

Brain Developments

Although the rhythms of neurologic growth indicate the beginning of the next growth spurt around age six, this very sensitive neurologic growth may occur any time from age six to eight. This is not a reflection of intelligence but merely a personal hereditary timetable for continued brain growth. For boys, it is likely to be later than girls. Environmental elements contribute to the speed and intensity of growth once this process begins.

The growth spurt is triggered by the development of a more elaborate set of spinal pathways. This initiates a dramatic growth spurt in many areas of the brain as brain-to-brain connections between visual, speech, and motor regions are made. The growth is so great that midway through the spurt, the skull gives way and grows in size.

Around eight years of age, the brain growth spurt slows down for most children, but two areas continue their growth. The auditory area begins a new two-year growth spurt enhancing auditory processes, and corpus callosum myelination continues until it is finally completed around ten or eleven.

The frontal lobes are the final areas where the corpus callosum myelinates. Upon the completion of the myelination, there will be a major change in the processing of the left and right brain hemispheres. Until this time, the brain hemispheres have duplicated efforts to a great degree to compensate for the ineffective communication system of the unmyelinated corpus callosum. When the neurologic bridge is completely myelinated, hemispheric specialization of skills and thought processes become much more distinct.

Learning Potential

Movement, language, and perception have taken shape for six-year-olds, and between the ages of six and ten children begin learning to process thoughts internally and understand the flow of logic. Piaget called this stage concrete, as the child's thought patterns reflect only what is experienced directly. At this point, since children cannot create their own abstract ideas, abstractions must be made concrete by physical demonstration.

Because of new connections between brain areas, the child can now link the visual stimuli directly to the auditory stimuli without having to process through the body first. This ability assists in the process of inner speech development, which must be in place to fully begin internal thought processes. When this occurs, between the ages of seven and nine, the child can begin to understand codes and symbols such as math, phonics, and music notation, a function called equivalency or exchangeability. The development of concrete reasoning skills depends upon the attainment of this function.

155

Skull growth occurs at the midpoint of the brain growth spurt and is a good indicator that brain connections have developed adequately enough to begin teaching code work. Since there is great age variation in this growth spurt, postponing codework until age eight will insure that most children have the neurologic capability to grasp the reasoning behind symbol systems.

The emphasis on early acquisition of reading, writing, math, and other symbol systems may actually cause children to develop awkward and inappropriate methods of understanding these symbol systems. Presenting this information before the necessary neurologic structures are in place does not develop intelligent thought, but instead encourages rather meaningless memorization of facts. Premature presentation may force code skills to be developed in the rear associative areas, which is not as beneficial to future cognitive developments as involving the frontal lobe structures in the process.

"A mind once stretched by a new idea can never go back to its original dimension."

—Oliver Wendell Holmes

Children can benefit from active play with code systems between the ages of six and eight. Based on imitation, rhythm, and movement strategies this type of play can bond information to the body and lay the groundwork for later understanding of symbol systems. When the code work begins, the order of presentation of symbol structures is best accomplished moving from the simplest (music notation) to the most elaborate (math, phonics), and the concrete (number based) to the abstract (letter based). The child's ability to handle music rhythm notation skills can serve as a readiness test for moving on to the next level of complexity.

156

The plateau period at nine or ten offers special opportunities, particularly in the arts. Because of the redundant nature of hemispheric processing prior to the completion of the corpus callosum myelination, access to right-hemisphere processing techniques is easy. Later on, after age eleven, the hemispheres process much more independently, and the left hemisphere develops inhibitory tendencies over the right. At nine or ten, the easy access to right hemisphere characteristics provides the inspiration to be creative while the newly attained concrete reasoning skills result in gains in technical skills. A longer attention span at this age adds the additional benefits of determination and dedication to practice. The combination of these factors allows significant advances in the arts, sports, and many other areas of study.

At nine or ten, the ability to recognize and copy subtle nuances of tone develops due to enhanced auditory discrimination and vocalizing capabilities from the continued growth in the auditory areas. Vocabulary can be greatly enriched, and students can learn to speak foreign languages without an accent. In this brain growth plateau period, practice through imitation is appropriate. This plateau period is not the time to attempt the mastery of any language system, but introduction and practice through imitation is possible. The study of dramatic voices through choral readings, Shakespearean pronunciation systems, or dialects is appropriate.

In music, students are able to combine parts, to attain command over their singing voices, and even to sing in harmony. They have the ability to blend sounds within a group and will improve with rehearsal. Dramatic abilities increase as well. Musical discrimination of sound and experiments with timbre of voice and instruments are productive. In all art forms, the student at this age is generally enthusiastic and will be eager to participate.

Finally, Piaget has accurately identified the beginnings of an understanding of rules at this age; rule-based games, guidelines for behavior, protocol in music performances, grammar, and punctuation may be introduced.

Problem Solving:
Discovering the Answers

10 to 14 years
Growth Spurt: 10 to 12 years
Plateau Period: 12 to 14 years
Piaget Developmental Stage: Formal Operational (ages 11 to 14)

Brain Developments

In the ten- to twelve-year-old there is measurable growth in skull size, from developments in the nonspecific associative areas of the brain. The growth in girls at this time is nearly twice that of boys.

The completion of corpus callosum myelination brings an end to the dual nature of hemisphere processing and the easy access to the right brain. The development and strengthening of the left brain now permits the child to handle logic and abstract ideas.

158

Learning Potential

The ten- to fourteen-year-old child now is developing the brain connections to discover how abstract thought can emerge from logic. Independent thought leads the student into an intense process of discovering how to solve problems. While younger children often have a solution for almost everything, the student between ten and fourteen will use logic and abstraction to make elegant solutions.

Between the ages of ten and twelve, the brain growth spurt allows facts and information to be brought into new levels of cognitive skills. During this growth spurt, students will begin to understand the detail of step-by-step logic. Theories of science, music, processes of history, and other sequential studies will be accepted. At the same time, it is important to nurture the intuitive, global, and experiential learning aspects that continue the development of right-brain processing abilities. Education can begin to teach the qualities and usefulness of both logic and intuitive thought processing. Skills in knowing how and when to use these processes should be introduced at this age. The following brain growth plateau between twelve and fourteen is most suited for consolidation, refinement, and maturation of the cognitive skills attained in the previous two years.

Piaget describes this stage as the onset of abstract reasoning. While the development of abstract thought is possible, research by Herman Epstein shows that formal reasoning has not been a natural outcome of our current educational process during this stage. At age eleven, only 5 percent of the population is at a formal reasoning level. By age fourteen, only one quarter of the population is at a formal reasoning level. In adults, we find that only half are fully functional formal thinkers. The percentages may be even lower for cultures that operate in a less linear mode, relying more on right-brain processing qualities of thought.

If these figures are an accurate representation of the condition throughout our country, only one-fourth of students actually develop formal reasoning skills by the age of fourteen, when Piaget determined these skills would normally be attained. Many adults still operate at the concrete level and handle only one variable at a time. This failure to develop formal reasoning skills may be the result of a failure to fully develop the concrete and preoperational stages. The need to change the methods of teaching formal reasoning skills is obvious.

The curriculum structure of seventh and eighth grades in most schools consists of a continuation of the development of higher abstract reasoning, requiring students to produce thinking skills incongruent with their brain development. This is a time when greater cognitive advances are not in the students' brain growth timetable. Between the ages of twelve and fourteen, students need the opportunity to incubate their knowledge and focus on emotional and physiological changes.

Between twelve and fourteen, the student is dominated by physiological and emotional rhythms. New facts and information can be learned during this brain growth plateau but must not be aimed at higher-level cognitive skills than the student has already achieved. To facilitate this, researchers Conrad Toepfer from SUNY at Buffalo and Herman Epstein suggest that students be tested around age twelve to determine their cognitive skill level. Much the same as kindergarten readiness tests, the test results could be used to insure appropriate cognitive advancement. A retest around age fourteen would again help determine optimal educational planning.

The ages between twelve and fourteen are an excellent time to expand and nurture the attributes of global awareness, social consciousness, and intuition in living skills, as well as the reinforcement of empathy and altruism now emerging. As a method of practicing logic skills from the previous growth spurt, the years between twelve and fourteen present a wonderful opportunity for an extension of these skills by allowing for practical experience in real-life situations. The student can incorporate logic principles into life skills in many ways: by looking at history in the context of patterns of creative human existence and futuristics, applying math principles to human problems and daily needs, and by using scientific principles in community service projects such as working with the elderly, in child development centers, with local gardening projects, or in ecological management programs. This approach nurtures student self-esteem while consolidating skills.

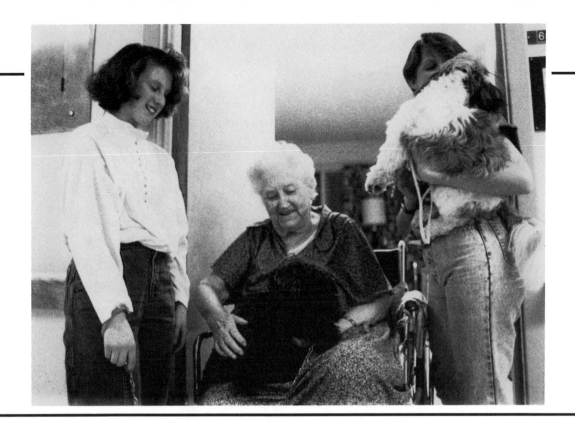

At thirteen and fourteen, bonding and creating a sense of trust are essential if learning is to occur. When asked what the most important teaching tool for this age is, a veteran junior high teacher of thirty-five years responded, "Cruising. That's what I call walking around the room while students are studying or working independently and spending one-on-one time with as many students as possible."

Because the twelve- to fourteen-year-old student is heavily involved in the development of the social self and affected by unpredictable emotional rhythms, a sensitivity to the emotional and social rhythms of the classroom is essential. Learning can begin only when these rhythms are brought to focus or used to create an understanding of the subject matter in relationship to the student. Curricula that are closely associated with student interests will enhance the acceptability of learning.

Creative teaching techniques may help to draw the intensity of the developmental rhythms of the age into subtlety and away from the self. The use of hats, masks, costumes, special lighting effects, story-telling, plays written by the students, and guided fantasy warm-ups draw the student away from the self. These techniques are beneficial for decontaminating a room and creating a special mood and excitement that stimulate the brain and enhance learning. At other times, emotional expressions may be safe and fulfilling as in the use of dramatic, emotionally powerful music, especially styles that speak to this age - a delicate age for protecting the rhythm of discovery.

Cognitive development enters a critical time period during this cycle. If the pace of the educational system is not in rhythm with students' brain development, they may experience apathy, resentment, or "turnoff" to learning. Current student problems indicate the futility of forcing continued cognitive advances between the ages of twelve and fourteen. The dropout rate is higher than desirable, especially in city schools. Suicide has become a disturbing issue. Formal reasoning is not being generally attained.

Our rhythms of educating are not blending with the rhythms of learning. The chaos of sound within our society and much of its music reflects the chaos created within the individual by this disharmony between the inner and outer worlds. We have the knowledge and tools to create a counterpoint of harmony between these worlds. Now we must learn to listen to the inner world and develop an educational process to bring the inner and outer rhythms into resonance.

Problem Finding:
Discovering the Questions

14 to 19 years
Growth Spurt: 14 to 16 years
Plateau Period: 16 to 19 years
Developmental Stage: Problem Finding (not defined by Piaget)

At this time, all major fibers in the rear associative network complete the myelination process, which triggers a new growth spurt, noted by the final growth in skull size. These changes enable young people to improve their abstract reasoning skills. The growth initiates the beginning of problem-finding skills as students develop the ability to identify issues and ideas independently. They are able to analyze and critique their own work, and envision and integrate their part into the whole picture. By age nineteen most students have the ability to develop their own personal interpretation of information and style of presentation.

"I'd rather know some of the questions than all of the answers."
—Unknown

This is the age of envisioning new questions that need answers, a discovery that is the spark that can lead to a continuous cycle of lifelong learning. Learning approached from a problem-finding basis will enhance skill development in this area. Student participation in presentation of material develops the ability to synthesize and consolidate information and is valuable as a monitor for self-improvement. Studies, reports, and projects performed with a group provide students with practice in cooperation, a skill often needed in outerworld situations.

At this stage, creative thinking emerges as the student finds new ways to combine logic and intuition. The age of communication and technology has created a condition of rapid advances. Knowledge of facts is no longer as important as creative, flexible thinking and the ability to adapt to changes and new technology. Flexible, creative thinking is an important life skills technique to nurture during these final secondary school years.

The years between fourteen and nineteen are a time when young adults are moving toward accepting full responsibility for the form their life will take. Decisions about career, vocation, and family need answers, and now young adults must begin to ask themselves questions about their goals. What are my goals for life? What are my options? How can I meet my goals? If a student's education has developed creative problem-solving techniques, the young adult will now be able to approach these important decisions with a creative intelligence.

Discovering a Global Vision

Around age twenty-two, frontal lobe development initiates a global outlook on life and encourages further development of empathy and altruism. This growth has not been found in all adults, but those at this age who experience a sense of understanding of the patterns and connections of life have probably realized this last burst of frontal-lobe growth.

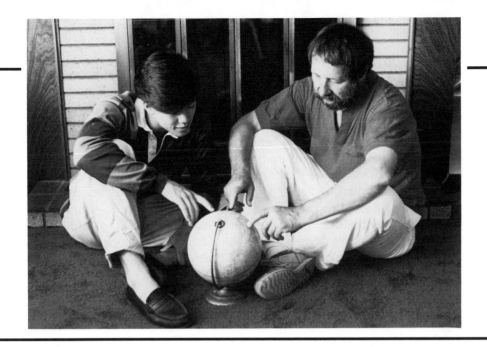

Thoughts begin to broaden in perspective after twenty-two, as a holistic view of the interconnections of life become apparent. Discovery becomes a reawakening to these connections leading to an ever-deepening search for greater meaning and understanding.

Patterns that were recognized so naturally in the preoperational stage now reappear in this stage of global thought. Combined with the skills of logic and abstract reasoning, the potential for insightful and creative intelligence is powerful. Each of the gifts from the entire triune brain complex may be honored: the sense of connection deep within the reptilian brain, the Aha! and sensitivity of the emotional limbic brain, and the potent complexity of neocortical reasoning. The empathy and altruism developed in the frontal lobes has added a moral aspect to logic. Ethics of life and the importance of the interrelationship of peoples and the earth come to fruition in this stage.

At approximately age thirty, the sensory motor fibers connecting the frontal lobes to the extremities myelinate, creating a refinement of fine motor control in fingers, toes, and facial muscles, as well as in subtle nuances of the voice. This development ushers in a golden era for skills requiring fine motor control. Adult musicians, artists, dancers, actors, woodworkers, jewelers, and others whose work or hobbies involve fine muscle control will enjoy a sense of elegant improvement in their abilities that is brought about by this motor development.

By age forty, frontal-lobe and other brain growth concludes. This does not represent the end of learning, only the end of brain growth. The brain structures are now fully developed, and the realm of thinking possibilities is great. New connections between neurons can still occur by the billions, and science is now recognizing the possibility that worn-out connections may even be replaced throughout life. There is some evidence that the connections between neurons naturally weaken and deteriorate approximately every seven years. When this occurs, our paradigms and views seem to need restructuring, reflecting the need for strengthening and restructuring within our neural connections. Many of our life activities appear to coincide with this pattern. Relationships, work, habits, and even spiritual ideals seem to fall in this seven-year cycle of development, growth, and re-evaluation.

"To raise new questions, new possibilities, to regard old problems from a new angle requires creative imagination and marks real advances."
—Albert Einstein

In the past, the formal operational thinking stage has been considered as the final stage in cognitive development. We are today recognizing a stage beyond this level. This new stage has been called postformal, problem-finding, dialectical, general-systems thinking, or global thinking, and is the culminating stage in the evolution of creative intelligence.

Postformal thought encompasses the ability to envision new questions and the skills to relate all of these into new personal and cultural paradigms. This is the thought process of the great scientists and visionaries of the past. Some of the work in researching this stage comes from H. E. Gruber, who analyzed the development of creative thought using case histories of individuals characterized as geniuses. The results are based in part on a thirty-eight-year study of intelligence development from preschool to middle age, revealing that adults do continue to advance in cognitive development past Piaget's formal reasoning stage. As education moves towards orchestrating this creative intelligence, the potential for accelerated and lifelong learning becomes more available.

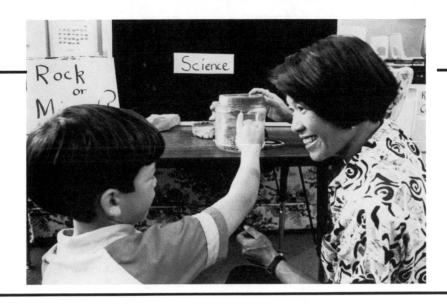

Sharing Discovery

Throughout the process of cognitive development, the act of discovery moves the learner into new levels of thought. At each cognitive step, discovery focuses in new ways.

Administrators, teachers, and parents have the opportunity to travel with students as members of their co-discovery learning teams. Each new exploration can be envisioned as an opportunity to begin the discovery cycle and travel with the student as far as his or her present level of cognitive skills can support. The more students practice moving through the discovery cycle, the more discovery is reinforced in the process of thought.

The rhythms of discovery have greater relevance to optimal learning than any method, technique, or curriculum. Teaching through the discovery process allows students and teachers to travel together on the learning journey with whatever curriculum is available. The only necessary tools for successful discovery are a sensitivity to the students' individual learning timetable and permission for students to follow their discovery process to its natural outcome. When we allow ourselves the freedom to simply be with the joy of discovery, without worry of meeting specifically set curriculum goals, the co-discovery journey can be exciting, productive, and nurturing. Lifelong learning patterns are built as the inner and outer worlds are connected by the rhythms of discovery.

"There are two ways of spreading light: to be a candle or the mirror that reflects it."
—Edith Wharton

167

Activities for Teachers

Tuning Up Our Teaching

The awareness of individual learning timetables based on neurologic brain growth validates teaching through the discovery process in education. Tuning up our teaching requires only that we develop a sense for the rhythms of discovery. Teaching actually becomes easier as we release the burden of instructing and adopt an attitude of co-discovery in our classroom. The information provided in this chapter can serve as hints to understanding learning behavior when you are unsure of a child's learning process.

The following activities offer discovery opportunities for the teacher. Approach them with the same sense of wonder you look for in your students. Allow yourself to experience learning discoveries. The insights you gain in your own discovery process will be among your most valuable tools.

TEACHING CIRCLE

Often, we do not acknowledge our goals, or we become lost in the process of attaining them. Sometimes, the frustrations we experience in teaching cause us to become disillusioned. We may not realize how much we have accomplished and how successful we have been in reaching our goals. This activity will help to reveal how we feel about our work and provide us with insights into our future.

❖ Make three circles approximately 3" to 5" in diameter.

❖ Think back now to when you first started teaching. How did you feel? What were your goals and aspirations?

❖ Using colored markers, draw these feelings in the first circle with color, line, and shape.

❖ How do you feel now about teaching? What color best depicts your emotions toward your profession? Are the lines soft or jagged or both?

❖ Draw these feelings in the second circle.

❖ Close your eyes and envision the future. How would you most like to feel about teaching? Imagine how you would feel if your teaching experience was the best it could be.

❖ Fill in the last circle with the vision of future goals.

When you are finished, spend a few moments reviewing your circles. What is the progression through your teaching experiences? How can you best make your present circle and experience match the future vision?

OBJECTIVES
To present a visual image of past, present, and future teaching goals; to allow the expressions of the right brain and limbic centers of the brain to be seen

DESCRIPTION
The teacher will recognize past, present, and future feelings about his or her teaching goals and will draw these feelings with line, shape, and color.

MATERIALS
An 8 1/2" x 14" sheet of unlined paper, colored markers

SCHEDULING
15 minutes

LEFT BRAIN, RIGHT BRAIN

OBJECTIVES
To gain an understanding of the functions of the right and left brain hemispheres; to explore how the use of rhyme and rhythm can make learning facts and information fun and easy

DESCRIPTION
The teacher will read a rap.

SCHEDULING
5 minutes during a quiet time

Jean Houston's song about the brain is an effective and rhythmic chant that easily explains some of the right- and left-hemisphere functions.

✧ Read the rap silently.

✧ Read it again aloud while tapping your foot or clapping your hands. The ° sign indicates a slight rest or a place to clap. Notice how different the meaning is when you read rhythmically.

> *Left brain, right brain ° get your head together.*
> *Left brain, right brain ° get your head together.*
> *Get ° ° ° your head ° ° ° together.*

The left brain discusses what your eyes can see,
Teaches you to read and the one, two, three.
The left brain helps you structure your day.
If you didn't have a left brain, you couldn't say
That the right brain paints pictures,
Right brain loves stories,
Right brain makes scriptures,
And the right brain dreams glories.

> *Left brain, right brain ° get your head together.*
> *Left brain, right brain ° get your head together.*
> *Get ° ° ° your head ° ° ° together.*

The right brain intuits things as a whole,
Synthesizes, integrates, believes in the soul.
The right brain visualizes patterns so strange,
If you didn't have a right brain, you'd never change.
And the left brain clock watches,
Left brain loves order.
Left brain hates blotches, and the
Left brain makes borders.

170

Left brain, right brain ° get your head together.
Left brain, right brain ° get your head together.
Get ° ° ° your head ° ° ° together.

And the corpus callosum acts like a road
For the two brains to share each other's load.
In any given second there's a quadrillion things
That the brain puts together and that's how it sings.
Whole brain wants teaching.
Whole brain needs learning,
Whole brain's outreaching.
The whole brain is yearning.

Left brain, right brain ° we'll get our heads together.
Left brain, right brain ° we'll get our heads together.
We'll get ° ° ° our heads ° ° ° together.

—Jean Houston

PERCEPTUAL I.Q. TEST

Teaching today is a complicated task. In order to best meet student needs and teach with emotional I.Q. in mind, we must have an understanding of how each child perceives information. Twenty to thirty students in a classroom can make this an arduous and time-consuming task. Here is a quick test for your students to provide you with insight into how they think.

❖ Talk to your class about the different ways we process information. Explain that some of us see images in our mind, others tend to hear the words, and some may spell or define words in their mind.

❖ Tell your students:

> "I am going to read a list of words to you. When you hear a word, notice how you perceive that word. For instance, if I say, 'airplane,' do you see a picture of an airplane or the word airplane in your mind?. . . Or do you have a feeling about an airplane?. . . Do you spell the word in your mind?. . . Or think of the word's definition?"

OBJECTIVE
To provide teachers and students with insights into students' preferred modes of perception

DESCRIPTION
The teacher will give students a test to provide insight into learning preferences.

GRADE LEVEL
4 through adult

MATERIALS
A chart of the word key displayed on a chalkboard or chart

SCHEDULING
20 minutes

171

✧ Ask for responses. Then read the following key as it is displayed on a chart or chalkboard:

IF YOU:	WRITE
See a picture of the word	the letter A
Have a feeling about the word	the letter B
Hear the spelling of the word	the letter C
Think of the word's definition	the letter D

✧ Tell your students:

   "Remember, write the letter A, B, C, or D to show how each word first appears in your mind when I read the word."

WORD LIST

1. playing	11. cat	21. bread	31. paper
2. helping	12. potatoes	22. drum	32. desk
3. rhinoceros	13. running	23. elephant	33. fighting
4. toe	14. truck	24. jewel	34. sister
5. swimming	15. eating	25. monster	35. TV
6. rose	16. pencil	26. clock	36. flute
7. book	17. blood	27. angry	37. dirty
8. grandmother	18. peaches	28. shoe	38. opossum
9. building	19. doctor	29. shower	39. exercise
10. fishing	20. music	30. raining	40. gold

✧ After reading the entire list, have students total the number of each letter. The distribution of the letters should reveal how the student processes thoughts. Students with a high number of letter A's have a visual and right-brain strength in their processing. Those with a great number of B's are strongly emotional with strengths in their limbic and right-brain processing. The students who had a high number of letter C's are very auditory. Those who responded with many D's are strongly analytical, left-brain thinkers.

✧ Share the results and learning implications with your students.

BODY STATEMENTS

The Perceptual I.Q. test provides teachers with insights into student's preferred modes of perception. Learning states are temporary physical, mental, and emotional conditions. Throughout the course of a day, a student's learning state may change. Some students may remain in one state, while others have rhythmic patterns of change, and still others change frequently as they adapt to the teaching style presented. A teacher who is observant of his or her students will be able to perceive learning states by observing student body language. Student posture, breathing, emotional expression, and eye movements provide clues to the student's current state of receptivity.

✦ During the school day, observe your students for the following body clues:

Is breathing shallow, moderate, or slow? Is the breath from the upper or middle chest, or from the abdomen?

What is the students' posture? Are shoulders back or low and rolled forward?

Are their speaking voices quick and high with little variation in tonality, moderately paced with a great range of tonality, or slow?

Are students leaning forward to hear you, fidgeting, or nodding in agreement?

Do their facial expressions say "I'm confused," or are they engaged?

Does the tonality of their voices say they are interested, or that they wonder why they have to learn this concept?

Observe student eye patterns: Do they move their eyes from side to side, are they looking up or down and to one side?

OBJECTIVE
To provide teachers with techniques of observing students' body language as a tool for discovering their learning state

DESCRIPTION
Teachers will observe student body language, breathing patterns, and emotional expressions.

SCHEDULING
Throughout the day

✧ After you have become more aware of body cues, notice how the cues combine in the following manner to create a learning state:

Visual: Good processing state for pictures, charts, movies, other visual tools, and for spelling

shallow breathing
breathe from upper chest
quick speech
high, monotone intonation
eyes up

Auditory: Good listening state

highly verbal
moderate breathing pace
breathe from midchest
moderately paced speech
wide range of tonality and texture in voice
eyes moving from side to side

Kinesthetic: Responsive to environment and personal feelings

often manipulate objects around them
slow breathing pattern
breathe from the abdomen
slow speech pattern
shoulders dropped low or forward
eyes down and to one side

✧ Familiarize yourself with these states. They will help you know when students are ready for highly verbal or auditory teaching tools, when a change of pace is needed to change the energy level of the class, and why certain students may be having trouble focusing on the task at hand.

TEACHING PATTERNS

Your patterns of breathing, speaking, tempo, and posture will affect your students' attention depending on their learning state. You can hold students' attention by matching their state, entraining them to another state, or varying your method of presentation to fluctuate between the different learning states. Here are some ideas for teaching to the different learning states:

✦ Auditory

Vary the tonality, tempo, and volume in your speaking voice.
Use vocal sounds other than speech.
Use auditory verbs:
> How does this sound to you?
> Let's tune into this.
> Does this ring a bell?

✦ Visual

Present material with visuals: on the board, videos, handouts.
Use your own body language and facial expressions to emphasize your presentation.
Use visual verbs:
> Do you see what I mean?
> Let's look at the next step.
> Now we have a clear perspective of this.

✦ Kinesthetic

Slow your speaking voice down.
Use kinesthetic verbs:
> This should give us a better handle on things.
> How does this feel?
> Do you have a sense of how this fits together?

✦ When working with one or two students at a time, you may want to match their learning state. In larger groups, a range of different verbs, changes in tempo and pace, and voice tonality should hold the attention of most students. Experiment with changes in your presentation to match the different learning states.

OBJECTIVE
To provide teachers with methods of speaking and pacing their tempo to address various student learning states

DESCRIPTION
Teachers will experiment with different speaking paces, breathing patterns, and postures.

SCHEDULING
Throughout the day

SMALL TECHNIQUES WITH GREAT RESPONSES

OBJECTIVE
To provide the teacher with techniques to improve student reading abilities through new reading patterning perspectives

DESCRIPTION
The teacher will use various visual, movement, sound, and rhythm techniques to assist in developing students' reading skills.

GRADE LEVEL
2 to 7

SCHEDULING
During regularly scheduled reading sessions

We all need a pocket full of techniques that allow us to move students' activity into diversity and new realms of attention. These techniques, based on research of eye, hand, and vocal coordination, have been developed for teaching reading. Students can suddenly perceive differences in vocal flow and comprehension when their patterns of reading change.

Experiment with these techniques to enhance a student's reading ability:

- ✧ Read aloud into the child's right ear, then the left ear.

- ✧ Have the child hold a hand from chin to ear while reading aloud.

- ✧ Keep a tapping rhythm going while the child reads.

- ✧ Turn the paper upside down and have the child read.

- ✧ Have the child read through the paper, so the words are backwards.

- ✧ Have the child read upside down and backwards.

- ✧ Printsentenceswithnospacesbetweenthewords and have the child read.

- ✧ Let the child have a worry bead, clay, or something to keep the index finger and the thumb busy while reading.

- ✧ Keep the child's right hand in a fist near the mouth as if holding a microphone.

- ✧ Change the rhythm of your voice and have the child echo as you read.

- ✧ Change from high to low vocal pitches and have the child echo.

- ✧ Read the sentences like a rap in a variety of rhythms and have the child echo.

- ✧ Spell words in rap.

Activities for Students

Tuning Up with Students

For many students, the process of learning through discovery has been replaced by waiting to be given the right answer. When students lose the ability to learn through personal discovery, they lose their own sense of trust and self-esteem. Bringing discovery back into learning may require rebuilding your students' ability to feel and see connections between their inner and outer worlds.

These activities are provided for the simple purpose of enjoying learning experiences and enhancing the process of discovery. They encourage perceptive thought and individual experience of mind, body, and emotions. Join with your students in the elements of discovery in these activities.

LEARNING CIRCLE

To express feelings about the learning process; to create a visual image of feelings; to allow the expressions of the right brain and limbic centers to be visualized; to provide the teacher with insight into student attitudes about learning

DESCRIPTION
Students will draw using line, shape, and color to express their feelings about their learning process.

GRADE LEVEL
3 through adult

MATERIALS
For each student: an 8 1/2" x 14" sheet of unlined paper, three or four colored markers, and a paper cup

SCHEDULING
10 minutes (This is an interesting activity to do at the beginning, the middle, and the end of the year. Save and compare the circles.)

Both students and teachers will gain valuable insights into each student's attitude toward his or her learning.

✧ Have the students draw a circle using the paper cup to trace around.

✧ Ask students to close their eyes and image the colors and shapes of their feelings while you ask them the following questions:

How do you feel about your learning experiences?
What part of learning do you like best?
What part of learning do you like least?
What colors and shapes illustrate your feelings about learning?

✧ When students have had a moment to image, ask them to draw their images in the learning circle using line, shape, and color. Allow several minutes to complete the drawings. You may want to share the results.

DISCOVERY MAPS

We all feel more comfortable when we know what to expect next. In learning, information may have more relevance if we understand how the information fits into the total picture. A road map that highlights the important steps along a learning journey will provide students with an understanding of the process and encourage them to recognize the importance of personal responsibility in learning. Some of your students will appreciate the use of symbols and pictures rather than a straight outline. Use this activity to let your students know where their learning path may take them.

✧ From your lesson plans, outline the four to six most important signposts along the discovery journey within a particular unit.

✧ Using colored chalk on a chalkboard, or colored markers on a large sheet of drawing paper or flipchart, draw a road. Title the road map with the subject you plan to outline. Label one end Start . . . the other end Finish, and along the road, label signposts with your main points. You may want to decorate the roadway with trees, buildings, streams, or whatever feels appropriate. For example, the following map might be used to introduce a science unit on volcanoes:

OBJECTIVES
To provide students with a visual road map of the discovery path for a curriculum unit; to give students an idea of their learning goals; to create a feeling of comfort in knowing what the flow of discovery will be for a particular unit

DESCRIPTION
The teacher will draw a road map depicting the important steps and goals from the beginning to the end of a unit.

GRADE LEVEL
2 through adult

MATERIALS
Colored chalk and a chalkboard, or a flipchart with a stand and colored markers, or large sheets of drawing or butcher paper and colored markers

SCHEDULING
5 minutes to draw the map before the start of a new unit

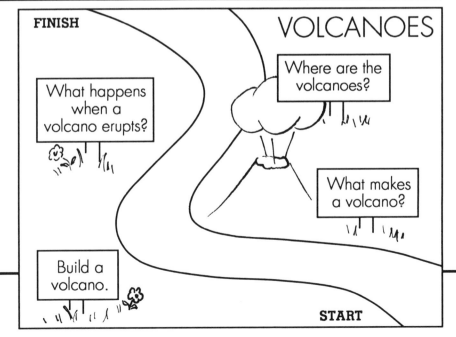

FINISH

VOLCANOES

Where are the volcanoes?

What happens when a volcano erupts?

What makes a volcano?

Build a volcano.

START

❖ Explain to your students that this is their road map on the discovery journey for the next learning unit. Refer to the map periodically as you travel through the lessons, or keep track of your progress on the map by coloring in the road as you progress on your learning journey.

❖ You may want to do a road map for more than one subject. To save chalkboard space, draw the maps on large sheets of butcher paper or drawing paper, or on a flipchart, and display these during the corresponding lesson.

❖ A road map can be made to outline the flow of the day as well.

TRACKING YOUR DISCOVERIES

A new discovery can be an exciting and rewarding experience. When we take the time to honor a discovery, we develop a sense of pride and a feeling of moving forward. By taking the time to name and identify a learning discovery, the event gains more importance, and the brain will more easily remember the discovery later. The accumulation of discoveries seen in a visual format can give students and teachers a feeling of direction and may reveal areas where more work is needed.

❖ At the beginning of a week, give each student five discovery charts. You may want to have students use construction paper to create a discovery folder to hold their charts.

❖ At the end of each lesson, ask students to review what they learned in the lesson and think about the discoveries they made. Give them a minute or two to write their most important discoveries on their chart. This can be done while you prepare for the next lesson.

❖ You may want students to review their discoveries for a moment at the end of the day, or share them with a partner. A review can be done at the end of the week as well. Do this activity for one week or continue it longer. (For older students, you will want to design your own chart with the appropriate subjects.)

OBJECTIVES
To allow students to appreciate their learning process by recognizing how much they are learning; to enhance memory retention by emphasizing their learning discoveries; to provide a visual of each student's learning process for parents, teacher, and student to see

DESCRIPTION
Students will keep a daily record of their learning discoveries.

GRADE LEVEL
4 through adult

MATERIALS
For each student: a copy of the discovery chart for each day of the week, a 10" x 20" sheet of colored construction paper (optional)

SCHEDULING
2 or 3 minutes after each subject and 5 minutes at the end of the school day

My Discoveries

Name ————————————————————— **Date** —————————————

Today I made these discoveries:

Reading	
Spelling	
Language Arts	
History, Social Studies	
Science	
Math	
Music, Art	
P.E., Health	

CHALLENGING DISCOVERY

Discovering new methods of evaluation is an important part of encouraging joy in learning and student motivation. Challenging a student to learn more about a subject provides opportunities for students to expand their knowledge. Here is a method for challenging students:

✦ Write a multiple-choice or true-and-false test for a specific lesson.

✦ Before you begin the lesson, give each student a copy of the test, but call it a challenge. Allow students five minutes to complete the challenge. Review the answers and have the students keep these in their desks.

✦ Present your lesson.

✦ Then, have the students retake the same challenge. Allow them five minutes to complete the challenge, and review their answers.

✦ Check with students to see how many they now have right. Ask them if they answered more questions correctly during the second challenge. Do your students realize how much they have learned? Encourage their feelings of accomplishment in gaining their new learning discoveries.

Providing students with a pretest gives them an opportunity to see the terminology and concepts they will be learning. When students retake the challenge, they experience a sense of accomplishment upon realizing how many discoveries they have made. Students can evaluate themselves based on their increased discoveries.

OBJECTIVES
To allow students the opportunity to realize how many discoveries they have made in a lesson; to start students thinking about a subject; to familiarize the students with terminology and concepts in a subject area

DESCRIPTION
The teacher will give students pre- and posttests to help students realize how much they have learned in a lesson.

GRADE LEVEL
3 to adult

MATERIALS
Pre- and posttests

SCHEDULING
5 to 10 minutes before and after a lesson

183

SOUND CHARADES

OBJECTIVES
To explore the subtle ways we can communicate with sound; to encourage students to think about the sounds they hear; to provide an exercise in creating form from sound; to experiment with making sounds

DESCRIPTION
The teacher will give students a scene to portray in sound and ask some students to create an auditory soundscape of the scene while other students guess what scene the sounds depict.

GRADE LEVEL
2 through 8

MATERIALS
Suggestions for sound scenes written on cards or small slips of paper

SCHEDULING
20 to 40 minutes depending on the size of the group

✧ Have students form groups of two or three.

✧ Explain to your students:

"You are going to create sounds that describe a scene I will give you. Use only sounds, and not actions, to describe your scene. You may not use recognizable words in your sound scene, but you may use your voice, your body, or objects you find in the classroom to make your sounds. Be sure to keep your scene a secret. You will perform your sounds for the class and students will guess what your scene is. You now have five minutes to create your sound scene."

✧ Give each group a card with the name of a scene to portray in sound. Select scene suggestions from the list below or make up your own.

    a circus
    the county fair
    the bus ride to school
    waking up in the morning
    two friends meeting who begin visiting and then get
      into an argument
    a mother scolding her child
    a child consoling her sad friend
    two friends walking up to a door that has something
      scary behind it

✧ Have students find places in the room or hall where they can create their sound scenes. Move from group to group to assist with ideas.

✧ After five minutes, have the groups come together to present their sound scenes. If you can place the performing group behind a screen, students may be less inhibited about making sounds and will not give away the scene with any actions. Students may need to repeat their scene more than once while the other students guess.

✧ Students enjoy this activity and may want to repeat it with new scenes. You might ask them to think of their own sound scene ideas.

MUSIC - BODY - RHYTHM

Rhythm, movement, and physical activity are essential tools in developing vocal patterning in language.

✦ Have students practice saying single syllable words that designate a specific part of the body. Guide them in this manner:

> *"While you stay in your seat, imagine yourself walking slowly and saying these words in groups of four:*
> *knee, knee, knee, knee*
> *head, head, head, head*
> *chest, chest, chest, chest*
> *feet, feet, feet, feet*
> *lips, lips, lips, lips*
> *chin, chin, chin, chin*
> *hips, hips, hips, hips"*

✦ Keeping the words in groups of four, repeat groups in any order.

✦ Say the groups of four words aloud and have the children echo the words, this time using their hands to tap those places on their body. For example:

> teacher: *knee, knee, knee, knee*
> (with no hand movement)
> students: *knee, knee, knee, knee*
> (tapping their knees with echo)

✦ Change the dynamics of the words: soft, very loud, whisper, abrupt. Continue the echo process as above but allow the tapping and movement of the hands to match the dynamic level of the word.

✦ Change the tonal center of the word. Make the word very high, then very low, then in the middle. Try swooping the sound up, then glide the sound down.

✦ Give the students two paper plates to tap on their body while saying the words. This time, play march music in the background.

OBJECTIVE
To use rhythm and movement for developing vocal patterning in language

DESCRIPTION
Students speak in a rhythmic manner and physically move or imagine moving to the pulse.

GRADE LEVEL
Kindergarten through 4

MATERIALS
For each student: two paper plates. For the teacher: marching music and a cassette player

SCHEDULING
20 minutes

MUSIC - BODY - MOVEMENT

OBJECTIVES
To use rhythm and whole body movement to develop vocal patterning; to release body tension and encourage freedom of movement

DESCRIPTION
With musical accompaniment, students will echo the teacher's spoken movement words and move accordingly.

ENVIRONMENT
A room with space to move

GRADE LEVEL
Kindergarten through 4

MATERIALS
For the teacher: lively folk music and a cassette player

SCHEDULING
5 minutes

Good folk music in 4/4 time played in the background makes this an easy and interesting improvised rhythm movement session.

✦ Ask students to stand and repeat movement words while making the appropriate movement. For example:

walk, walk, walk, walk
tip, toe, tip, toe
side, side, side, side
jump, jump, jump, jump
slide, slide, slide, slide
clap, clap, clap, clap

✦ Repeat each line two to four times. Be sure to keep the single words in groups of four.

WHO IS HARVEY WHOLE NOTE?

By incorporating the whole body into the lesson, the young child remembers music notation with greater ease. This activity is fun, provides an energetic addition to the school day, and is extremely helpful in learning notation. It all begins with Harvey:

✦ On a chart or chalkboard, show a whole note.

✦ Tell your students:

"Harvey is a whole note who looks like a hole. We can look like Harvey by putting our arms in a circle above our heads. Usually Harvey moves by jumping once every four beats, but at times he moves forward for four beats and then backward for four beats."

OBJECTIVES
To learn basic note values; to provide an energizing experience

DESCRIPTION
Students will make body shapes and movements to define whole, half, quarter, and eighth notes.

GRADE LEVEL
Kindergarten through 4

MATERIALS
A chart or blackboard with whole, half, quarter, and eighth notes and a quarter rest drawn on it

SCHEDULING
15 minutes

187

◇ While the herds of Harveys are moving appropriately, sing
  or chant this song:

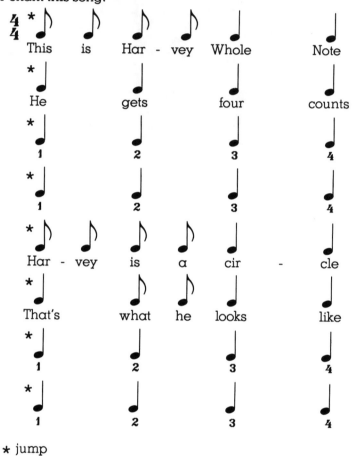

★ jump

✧ On a chart or chalkboard, show half notes.

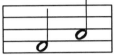

✧ Tell your students:

"Now, Harriet Half Note is that poor girl who fell into the hole. She cannot jump for as long as her friend Harvey. As a matter of fact, she receives two beats when she moves. Harriet's arm is sticking straight up out of the hole and the other arm makes a wide circle around her head with her hand touching the wrist of her straight arm."

✧ Move with the students like Harriet and chant or sing this song:

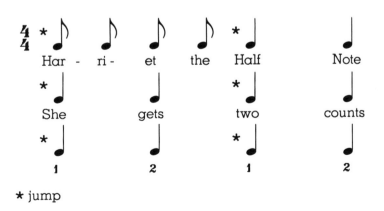

* jump

✧ On a chart or chalkboard, show quarter notes.

✧ Tell your students:

"Kathy also fell into a hole, stuck her arm out and some mean kid came along and filled the hole with dirt. Alas, Kathy the Quarter Note gets one beat. With one arm sticking straight up and the other close around her head holding the straight arm's elbow, Kathy is ready for action."

✧ Move with the students like Kathy and chant this song:

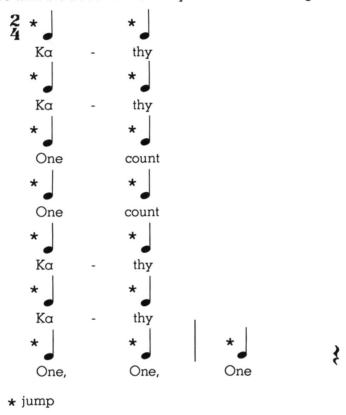

Ka - thy
Ka - thy
One count
One count
Ka - thy
Ka - thy
One, One, One

★ jump

✧ On a chart or chalkboard, show eighth notes.

✧ Tell your students:

"Now, if you are not suffi-ciently exhausted from hop-ping like Harvey, Harriet, and Kathy, here is Henry the Eighth Note. He is the most energetic. Henry is the hole filled with dirt, sticking out his arm and waving a flag."

Usually when you jump the Henry pattern, physical chaos overtakes the group and a rhythmic chant is in vain.

After five minutes of this activity, everyone will welcome the arrival of Ricky Rest, who likes to lay down on the floor amidst groans and moans of exhaustion!

✧ Show a quarter rest on the chart or chalkboard.

CHAPTER V

EMOTIONAL I.Q.

Rhythm and Emotion

Consider that emotions have an I.Q. just as cognitive thought does. Emotional I.Q. is regulated by our limbic brain and encouraged by the willingness of our society to nurture emotional awareness and expression. One of the most essential skills to learn is the ability to perceive and nurture the emotional rhythms of the inner world.

The development of intelligence is dependent on a healthy emotional I.Q. Even with a high I.Q. in logic, music, spatial, kinesthetic, intra-personal, interpersonal, intuitive, or linguistic intelligences, the ability to manifest useful and fulfilling actions based on these abilities is difficult without the reinforcement of a harmonious emotional I.Q. A low emotional I.Q. prevents an accurate perception of personal potential and inhibits the ability to live fully in either the inner or outer world. It denies the self-esteem needed to move from an attitude of survival into the attitude of curiosity that is necessary to learning. The richness attained from a healthy emotional I.Q. builds a richness in cognitive intelligence.

Emotional I.Q. is shaped by the emotional rhythms adopted throughout life. Even before birth, emotional reference points are established through the feeling tone and emotional context of the voices and sounds a fetus hears. The rhythm of emotion behind the spoken word becomes patterned within the inner world and represents the first association with the feeling realm. Childhood experiences frame these emotional patterns into a repertoire of feelings that guide behavior and attitudes. As emotional rhythms are passed from parent to child, parental modeling is responsible for much of a child's emotional repertoire. Through these reference points, emotional associations are developed for friends, family, self, activities, home, personal belongings, learning, pets, and nearly every other contact we make. Our lives become imbued with emotional rhythms.

The emotional rhythms of the inner world are a communication link to the outer world. How we say or do something often means more than what we say or do, for the emotional countenance that we present to the outer world literally determines how we are received. Often, the outer world response does not match the inner needs. The inner rhythms are not always appropriate in the reality of the outer world. A high emotional I.Q. is the result of a sensitivity to emotional rhythms and a knowledge of how to blend the inner and outer worlds. The ability to understand emotions well enough to respond positively, or as director of the Foundation of Mind Research Dr. Jean Houston says, our "response-ability" allows positive interaction between individuals, families, communities, governments, and cultures.

Strong, supportive emotional health begins at home with parental bonding and modeling. Children tend to adopt the prevailing reality including the emotional context that surrounds them. We are currently seeing children who model the emotional rhythms of parents overwhelmed with the confusion, frustration, and stress present today. In schools throughout the country, teachers are finding themselves faced with the impossible task of teaching students whose inner rhythms express fear, anger, frustration, disillusionment, and other negative emotions. Learning for these children is defeated even before it begins unless their emotional rhythm can be altered. The loss of learning abilities that occurs with an underdeveloped emotional I.Q. can have a great effect on children's cognitive abilities and even on their competency in life skills.

A low emotional I.Q. may dispel intellectual potential by forcing individuals into a situation in which they are so actively perceiving the world around them that they cannot move into conceiving ideas and creating intelligence. In other situations, a student may shut out the outer world because perceiving is too painful. It is essential for parents to address this issue as they have the greatest ability to make effective changes.

> Seven-year-old Steven had been in Special Education for two years. He was labeled "learning disabled," but his behavior was the real problem. He was unmanageable in the classroom. Among other attention-seeking activities, he would often chant four-letter words for minutes at a time. Mark quit coming to school at age eight, of his own accord. His mother was uncooperative, saying he was the school's failure and problem. Mark was later arrested for stealing and attempted suicide.

What did Steven and Mark learn in their school experience? Their Special Education teacher said that they learned very little and attained few skills because their needs were too great to be met in the classroom. Their emotional I.Q. was so low that cognitive training was not possible. These unfortunate but true stories are extreme cases that bring to light the importance of emotional I.Q.

Emotional I.Q. is unhealthy when :

- ✧ there is a lack of opportunity to develop and express emotional rhythms,
- ✧ the expression of one or a few rhythms becomes overwhelming and the individual cannot move out of them, or
- ✧ the expression of an emotional rhythm inappropriately manifests toward others.

A healthy emotional I.Q. emanates from the experience and understanding of many varied emotions. Sadness, anger, fear, and frustration are just as important to explore and learn to express appropriately as are joy, love, empathy, excitement, and other positive rhythms. If emotional development does not occur at home, the school system is faced with the task of teaching emotional response-ability: the ability to perceive, understand, control, and respond to a variety of emotional rhythms.

A rich emotional I.Q. lays the foundation for high intellectual I.Q. The experience of intense emotional extremes such as terror, passion, ludicrous humor, or exuberant joy establishes patterns for the ability to sense the obvious and basic rhythms of life. The development of a sensitivity to subtle nuances of feeling such as those expressed in compassion, awe, serenity, whimsy, triumph, and melancholy provides insight toward a greater depth of understanding. These subtle nuances expand the repertoire for self-expression and the perception of a greater variety of emotion in others, enhancing communication and social skills.

The ability to fine-tune feelings also transfers into an ability to fine-tune mental perceptions. There is a correlation between the ability to understand subtle feelings and the ability to perceive complex ideas in subtle ways. The ability to determine subtle patterns is a skill we can use in both emotional and cognitive contexts.

The Triune Brain

The development of the triune brain model in 1952 has provided great insight into our behavior, ability to learn, and emotional I.Q. Dr. Paul MacLean, chief of the Laboratory for Brain Evolution and Behavior at the National Institute for Mental Health in Bethesda, Maryland, created the triune brain model, which delineates three functional brain regions. The three brain regions govern specific behaviors and functions and are neurologically distinct yet are interconnected by neural pathways. Both intellectual and emotional I.Q. rely on balanced interaction between the reptilian, limbic, and neocortex brain regions. (See diagram on page 139.)

The reptilian brain functions at a basic level of instinctive survival actions including territoriality, the development of social hierarchy, rituals, and aggression. Self-preservation, activities of hunting, foraging, hoarding, and mating are centered here. The reptilian brain regulates basic physiologic functions.

The limbic system governs the emotions, the formation of long-term memory, short-term memory, conditioned reflexes, and attention, as well as metabolism, the immune system, and the hormonal system. The social and family sense of concern and protection is seated in this area. Limbic brain behaviors are inclusive of others. Strong emotional convictions arise from the limbic region. Under stress, the limbic brain response is a fight, flight, or freeze action. Current research suggests that the limbic brain regulates much more of our thinking and behavior than we have realized in the past.

The neocortex of the brain contains about 70 percent of the brain's approximately 100 billion neurons and controls high-level thought processes such as logic, creative thought, language processing, and the integration of sensory information. The neocortex includes the frontal lobes of the brain, and is responsible for altruism, compassion, pattern recognition, high-level physical/mental coordination, and planning for the future.

Each of these brain regions has essential functions. Knowing how and when to use and integrate the brain regions can lead us to greater understanding of ourselves and others.

Learning through Emotion

The neocortex has been the focal point as the center for cognitive intelligence in public education, but there is now a growing awareness of the many ways other brain regions contribute to learning. When we have the use of all areas to process information, there is a greater ease and retention in learning.

Emotions are to the limbic brain what facts are to the neocortex. Santiago Ramon y Cajal, often called the father of neuroanatomy, determined that feedback stimulus from one's own expressive activities was the primary factor in physical growth and development of the brain. Providing students with the opportunity to express and understand emotions is one of the greatest tools for expanding emotional and intellectual I.Q.

The limbic system functions as the regulator of emotions and is also essential to memory. We now know that approaching subject material within an emotional context enhances memory. Personally, we can recognize our facility at remembering events that are emotionally charged. D. A. Rappaport has provided research to indicate that emotions may very well be the medium through which memory patterns are organized. Memory of cognitive material can be heightened when structured within an emotional context or in such a way as to elicit an emotional response.

"Feeling is just a different form of thinking."

The experience of feeling positive about learning is, in itself, a stimulus to encourage excitement about the learning process. When sensory input has a positive emotional reference point, the brain triggers the release of a pleasing opiate type of chemical that creates a state of heightened awareness and well-being. Within this state, learning becomes pleasurable and is accomplished with greater ease. Physiologically, this can explain the benefits of using music and art to develop an optimum learning state and assist in memory enhancement.

In the cycle of interaction between the inner and outer worlds, the limbic system represents an essential link between mind and body. We receive as many as a million sensory impressions each minute, but only a select few reach our conscious attention in the neocortex. The limbic system acts as a switchboard, reading the sensations from the body and deciding which to send on to the neocortex for expanded awareness and action. Through this editing process, the limbic system has a significant role in directing our conscious thought.

The creative thought process incorporates the limbic brain with the right and left regions of the neocortex, joining the spark of the Aha! illumination with the cognitive and intuitive intelligence of the neocortex. When we strengthen the neural pathways between brain centers, future communication ability strengthens. This phenomenon has been identified by educational researcher Win Wenger of the Institute for Visual Thinking, and is known as "pole bridging" (Wenger 1987). It occurs when any distinct regions of the brain work closely together in an intense synthesis activity. Pole-bridging activities have been observed to develop pathways to greater intelligence and thinking potential and even reduce the time required for the brain to make future connections. Using the creative arts to facilitate cognitive instruction provides an opportunity for information to bridge between the logic and intuitive areas of the neocortex and the limbic system.

Greater flexibility of thinking and feeling abilities becomes available through processes that involve the emotions in the learning experience. Emotional repertoire can be expanded through creative stories and assignments that focus on the subtle emotions. Games or activities that play with emotional context, such as "Sound Expressions" on page 216, encourage experiences within various emotional contexts. Other activities within this book provide models for teaching cognitive concepts through music and art mediums.

Stimulating vs. Awakening

Education (*educare* in Latin) means to "draw out." It implies the process of awakening the inner world to its potential. Instruct (*instrure* in Latin) means to "pile upon." When we pile upon, we do not honor the creative process, for we do not allow time and space for incubation, illumination, or the synthesis involved in creative intelligence. When we instruct, we merely provide facts and answers. Educating implies a drawing out, an active participation in creating intelligence, and an awakening of inner thought processes.

Today we see many aspects of society that are adrenalin producing. Home life may be a barrage of video movies, Nintendo®, battery-operated active toys, TV, and other highly stimulating activities. The range of possibilities for extracurricular activities is so great that we sometimes see children who find themselves frantically running between sports practices, arts classes, church meetings, drama activities, and any number of other extras. While these can be enriching, too much activity creates a sense of stress and does not allow the inner world to incubate and find time for the critical Ahas! of living.

Added to these stresses is the growing disharmony found in many homes today. The result can be a child with low emotional I.Q. who operates within high levels of adrenalin much of the time. Adrenalin puts the body in a survival mode of fight or flight, a state that tenses the body for quick action. In this state, long-term memory is inhibited. The eyes become tense, and peripheral vision is narrowed, which makes activities such as reading difficult. Focusing on an activity may be hard, and one-to-one personal communication is difficult.

Under stressful situations, thought processing tends to downshift into the survival-oriented reptilian brain functions or the emotional limbic system. When behavior is limited to these areas alone, significant input from the logical and abstract neocortex and the frontal lobes can be eliminated. Thinking becomes highly limited when access to these brain regions is blocked, and the integration of the abilities and functions of the whole brain cannot occur.

Children may respond to overstimulation in one of two ways. They may shut out the outside world by not responding or by even falling asleep. Or, they may become even more stimulated and emulate hyperactive behavior (similar to the infant who cries when overstimulated). In either case, learning is not feasible. These are the children in the classroom who are restless, unable to focus, or wholly unmotivated.

The reaction to these children often comes in the form of discipline and disapproval. For those that appear unmotivated, we may seek to create more exciting teaching methods in the hopes of gaining a response. Neither alternative provides the respite the student needs, and both methods incur frustration for the student, teacher, parent, and administrator.

There are many aspects of current classrooms which students may find threatening. Fear of failure, discomfort, peer pressure, disapproval, and other negative emotions may cause the classroom environment to induce downshifting and learning disability. We can nurture the emotional I.Q. of children by first providing an environment of emotional safety and acceptance. A mind and body that are relaxed and without fear will be more available for an educational experience.

As educators and parents, we must recognize our own emotional rhythms and become aware of the emotion that is carried within our voice. There is great power within the voice. If it carries stress, the voice may very well trigger a stressful reaction, causing the release of adrenalin within others. While excitement and heightened interest involve positive stress and can provide improved learning results, too much stress can reduce the effectiveness of learning. Here is an example:

As a third-grader, Sue was assigned to a teacher who had an extremely powerful voice. It was shrill and loud, and carried a sharpness in it. Coming from a home where this tonality was only rarely used under extreme stress, this teacher's voice was extremely disturbing to Sue. In fact, her first two months of third grade were spent in great discomfort. These feelings were magnified when the teacher was angry at another student. The stress was too much, and school became unbearable. When the teacher reprimanded another student, Sue would cry. After three months, the teacher became aware of Sue's distress. The teacher gently explained to her that she was not angry with her when she reprimanded other students. After this, Sue was greatly relieved, and felt more comfortable in the classroom.

The emotional rhythms we present within our voice and teaching methods can powerfully motivate the child and increase learning potential. The use of a carefully modulated nonadrenalin voice can be the beginning of bringing a stressed child into a state in which learning can occur. At the same time, we can create a sense of excitement with our voice when it is needed to stimulate the classroom rhythm and generate interest.

Musical tone can also be used to create the sense of safety and trust that will awaken the child's learning potential. The language of expression used by both the limbic and reptilian brain systems is emotive and not linguistic. Music can elicit a wide variety of emotional responses and nurture the development of subtle nuances of emotion. Music can be a catalyst for emotional expression and can provide another mode for the establishment of new emotional reference points. The high level of emotional charge in music can have a strong effect upon the emotional rhythm of the entire classroom and help in activating tired students or in relaxing the classroom pace.

Developing the Emotional I.Q.

Cultures around the world have explored different methods of developing thought, reflecting the priorities of their society. While some have focused on cognitive thought, others have nurtured the intuitive process. Both approaches are valuable and offer pathways to the development of fulfilling lives.

In recent years, public education systems have focused attention on the development of rational, intellectual thought. Piaget provided great insights into the evolution of cognition from birth through formal reasoning. With the realization that many valuable intelligences exist comes the recognition of the need to develop learning processes that nurture and build different ways of knowing, moving beyond formal reasoning.

We can find insights into ways of educating the various intelligences by looking at cultures with an intuitive approach to learning. In this same way, we can look closely at the students labeled "failures" within our school systems, students who often have great abilities within the neglected intelligences. The blend of the development of cognitive reasoning with intuitive, creative skills is the unification of intelligence that can bring us into the global, problem-finding stages of creative intelligence.

Phase Forward Education empowers the administrator and teacher with a repertoire of creative methodological and psychological rhythms that communicate through the curriculum and thus interacts with students. Thus teachers and administrators can develop a sensitivity to student rhythms that can help determine the emotional needs of the student and promote a balanced counterpoint and harmony within the educational framework. The development of a healthy emotional I.Q. may be one of the most important tasks that stands before our culture today.

Activities for Teachers

Tuning Up Our Teaching

The value of building self-esteem in the classroom has led many schools to implement programs that build personal awareness and confidence. Presentation methods that build the self-image through positive language and peripheral stimuli are currently being integrated in teaching methods as well. The extension of these concepts towards building the emotional I.Q. provides an even greater expansion of understanding our personal rhythms and developing the ability to successfully blend the inner and outer worlds while boosting other areas of intelligence.

As teachers, we can refine our teaching skills and develop our emotional I.Q. through the process of exploring our inner world. An understanding of our emotional processes provides great insights into the inner world of others. Activities in this section will assist in providing personal insights, becoming aware of the emotional states of others, and using our voice and body in ways that develop emotional expression as a learning tool.

UNDER THE SPELL OF TEACHING

OBJECTIVES
To affirm positive
aspects of teaching;
to empower teachers
with a verbal
reinforcement of their
teaching abilities

DESCRIPTION
The teacher will
repeat positive
affirmations about
teaching.

SCHEDULING
5 minutes

The repetition of an affirmation is very useful in preparation for an empowered day. Do not feel that you need to use or agree with all of these techniques. Use the ones that are comfortable and useful for you. In a few months, you may find some of the following affirmations more effective and wish to experiment with them for greater compassion and attentiveness in the classroom.

✦ Repeat these affirmations to yourself. For even greater reinforcement, repeat them while doing the cross-crawl described in Moving to Learn on page 219 or the lazy eight movement in the air from Drawing Connections on page 220, both described later in the student activity section.

   ✦ I am grounded in the information that I teach. It is essential to lifelong learning. I exemplify that in my enthusiasm.
   ✦ I share knowledge and wisdom from my life experience.
   ✦ There are many ways to learn and listen. I honor the differences.
   ✦ Every student is unique, and I honor each viewpoint, no matter how different from my own.
   ✦ I make a difference in every student's life.
   ✦ I am a model for each student. I am both flexible and clear.
   ✦ Every student offers a creative challenge.
   ✦ Through a variety of teaching styles, I empower every student.

EMOTIONS IN SOUND (OOOOH-AAAAH)

Communicating with the emotional centers of our being can reduce stress and give us a sense of well-being. Through emotions we can create a feeling of being bonded with others and safe within ourselves, or feel fearful with a sense of distance from others. We can reach a state of contentment in a safe and fully aware state of mind by consciously communicating with the midportion of the brain, sometimes referred to as the limbic system. This midbrain regulates the tone or emotion of the body and is where the most basic sounds of expression originate. These expressions are understood intuitively. When we use sounds to connect with our mind and body, we can stimulate this limbic area and consciously communicate with our basic natural rhythms.*

❖ Tune in to the inner world of emotions. Move quietly in your mind through the emotions of joy, sadness, anger, ecstasy, fear, and excitement.

❖ Using long vowel sounds, move again through these emotions, this time verbalizing the emotion through an extended sounding of the long vowels (*aaaaa, eeeee, iiiii, ooooo, uuuuu*) with each emotion.

❖ Experiment now with moving from one emotion to another, changing vowel sounds as you do. (*Aaaaa* [the ascending happy *a*]; *eeee eeee eeee* [the laughing *e*]; *you!* [the surprised *u*]; *ooooo* [the praising *o*]; *uh uh uh uh uh* [the *uh uh* way of saying no]; *aaaaa* [the inhaled breath of fear]; *uhmmmmm* [the satisfied *uhm*]; *oh oh* [the '*oh no*']; *eeeee* [the *whee* of the circus rides] - add your own.)

❖ Notice how the body and mind respond to these connections with emotions in sound. Is there a sense of the emotion within the body? Within the mind? What memories are triggered with the sounding?

OBJECTIVES
To consciously communicate with and stimulate the emotional center of the brain; to become attuned to the expressions of the inner world and their potential as tools for creating a desired state; to experience the release of stress and negative emotions through the use of emotions in sound

DESCRIPTION
The teacher will explore long vowel sounds within varied emotional contexts and become conscious of the physical, mental, and emotional responses elicited.

ENVIRONMENT
A quiet, safe room

SCHEDULING
15 minutes before or after school

* Refer to Don Campbell's *The Roar of Silence* for more details on toning.

"SYS-TEM": AN OUTER-WORLD RAP

OBJECTIVES
To explore the rap
technique; to look with
a new perspective at
the systems our society
creates

DESCRIPTION
Teachers will read
the rap.

SCHEDULING
5 minutes

Sometimes we feel caught in the middle of a pulse or rhythm in life that just will not let us go. We long for vacations, new positions, and change! Jean Houston's clever and relevant rap about *The System* is a help in relieving pressure brought on by inflexible systems. No matter how chaotic or rigid our life is, it's part of the human system.

✦ Start by tapping an even beat with your foot and repeat the word "sys-tem," until the rhythm is set in your mind.

✦ Maintain a beat and read the rap. Enjoy!

SYS-TEM, SYS-TEM, SYS-TEM, SYS-TEM . . .

This is the way the System goes,
How does it work? Nobody knows,
Where does it end? Where does it start?
Everyone must play their part
To smooth the way of the SYS-TEM, SYS-TEM,
  SYS-TEM, SYS-TEM . . .

This is the way the theories come,
Keynesian, Skinnerian, Freudian.
Charts, computers, test tubes, too,
Show exactly what to do
To smooth the way of the SYS-TEM, SYS-TEM,
  SYS-TEM, SYS-TEM . . .

This is the way we change the law
Cover the way we screwed up before.
Special interest lobby groups
Buy their way through legal loops
To smooth the way of the SYS-TEM, SYS-TEM,
  SYS-TEM, SYS-TEM . . .

This is the way we educate
Guidelines, deadlines, administrate.
Back to basics, that's the fad.
You're bored to death? Isn't that sad!
But that's the school of the SYS-TEM, SYS-TEM,
  SYS-TEM, SYS-TEM . . .

General Motors, General Foods,
General Pills for General Moods,
IBM and Xerox too,
Coca-Cola® provides the brew
To quench the thirst of the SYS-TEM, SYS-TEM,
    SYS-TEM, SYS-TEM . . .

The new idea that you submit
Just send it out in triplicate.
It's kicked upstairs to you know who.
The word comes down, Catch-22,
For that's the way of the SYS-TEM, SYS-TEM,
    SYS-TEM, SYS-TEM . . .

H. E. W. and D.-O.-D.
CIA and Washington, D.C.
Tweedledum and Tweedledoo
The IRS is after you
To pay your dues to the SYS-TEM, SYS-TEM,
    SYS-TEM, SYS-TEM . . .

Whatever you've done, whatever you've said,
Computer banks record your head.
How does it work? Nobody knows.
Where does it end? Where does it start?
Everyone must play their part
To smooth the way of the SYS-TEM, SYS-TEM,
    SYS-TEM, SYS-TEM . . .

Subsection one, paragraph three,
Item nine, Addendum B
See above, and what do you know?
It says up there to see below.
And that's the rule in the SYS-TEM, SYS-TEM,
    SYS-TEM, SYS-TEM . . .

This is the way the system lasts
Builds its future on its pasts
Bureaucracy ensures its own
Each and everyone a clone
You never escape from the SYS-TEM, SYS-TEM,
    SYS-TEM, SYS-TEM . . . (cont.)

A million billion years from now
a UNIVERSAL system . . . WOW.
And all the stars cooperate
And form in lines, nice and straight
The organized light of the SYS-TEM, SYS-TEM,
    SYS-TEM, SYS-TEM . . .

—Jean Houston

INNER-SOUND DYNAMICS

OBJECTIVE
To experience the physical, emotional, and mental character-istics that are present at different levels of inner sound

DESCRIPTION
The teacher will make an audible crescendo and decrescendo with an aaaaa sound and then make the sounds internally.

ENVIRONMENT
A quiet, safe place

SCHEDULING
5 minutes

Many students, particularly in the teen years, are filled with internal energy and sound. Sometimes, when these sounds are very loud, students can hardly hear the world around them. At times, their internal world totally encompasses their attention. Our inner world is much more controlled than that of a younger student. This activity will help you in remembering the dynamic range of the young person's internal world.

✦ Begin by making an aaaaa sound and see how long you can hold this sound before letting it gradually fade away. (In music, the gradual decrease in sound is called a decre-scendo.)

✦ Now begin as softly as you can and make the sound louder and louder; then hold a loud dynamic level until you can no longer extend the sound. You have just made a cre-scendo.

✦ Next, take these sounds inside for two minutes. You may want to close your eyes while you make an inner crescendo first and then a decrescendo.

✦ Rotate between the two a couple of times inwardly. Notice how your breathing patterns change with the internal soundings. Does your body feel different when you hear the quiet sounds than when you hear the loud sounds? Is your awareness level different in either case? Imagine what it is like to live with inner dynamics of different levels.

END OF A PERFECTLY EXHAUSTING DAY

It is easy to become tangled in an endless maze of cognitive thoughts and patterns. Our health and the health of our teaching demands a balance between our inner and outer worlds. When we listen, we can become actively aware of both worlds and allow the two to transform into a synchronized rhythm. *

—REVIEW THE DAY

✦ Begin by closing your eyes and concentrate on exhaling all fatigue from your body for a couple of minutes. Allow each inhalation to bring in more inner space and better acoustics. Allow each exhalation to release tension and cluttered or disorganized thought. Then slowly begin to tonalize the breath with the vowel sound *ah*. Continue to make the *ah* sound on the exhalation for a couple of minutes as you allow thoughts about the past twenty-four hours to emerge. Review the past day, by starting with this exercise and progressing backward through your activities and associations.

✦ Observe the emotions that arise when you ask yourself, "Was I heard? Was I understood?" The answer is not a "yes" or "no" but a nonjudgmental sensing. Remember to keep breathing naturally but deeply with the tonalized *ah*.

✦ Now allow yourself to go deeply into situations when you felt an imbalance. Think of a time when you felt less effective than normal. Go gently into this time and allow the *ah* to fill the place in your body where the awkwardness occurred.

✦ Allow the tonalization of the sound to release the emotion. Use the power of your breath and sound to balance that moment. Even though you may not have consciously felt the imbalance at the time, release it now with your voice.

✦ Bring your mind back to a calm place. Use the *ah* to fill your body and mind with a clear and vital sound. You may wish to image the opening of a window on a clear, beautiful day with the *ah* as fresh air clearing the room.

OBJECTIVES
To provide the teacher with a technique for resolving uncomfortable emotions and releasing the stress of the day; to initiate a positive rhythm and a fresh approach to new challenges

DESCRIPTION
The teacher will review the day and use vocalized sound to release any unbalanced events and emotions that may have occurred.

ENVIRONMENT
A quiet, safe place

SCHEDULING
10 to 20 minutes at the end of a day

* Refer to Don Campbell's sound cassette "Healing Yourself With Your Own Voice" for details on vocal techniques.

Activities for Students

Tuning Up with Students

Building an emotional I.Q. within the classroom can provide students with the comfort of understanding and expressing their inner world. When personal expression feels safe, there is greater freedom to move into explorations of the outer world. Cognitive levels of understanding can reach new depths and subtleties as the emotional I.Q. expands. With heightened emotional I.Q. comes the ability to explore new states of learning and to use and integrate the skills of different brain regions.

The following activities for students explore subtle arenas of emotion and its expression, creating opportunities for the integration of brain functions. The experience of fully available and integrated brain functions can elicit new excitement from successful learning experiences. As the creative learning process is repeated, we can begin to see the development of creative thinking skills. Teachers, too, will enjoy these activities and find new insights into thinking and feeling skills.

SOUND FEELINGS

Suggest to your students:

"Imagine that we have been transported magically to a new world where no words are spoken. All communication comes from the feeling within your voice and only long vowel sounds are used. We will now experience the expression of emotions in sound." (You may want to use only one or two small parts of this activity at a time.)

❖ Ask students to repeat *aaaaa, eeeee, iiiii, ooooo, uuuuu* after you with an extended long vowel pronunciation and a happy inflection.

❖ Repeat the extended vowel series again, this time in a fearful manner.

❖ Repeat the extended vowel series again experimenting each time with a different emotion: anger, sadness, excitement, praise, discouragement, and wonder. Notice the bodily changes with each new emotion. Do their bodies reflect changes of posture associated with the emotions? Do their facial expressions change? Do their voices reflect an emotional charge?

❖ Now, have students repeat after you a happy sounding of *aaaaa*, followed by a sad sounding of *eeeee*, an angry *iiiii*, an excited *ooooo*, and a fearful *uuuuu*. Experiment with different combinations of vowels and emotions.

❖ Ask children to lead each other in these soundings.

Observe your students as they move through the emotions. Do you notice a release of tension within your students? Observe the changes in students' rhythms when the activity is completed compared to their rhythm prior to the activity. Are their minds and bodies refreshed and ready for a heightened learning experience? Are they more responsive to the learning experience? Discuss the differences of responses and how playground time can be used to relieve any stress or frustration experienced in the classroom.

OBJECTIVES
To explore the voice as a mode of expression; to access various emotional states and expand the potential range of feelings; to allow students and teachers to develop an awareness of the cues for perceiving rhythms within themselves and others; to explore the energizing potential of the voice

DESCRIPTION
Students will use long vowel sounds to explore and express various emotions.

ENVIRONMENT
A room that is free from distractions

GRADE LEVEL
Kindergarten through adult

SCHEDULING
5 to 10 minutes

SOUND EXPRESSIONS

OBJECTIVES
To explore the dynamic and harmonic properties of emotion within the voice; to help students develop a sense of moving personal expression outward

DESCRIPTION
The teacher will read a gibberish poem with varying emotional intonations, and students will guess the emotion.

GRADE LEVEL
1 through 9

MATERIALS
A gibberish poem such as "Omapoli"

SCHEDULING
15 minutes

Our voices are reflections of our emotional state. When we are happy, our voices are rich and vital. Sadness creates a low-pitched voice with a lack of energy. Anger, fear, excitement, suspicion, and curiosity all have unique vocal characteristics as well. This activity helps to develop an awareness of emotional expression within the voice.

✦ Read the following gibberish poem to your class three times: the first time in an angry voice, the second in an excited manner, and the third fearfully. After each reading, ask students to guess which emotion you are expressing.

> OMAPOLI
> Aso mata boomera zu
> Frapoli fufu ee hoo-lululu
>
> Umani, pumani ick ick von gick
> Ala shoop ala shing ala suma baloo
>
> Razaly roo ona ee ee magroo
> Hacow nee oof ees homa baloo
>
> Soto nunu om apoli goo
> Eiya zoozoo, om apoli stu.

✦ Discuss the power of our voice and how much of our communication is through tone rather than words.

You might repeat the activity later and extend the range of emotions. Students will enjoy taking a turn reading various expressions of the poem as well.

216

MOTION PICTURES

✧ Give each student a large sheet of unlined paper and markers.

✧ Explain to your students that they are going to draw with their eyes closed. Their drawings will reflect the musical rhythm spoken through their bodies, not as a picture but as a reflection of the motion of the music.

✧ Ask students to close their eyes and listen as you play one of the musical selections listed in Group 1.

✧ When their bodies feel ready to move to the music, students may move their markers on the paper in response to the musical rhythm. Remind them that their eyes must remain closed.

✧ When students are finished, tell them to open their eyes and write the number one on their papers.

✧ Repeat the process with new paper and a music selection from Group 2. The paper should be marked number two. Repeat again with a selection from Group 3. This paper should be numbered three.

✧ Put the number one drawings on one wall of the room, number two on another, and number three on a different wall. Ask students if they can tell the differences in the music by looking at the drawings. Compare the shape, size, and intensity of the lines in each category. How did each type of music feel to your students? Do the drawings convey a mood?

(cont.)

OBJECTIVES
To allow a midbrain response to different emotional stimuli; to see the emotional response in a visible art form

DESCRIPTION
Students will close their eyes and draw freely in response to three different musical stimuli.

GRADE LEVEL
Kindergarten through adult

MATERIALS
For each student: three large sheets of unlined paper and colored markers. For the teacher: a musical selection from each of the suggested lists and a cassette player

SCHEDULING
10 to 15 minutes

—GROUP 1: Music with a Swinging Rhythm

The Mozart Effect. Music for Children, Vol II, Relax,
    Daydream and Draw
Bach, J. S. "Jesu, Joy of Man's Desiring"
Bach, J. S. "Little Fugue"
Grieg, Edward. "Morning," from *Peer Gynt Suite*
McFerrin, Bobby. "Don't Worry, Be Happy"
Pachelbel, Johann. *Canon in D*
A Strauss waltz
Vangelis. "Chariots of Fire"
Any Irish jig

—GROUP 2: Music with Strong Accents

The Mozart Effect. Music for Children, Vol. III, Mozart
    in Motion
Bizet, Georges. "Toreador Song" from the opera
    Carmen
Brubeck, Dave. "Take 5"
Ravel, Maurice. *Bolero*
Strauss, Richard. "Also Sprach Zarathustra" (2001
    theme)
Williams, Mason. "Classical Gas"
Breakdance music
Dixieland jazz
Flashdance theme
Jaws theme

—GROUP 3: Music with Few or No Accents

Campbell, Don. *Essence*
Debussy, Claude. *Afternoon of a Fawn*
Halpern, Steven. *Comfort Zone*
Horn, Paul. *Inside the Great Pyramid*
Horn, Paul. *Inside the Taj Mahal*
Kobialka, Daniel. *Celtic Fantasy*
Close Encounters of a Third Kind theme
Gregorian chant

MOVING TO LEARN

When our minds and bodies are in balance, our learning becomes easier. The cross-crawl technique evolved from 1930s studies about the educational importance of crossing the body's midline. Educational kinesiology has expanded this information to develop simple and enjoyable movements and activities that enhance whole-brain learning. These activities have been found to make all types of learning easier.

This activity is from *Brain Gym* by Paul and Gail Dennison. It is an important learning tool and a good warm-up in the morning or before difficult learning tasks.

✧ Ask students to stand where they have room to move.

✧ Play one of the suggested musical selections or find one from your collection at home that is a medium-paced 4/4 tempo. You may want to have students bring suitable tapes from home after you have done this activity in class.

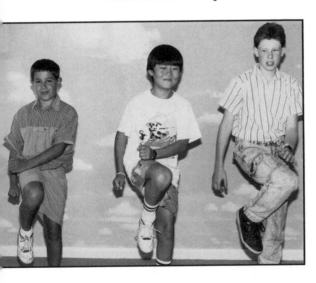

✧ Ask students to move to the music and alternate body movement so that an arm from one side of the body is moved at the same time as a leg from the other side. First, touch a raised knee with the hand from the opposite side, then touch the other knee with the other hand, always crossing the midline of the body.

✧ After this technique is accomplished, you can experiment with other ways to cross-crawl: reaching one arm up while the opposite leg moves out from the body, reaching behind the back to touch the opposite raised heel. Students may stay in one place or move about the room, as you choose.

OBJECTIVES
To prepare students for learning by integrating the brain hemispheres and body; to provide a sound break or refocusing activity

DESCRIPTION
Students will move to lively music and learn the brain and body integrating action of cross-crawling.

MATERIALS
A cassette tape of lively music such as a march or one of the following selections: *Kids in Motion* by Gregg and Steve, breakdance music, Phyllis Weikert's folk dance recordings, or the Pointer Sisters; and a cassette player

GRADE LEVEL
Kindergarten through adult

SCHEDULING
One minute for kindergarten through grade 2, two or three minutes for grade 3 through adult

DRAWING CONNECTIONS

OBJECTIVES
To integrate the mind and body; to activate brain centers by stimulating the total visual field; to develop hand-eye coordination

DESCRIPTION
Students draw a large figure 8 shape on its side (an infinity sign) while following the movement with the eyes. Students do the movement three times; they use each hand independently and then both hands together.

GRADE LEVEL
2 through adult

MATERIALS
For each student: a 20" x 16" sheet of unlined paper, colored crayons, pencils, or markers

SCHEDULING
4 to 5 minutes

Developed by educational kinesiology researchers, this activity combines two important integrating actions: crossing the midline and activating brain centers through eye movement. We are now aware that different positions of the eyes trigger different areas of the brain. In this activity the eyes will move to cover the total visual field.

❖ Give students a large sheet of paper and a colored marker or crayon.

❖ Ask students to stand at their desks and draw a large figure 8 on its side several times in the same place on the paper. Tell your students that their eyes should follow their hand movements carefully. Stress that they should move their marker up through the center of the eight each time they come to it, as shown below:

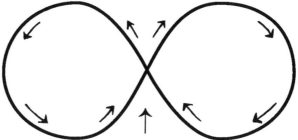

Always move up through the center of the eight.

❖ Ask them to switch hands and repeat the process, drawing over their first eight.

❖ Now ask them to hold the marker in both hands and repeat.

❖ As a variation, students can do the activity on the chalkboard.

❖ Another variation: Do the activity without paper by holding the arm straight out in front, making a fist with the thumb pointed up, and moving the arm in the same pattern in the air. The eyes must follow the thumb and the head moves only slightly. This is an excellent activity to do before reading, writing, art, or verbal presentations.

SOUNDING OFF

Often we learn and work better when we take a moment or two to release tension and energize ourselves. The following techniques are one-minute methods for relieving tension and changing energy patterns that are low or have habituated.

Have students stand while you lead them in any one of the following ways:

✦ Take an *aaaah* break by vocalizing loud sighs. Lead students in the *aaaah* break by starting with a barely audible sigh and increase the length and volume on each sigh. Extend the pitch slightly higher and much lower with each sigh. Seven or eight sighs should be sufficient to provide a quick, refreshing break.

✦ Do a body "blither." Start by vigorously wiggling your hands, then add shoulders, hips, legs and feet, and finally your head. The accompanying *bllbllbllbll* sound that occurs when you relax your mouth and cheeks while vigorously shaking your head is fun and energizing, too.

✦ Enjoy an energized hip, hip, hooray for school, learning, Friday, or other appropriate event.

✦ Sound a high pitch and sweep it downward as low as you can go and then back up again. Repeat the fire engine sound two or three times.

✦ Play an energizing tape and ask students to cross-crawl to the music for one minute. Experiment with finding new ways to cross the midline.

✦ Play two minutes of march music while students stand with closed eyes. Without moving, have them imagine marching through their learning tasks with great enthusiasm and success. Use the dynamic power of your voice to create excitement as you lead the imaginary march through various subjects and daily activities. You can use lilting waltz music and imagine dancing through the day as well.

OBJECTIVES
To provide students with a quick stress-releasing break; to give teachers a technique for changing classroom energy levels

DESCRIPTION
The teacher will use sound and movement techniques to release tension and perk student energy levels.

GRADE LEVEL
Kindergarten through adult

MATERIALS
An energizing cassette tape from the active styles list on page 255 or Group 2 from the "Motion Pictures" activity in this chapter, a selection of march or waltz music, and a cassette player

SCHEDULING
One minute as needed

STRETCHING YOURSELF

OBJECTIVES
To kinesthetically experience stretching and the extension of the body; to determine a personal goal; to create a mental state acknowledging the ability to accomplish a goal

DESCRIPTION
Students will experience stretching in physical ways and then envision themselves stretching mentally toward a positive goal.

ENVIRONMENT
An open space with freedom for movement

GRADE LEVEL
3 through adult

MATERIALS
For each student: polyform clay.
For the teacher: selections from the passive or relaxation lists on pages 254 and 255, and a cassette player

SCHEDULING
15 to 20 minutes

Our success in the classroom and in life is greatly determined by our personal vision of ourselves. When we learn to expand our boundaries within our own mind, we may then be able to expand them in reality. The use of clay and the kinesthetic body movements in this activity help to create an internal image of stretching to greater heights.

✧ Tell your students they are going to stretch themselves in mind and body.

✧ Begin by having students work clay in their hands till it is soft.

✧ When the clay is soft, ask students to see how many ways they can stretch it. Experiment with making it longer, taller, wider, fatter, and pulling it into peaks. Work with the clay for 4 or 5 minutes.

✧ Next, ask your students to stand and close their eyes.

✧ Start the music and tell students to reach as high in the air as they can, even standing on tiptoes.

✧ While the music plays, ask students to reach down and touch the floor, then stretch to each side. See how far they can reach behind them.

✧ Let them explore their space by reaching as far as they can in as many directions as possible. To help your students, suggest that they imagine stretching in the same ways that they stretched their clay.

✧ Ask students to stop moving and, with eyes closed, imagine their body reaching as far as it can in all directions.

✧ Now, ask your students to envision a goal they would like to accomplish.

✧ Tell them to quietly imagine themselves reaching toward their goal until they have attained it. Let them enjoy and experience this vision for two or three minutes.

CHAPTER VI

ORCHESTRATING LIFELONG LEARNING

Reaching out to listen, perceiving and creating, personal tempos, memory patterns, the joy of discovery, the expression of emotion: each has its own rhythm of development and growth. Throughout this book we have explored the patterns of these rhythms in the mind, body, and emotions. They have led us on a personal discovery path to recognize patterns of learning within ourselves and in our students. These rhythms have provided us with tools for the development of rhythmic teaching techniques.

Successful, dynamic teaching begins with a sensitivity to the rhythms of learning and evolves into a rhythmic flow of teaching that nurtures discovery and creativity and emerges as understanding for the learner. The experiences of discovery through mind, body, and emotions instill lasting impressions upon the learner, while creative explorations of cognitive concepts provide the opportunity for deep expression of understanding. Rhythmic teaching invites the teacher to relax and move with students through their personal discovery cycle. The role of teacher becomes that of facilitator, co-discoverer on the learning journey, orchestrator of lifelong learning skills.

Orchestrating Learning Skills

Every teacher possesses the power to transform the quality of life and learning in themselves and in their students at any time. To believe less is to create less, to limit the learning process before it begins. The tools we use to orchestrate the rhythms of mind, body, and emotion are similar to techniques used in music therapy to direct conscious attention: entrainment, diversion, and the iso principle. Many teachers intuitively use these tools with success. Because these tools help to develop learning skills, they are as important as the information presented.

Entrainment is the ability to observe and enter into the rhythms of another. Usually students are expected to entrain with the teacher, no matter where they are in their personal rhythms. Most students quickly develop a sense of how to be with a teacher. They judge the comfort zones, the rough places, and the amount of freedom available. Some students do not develop the perceptual ability to "read" and entrain to others and may suffer academically. This ability is an important listening and communication skill necessary throughout life. It will be developed and improved as each individual explores the inner and outer rhythms of mind, body, and emotion.

A sensitivity to student and personal rhythms is the foundation of rhythmic teaching. Entrainment is the two-way street of communication. It is the avenue by which an exchange of information can lead to the discovery process. Many successful teachers intuitively entrain to their students. They use the pace of their voice, their mood, and timing to create a place of harmony, trust, and sameness that facilitates the discovery journey. When entrainment occurs, the rhythms of speech patterns, physical movement, and information are synchronized in such a way that the inner and outer worlds can converse. Entrainment can occur even when teachers are speaking or lecturing as they watch student response and adjust the pace, vocal inflections, and patterns of presentation to enhance the student's receptivity to information.

Habituation can occur when the rhythm within a classroom is so prolonged that there is no sense of newness. We quickly habituate to the sound of an automobile when we ride in it. We habituate to

background music when it is continually used. Although the sound is there, the conscious mind does not pay attention to it. If you have ever tried to record a conversation in a busy room, you may have habituated to the background sounds and not realized the level of ambient noise until the recording is played back.

Our ability to focus and concentrate turns our attention to things that are not habit. When habituation takes place in a classroom, the whole track of learning can slow down and become automatic. Learning can be replaced by boredom or frustration, which may elicit behavior problems. This book exemplifies ways to pay attention so that we do not habituate with ourselves, our students, or our methods. This vital key of awareness is essential for the empowerment and engagement that engenders long-range memory and knowledge.

Diversion is one of the most commonly used multisensory teaching techniques for stimulating the classroom away from habituation and boredom. The moments of losing enthusiasm and attention in the classroom can easily be modified with diversion methods that transform an atmosphere of habituation into attention. A simple change in the pattern of the voice, the dynamics of expression, or the tempo of speech can alter the classroom flow. Diversion can also be accomplished by rearranging desks, changing the typical flow in a lesson plan, or using a different teaching technique.

Many of the activities using art, music, and movement in this book will act as diversion techniques while enhancing the learning process. *Introduction to the Musical Brain* (Campbell 1983) demonstrates many ideas and exercises using music in the classroom for creative diversion. The wide variety of high-quality audiovisual aids can provide additional methods. Imagery activities, breathing exercises, stretching, and other simple yet effective diversions can easily bring a class back to a central focus. Teachers will find diversion techniques that most suit their personality and skills. Individual classes will have specific interests that provide opportunities for especially effective techniques as well.

The iso principle is one of the most natural and intuitive techniques for moving into a new rhythm. With the iso principle, a change in tempo and mood is accomplished by entraining to the present mood and slowly altering the pace in the desired direction. The teacher can use this technique to move an individual or even an entire class into a desired classroom experience, a place of release or rejuvenation, or a productive learning state. The music *Bolero* by Ravel exemplifies this technique as it moves from a quiet, simple sound to a forceful, complex sound, bringing the listener with it. Rather than a quick change to a fast or dynamic mood, the use of the iso principle moves the mood gradually, almost unnoticeably, into a different state. In the classroom the iso principle can be used to move high energy to a state of calm by gradually slowing the teaching pace through changes in voice speed and tonality, movement patterns, or playing music of progressively slower tempos. The students can be led to a state of greater excitement by reversing this process.

Many instruments are available to us for orchestrating learning. Those that create a harmony in learning integrate brain regions and provide greater access to thinking processes, understanding of concepts, and increased memory abilities. These learning tools lead to the development of strong learning skills, a bonding of the inner and outer world, and enhancement of the emotional I.Q.

Giving students tools they can use to orchestrate their own learning is an important aspect of teaching students how to learn. Every individual will find learning tools that suit personal abilities and interests. Some will work better for particular students and classes than others. Students will engage with the learning tools that speak to their personality and personal tempo. The role of facilitator in the learning journey allows the teacher to creatively explore these techniques and share them with the students.

Accelerated Learning: The Contributions of Lozanov

Many teachers have had experiences with accelerated learning methods based on the research of Georgi Lozanov. This Bulgarian psychiatrist studied the effects of suggestion on health and learning. His suggestopedic learning techniques, described in Appendix 3, were first used in foreign language teaching and have now been adopted throughout the curriculum at all age levels. Lozanov created a highly successful method that can be used to increase the ease and joy in learning facts and principles in nearly any subject. Lozanov's methods focus on both the conscious and unconscious perceptions that direct learning. His techniques are based on the idea that the learning process is accelerated when learning occurs through personal experience and multisensory integration.

Adaptations of the Lozanov method, called accelerated or integrative learning, have emerged. These methods are sensitive to the rhythms of learning and teach in a rhythmic manner. The relationship between stress, relaxation, listening, and attention are key elements in all systems of accelerated learning. A primary principle in these techniques is the establishment of a relaxed, passive learning state to reduce tension and enhance memory. These passive sessions of information input are blended with active learning sessions and activation exercises to enhance memory through multisensory associations. A benefit of these techniques is the capability they hold for reaching students within all learning styles.

Based on research indicating the enormous potential of the brain that is often unused, accelerated learning techniques view everyone as having a great capacity to learn. The removal of blocks to learning is one of the first steps accelerated learning takes toward tapping into this learning potential. Learning blocks are replaced with a perception of learning as a natural and joyous event available to everyone. Accelerated learning enhances the emotional I.Q. while providing engaging methods for learning information. Schools that have adopted accelerated learning methods are proving the validity of these ideas.

Accelerated learning techniques have evolved a rhythmic pattern of presentation that builds understanding, knowledge, and skills. Information is first presented and "decoded," followed by an active and passive concert reading. Activation exercises follow and are also used at various stages to elaborate upon the information and reinforce multisensory associations. This system presents a comprehensive and unified approach to learning that simply and powerfully integrates knowledge in the mind, body, and emotions. The flow of information in this pattern of presentation has been proven to accelerate the rate and depth of understanding in foreign language instruction and other curriculum areas.

While the accelerated learning format provides an optimal presentation method, benefits to learning can be obtained by using these techniques individually. Each of the techniques can be adapted and applied to meet specific classroom needs. One of the most important aspects of accelerated learning techniques is the freedom allowed for the teacher's creativity to emerge within the context of the presentation format, adding a personal and relevant spark to learning material. Teachers may also use their creativity to find appropriate ways to incorporate the accelerated learning presentation elements throughout the curriculum.

Verbal communication, drama, art, music, gesture, games, and movement are essential tools throughout the accelerated learning cycle. Music, rhythm, and vocal patterning are used as a primary means of activating the retention of information. Students gain their first familiarity with the sounds, tones, words, and meanings of learning material through oral, visual, and kinesthetic forms of presentation, building a strong foundation of understanding.

Accelerated learning may not be so much the process of "accelerating" learning as it is the process of filling in the gaps within teaching methods by making full use of time, sensory integration, and personal motivation. Many of the individual teaching and learning techniques used in the Lozanov method have already been incorporated in a variety of subjects by teachers who use general relaxation, concentrated focus, and multisensory activities. Some teachers already use background music and guided imagery with music as learning tools. A few of the techniques, such as using sing-along materials and rapping, have been used in elementary schools for years to assist in memory retention.

To develop a creative intelligence, it is important to blend accelerated learning techniques with the creative process in the flow of the discovery cycle. Lozanov's methods, developed primarily as a tool for teaching foreign languages, also provide excellent techniques for learning terms, facts, and content within any subject. But learning must not be relegated to simply knowing facts. The use of creative activities in accelerated learning assists in building confidence in personal expression as well as in developing abilities in the creative thought process. This can be carried further by providing experiences that develop creative thinking skills. As we become more aware of the rhythms of learning, we can develop an educational paradigm that uses creative methods for learning information and nurturing independent thinking skills.

Music and Learning

"Music enriches the human intellect and spirit. It can provide solace or joy, it can entertain or educate. And music is a universal language which helps to bind together the human community."
—Andrew Young

Music can be used in the classroom to accomplish the following goals:

- ✧ to create a relaxing atmosphere
- ✧ to establish a positive learning state
- ✧ to provide a multisensory learning experience that improves memory
- ✧ for the enhancement of active learning sessions
- ✧ as background sound for learning activities
- ✧ to increase attention by creating a short burst of energizing excitement
- ✧ to release tension by using music with movement
- ✧ to align groups
- ✧ to develop rapport
- ✧ to accentuate theme-oriented units
- ✧ to provide inspiration
- ✧ to add an element of fun

Music is recognized as a vital, easy, and simple tool for dynamic improvement in body and mental awareness. Sound can bring physical and emotional balance and integrate many parts of the brain. During the past decade, systems to enhance learning through music have emerged as we have discovered revealing facts about the neurology of learning and the different ways in which each person listens. These new systems are based on the theory that when auditory stimulation is blended with study, teaching, and cognition, there is an increased ability to memorize, learn, and think.

The brain accepts cognitive rhythms and patterns in a wide variety of ways. Each of us can notice how differently we react to learning every day. Our emotions, our health, our body English, and our ability to concentrate determine our keenness to learn. Music, vocal patterning, and tonal production give the teacher extraordinary opportunities to bring a group of students or an individual learner into his or her own pattern for optimal learning.

Music can be used to relax the body and mind yet activate attention, so there is more ease and trust in the learning process. Music assists in the focus, concentration, and ability to learn new words, sounds, and meanings. The experience of *hearing* music in a learning environment is very different from that of *listening* to the same music in a concert or home entertainment situation. In an accelerated learning format, the music is used for its ability to assist the flow of information and to entrain the learner into a positive learning state.

Music has the unique quality of integrating the emotional, cognitive, and psychomotor elements that activate and synchronize brain activity. Not only does music relax and stimulate the listener simultaneously, it also educates the learner in listening skills and the refined architecture of sound.

"Music to me is the essence of all that is living. Through music we see all that has passed before and all that is still to be. Music is a relationship with life itself."
—Bobby Vinton

> *"What is best in music is not to be found in notes."*
>
> —Gustav Mahler

Choosing Music

The accelerated learning techniques use classical music to enhance learning. Different forms and styles are used for specific effects based upon the way that rhythm, tempo, melody, and affect have been developed by the composer. The unique blending of these elements in each piece of music elicits a logical and emotional response that promotes specific learning consequences. Accelerated learning techniques use a variety of music with contrasting elements and effects to create a comprehensive, multifaceted learning experience. Georgi Lozanov and fellow researcher, Dr. Elena Gateva, have developed specific classroom methods for using the music of the Baroque, Classical, and Romantic periods.

Baroque music was written between 1600 and 1750 and is characterized by a predictable rhythmic and harmonic structure. This style of music creates a thinking environment for the student that integrates easily with inner speech and inner thought. The predictable characteristics of the music initiate a sense of stability especially beneficial in passive learning sessions. Gateva developed a highly effective learning technique that uses Baroque music in a learning session she calls "passive concert readings."

A common musical form of this time contains three movements: fast, slow, and fast. The slow movements generally have a pulse around 50 to 70 beats per minute and are entitled largo, lento, pastorale, or adagio. The pulse in these slow movements is similar to the rhythm of the human heartbeat and has been found to slow body functions, an important factor in orchestrating a relaxed learning situation. These slow movements are often used as background for passive concert readings, but entire concertos or symphonies are also used, including the faster movements (entitled moderato, allegro, allegretto, and sometimes vivace or presto). The varying tempos and affective aspects in the fast and slow movements provide contrasts in the emotional content of the music that stimulate a great depth of feeling and thought for the learner.

Music from the Classical time period (1750 to 1820) holds a continuity, clarity, and order within its sound but incorporates greater changes in rhythm, tone color, and harmony than music from the Baroque era. The tendency toward greater experimentation with musical elements was expanded in the era following Classicism, called the Romantic period (1820 to 1900). Freedom of expression and experimentation was prevalent during this musical time period and Romantic music has a dynamic, emotional sense often characterized by strong rhythms, unique sound textures, and changes in emotional context.

Selected works from the Classical and Romantic eras are used in accelerated learning for "active" concert readings. Music from these time periods has a dynamic sense of movement and, when used to enhance learning material, creates a broad range of emotional and cognitive associations. Entire works with varying movements are recommended in accelerated learning techniques for active concert readings.

The Impressionistic era (late nineteenth and early twentieth centuries) focused on the creation of free-flowing musical moods and impressions and was intended to evoke images for the listener. Impressionists experimented with new tonalities that even extended into the use of dissonance. There is considerable variation between impressionistic composers and selections; some of the music is intense and highly expressive, while other pieces imply subtle nuances of mood. Impressionistic music is not often used in accelerated learning techniques, but some selections have great value for their ability to relax and evoke images.

"Music may be termed the universal language of mankind, by which human feelings are made equally intelligible to all; whilst, on the other hand, it offers to the different nations the most varied dialects, according to the mode of expression suitable to the character of each nation."

—Franz Liszt

Some Baroque composers:
Vivaldi
Handel
Bach
Pachelbel

Some Classical composers:
Haydn
Mozart

233

Many proponents of accelerated learning believe that only fine classical music should be used because the powerful vocabulary of the great masters of Western music creates important poetic subtleties that enhance higher forms of thought. Accelerated learning teachers are currently discovering that some selections of ambient or attitudinal music, a style of music that greatly alters the sense of space and time, can also create this effect and elicit a state of relaxed alertness as well.

"All types of music should be explored; nobody should limit themselves. To do so would be like always having to view a tree without its leaves."
—Bobby Vinton

The music of the Baroque, Classical, and Romantic periods does have a great degree of orientation for our culture in its linguistic and poetic syntax. The melodic forms clearly hold great expression and inflection of dramatic oratory. Yet music is a symbolic language that speaks in many tongues. It is not just one universal language that can be hailed as understandable by all. There are as many musical languages as there are written languages in the world. We do not discount the validity of a rare dialect of Urdu in south India. We simply know that while we do not understand, much less speak, the Urdu language, it is a valid form of communication for those who speak it.

Some Romantic composers:
Tchaikovsky
Wagner
Debussy
Beethoven
Chopin

In the same context, how many of us understand Bach, Mozart, and Stravinsky well enough to speak (play, sing or compose in their styles) their languages? How many of us speak and understand Tibetan chanting, Japanese gagaku, or southern Italy's tarantella music? Gregorian chants and Austrian waltzes may be as familiar to us as country and western or jazz may be to others in our society. As we begin to explore the powers of music, of rhythmic sound stimulation, and the beauty of different forms of music, there is a realization that each is a unique language with a powerful emotive element.

Innovative teachers have experimented with more ambient forms of music for optimal learning environments. The music of Eno, Kitaro, Campbell, and other ambient composers has been successfully applied in accelerated learning. Both new forms of music and the classical styles are proving effective. If a teacher does not like newer forms of music, it is unlikely to be successful in the classroom. Any debate on teaching styles and musical tastes should be left with the results, engagement, and the joy of both the teacher and the learners.

There are many ways to use music in the classroom. The style of music used will be determined by the effect desired. Accelerated learning techniques have defined specific styles for particular uses. As teachers experiment in using music in their classrooms in new and different ways, they can explore a variety of forms to discover the most appropriate music for each use.

"Music is as natural as sun or rain. I'd hate to imagine our world without it, for my heart is a song."

—Big Bird

Because of the dangers of habituation, it is important not to overuse music and risk losing its effectiveness. A good rule of thumb is to use it no more twenty-two minutes per hour. A continuous twenty-two-minute selection is effective, yet shorter blocks of time distributed throughout an hour work well also. Three seven-minute selections at the beginning, middle, and end of an hour can be very effective. The length of music used during passive or active learning sessions will vary depending upon the amount of learning material. Active sound breaks, in the form of short musical activities that stimulate and empower the attention of the student, need only take two to three minutes.

The repeated use of music with one specific effect, even at various times throughout the day, is more likely to result in habituation than the use of varied musical styles and intentions. A comprehensive use of all of the accelerated learning techniques (active concert, passive concert, and activations) as well as sound breaks and appropriate music for background provides a variety of musical intentions and allows music to be used extensively as a classroom aid with little danger of habituation.

In most uses of music in the classroom, a moderate or low volume is effective and not distracting. Good sound equipment is essential for using music in the classroom. Music played on inadequate cassette playback machines does not even act as a placebo for enhancing listening and learning. A sound system with a clear, full spectrum will benefit the learning process.

Placement of sound also enhances the effectiveness of classroom music. When the sound system is placed toward the left ear, the music enters the left ear and right brain. The teacher's voice can then be directed more toward the leading language ear (the right ear) for increased effectiveness of the listening process. Memory improves when the cognitive and affective auditory information are unified.

While most students will become very comfortable with the use of music in the classroom, at times one or two students may be very annoyed by music. Placing those students to the far right side, halfway or to the rear of the room, away from the source of music, usually resolves the problem.

Instrumental music is generally more effective than vocal music for most uses in the classroom, as the presence of words distracts the listener. Vocal music in a foreign language, such as Gregorian chants, will not be distracting, however, as the mind will not focus on words it does not understand. Music used to accentuate a theme, inspire students, or as a sound break or sound cue may often have words that help to create the desired effect by evoking additional mental and emotional associations.

The music lists provided in this chapter are only a little of what is available. They contain music for use in the Lozanov techniques and other applications of classroom sound. You may already have most of the materials you need in your own private cassette library. Often, not all of the selections on a tape are appropriate for use. In this case, it is helpful to make your own tapes of those selections you wish to use. You can then play the desired selection at any time without having to search for it.

Background Music

Music provides effective background sounds that promote a student's general receptivity. Background music can be used to nurture concentration while students are working independently in reading, writing, studying, or participating in creative activities or lab times. Selections need to be made carefully as music holds elements that nurture particular moods and draw out specific emotions. Various styles of music will work for background music, including the music shown in the list for passive styles. As you experiment, you may notice that the time of day affects the best choice of music as well as its timing and use for better concentration.

—Selections That Help Concentration

Barzak Educational Institute. Music for Optimal Performance
Bear, Keith. *Echoes of the Upper Missouri* (Native Flute)
Campbell, Don. Essence
Campbell, Don. *Music for the Mozart Effect.* Vol. I, Strengthen the Mind
Campbell, Don. *The Mozart Effect.* Music for Children, Vol. I, Tune Up Your Mind
Daub, Eric. Pianoforte
Gregorian chant
LIND Institute. Relax with the Classics (Adagio)
Searles, Richard. Dance of the Renaissance
Peacock, Christopher. Oceans
Winston, George. *December*

Music used as a background for spoken instructional material can relax the student and create a passive learning state, or energize and create a stimulating, active learning state.

The Passive Style

Music can be used to create a passive learning state by playing fairly slow music as a quiet background while the teacher reviews information, reads, or lectures on new material. This use of music relaxes the student, initiates brain waves for an optimal learning state, and increases the student's attention span.

"I think of music as the ultimate form where thought and feeling, idea and instinct most effortlessly and naturally join."
—Arthur Miller

237

Accelerated learning techniques most often use Baroque music in passive concert readings. Following a short two- to four-minute relaxation exercise of imagery with music, there may be ten to fourteen minutes of background Baroque music while the teacher reads learning material. This is followed by three or four minutes of faster music to move students to a more active state.

In the foreign language accelerated learning format, the passive concert reading immediately follows the active concert reading. During the reading, the students' eyes are closed, and there is a sense of quiet and repose, a position of soothing receptivity. The teacher reads, stressing the inflection and flow of the foreign language.

"Music begins where words end."
—Johann Wolfgang von Goethe

There are many other beneficial uses of the passive concert reading techniques. Spellings and word definitions in any subject area may be read to passive music providing time after each definition or word for students to absorb the information and inwardly echo or think. The pulse of the music dictates the pace of the spoken material. Baroque or Classical music provides a predictable rhythmic pulse to guide the pace of speech and a stability of flow and temperament to encourage a passive learning state.

Passive concerts may also be in the form of a guided imagery journey, a metaphorical story, a review of important points of information, or even an explanatory section from a text. The teacher's voice moves slowly, with no conscious effort to match the phrases of voice and music exactly. The background music for these uses may include the Baroque, Classical, ambient, or occasionally carefully selected Romantic or Impressionistic styles of music.

To increase effectiveness, the teacher should listen carefully to music before using it for passive learning sessions to insure that the flow and intention of the music is appropriate. The selection must also be long enough for the reading, or more than one piece may be used if a consistency of flow is maintained.

The *Relax with the Classics* series that Charles Schmid of the Lind Institute has created explicitly for optimal learning environments is especially recommended for passive learning sessions. Each tape in the series provides a variety of selections with a specific tempo: adagio, andante, largo, or pastorale. The quality of the performances and recording is excellent.

Complete concertos or sonatas with movements of varied tempos can also be used for passive sessions. Almost any of the Baroque composers' music can be used for this purpose. The Optimalearning series from the Barzak Educational Institute provides cassettes with combinations of fast and slow movements. The contrast between the stimulating and relaxing movements of the Baroque music can help to focus the attention of the student.

Some Romantic, Impressionistic, and ambient music will work well for passive style guided imageries, stories, or text readings. The following list contains selections of passive style music with consistent slow tempos, musical selections with different tempos, and appropriate ambient style music.

—Selections for Passive Styles

Selections with consistent slow tempos:
Bach, J. S. "Jesu Joy of Man's Desiring"
Campbell, Don. *The Mozart Effect.* Music for Children, Vol. II, Relax, Daydream and Draw
Daub, Eric. Pianoforte
Halpern, Steven. Spectrum Suite
Kobialka, Daniel. Velvet Dreams
LIND Institute. *Relax with the Classics* (Adagio)
LIND Institute. *Relax with the Classics* (Largo)
Pachelbel, Johann. *Canon in D*
Satie, Erik. *Gymnopedies*
Speero, Patricia. Classical Harp

Selections with a variety of tempos:
Bach, J. S. *Brandenburg Concertos,* especially No. 2
Barzak Educational Institute. *Baroque Music No. 1 or 2*

(cont.)

Barzak Educational Institute. Mozart and Baroque Music
Barzak Educational Institute. Baroque Music to Empower
   Learning and Relaxation
Handel, George Frederick. *Water Music Suite*
Kobialka, Daniel. Celtic Quilt
Vivaldi, Antonio. *The Four Seasons*

Selections of ambient music:
   Bearns and Dexter. *Golden Voyage Nos. 1-4*
   Crutcher, Rusty. Macchu Piccu Impressions

Passive style music can be used to relax or rejuvenate students. At the beginning of an afternoon class, seven minutes of passive music played without speaking will relax and prepare a tired body and mind to receive concrete information. A short review of information using guided imagery and passive music during the afternoon, or after an intense study session, will provide a needed opportunity to refocus and relieve tension or stress. If the teacher is seeking to deeply relax students, or if students are tired and need a mini-nap, selections from the relaxation list would be appropriate for a six- to eight-minute time period. Many of the selections in the passive styles list are appropriate for short relaxation sessions. Listed below are other selections that work well.

"To learn the language of music—or at least to respond to it—one needs only an ear and a heart."
—David Mannes

—Selections for Relaxation

Campbell, Don. Essence
Campbell, Don. *The Mozart Effect.* Music for Children, Vol. II, Relax, Daydream and Draw
Chapman, Phillip, Anthony Miles and Stephen Rhodes. Music for Relaxation
Daub, Eric. *Pianoforte*
Debussy, Claude. *Afternoon of a Fawn*
Gardner, Kay. *Rainbow Path*
Goldman, Jonathan. *Dolphin Dreams* (deep relaxation)
Goodall, Medwyn. *Medicine Woman*
Halpern, Steven. *Comfort Zone*
Kobialka, Daniel. *Celtic Fantasy*
Kobialka, Daniel. *Path of Joy*
Kobialka, Daniel. When You Wish upon a Star
LIND Institute. *Relax with the Classics* (Adagio)
LIND Institute. *Relax with the Classics* (Classical Impressions)
LIND Institute. *Relax with the Classics* (Largo)
Locke, Kevin. *Dream Catcher* (Native Flute)
Narada Collection. *African Voices*
Robertson, Kim. *Wind Shadows* (Celtic harp)

If deep relaxation has been reached, play a selection from the passive styles suggestions to activate the iso principle and slowly initiate a return to an active attention state.

The Active Style

The passive, relaxed states of learning must coexist with active phases. Passive imagery without the active utilization of the information in the imagery does not provide the best use of sensory integration. Active concert readings and multisensory exercises or activations are needed to elaborate upon the information and integrate it within the mind and body.

In accelerated learning, an active concert reading by the teacher is often used to introduce new material. Emphasizing language dramatically and leaving space between words allows students to absorb the new language sounds more easily. The rhythmic flow of the sounds and speech is matched to the dramatic flow of the music.

"Music is always movement, always going somewhere, shifting and changing and flowing from one note to another. That movement can tell us more about the way we feel than a million words can."
—Leonard Bernstein

Just as the musical score of a movie is responsible for setting the mood and flow of action, music can be used to influence the mood and flow of a learning session. Music builds excitement, creates a sense of emotional engagement, and adds drama to cognitive information written in the form of stories, poems, and short plays. The appropriate use of music can also enhance learning sessions in which students are engaged in movement, drama, or art experiences that entail cognitive thought and listening patterns with an active brainwave state.

Active sessions can be in the form of a dramatic play in which the students participate in part reading. In accelerated learning foreign language instruction, plays are often used without music following the passive concert readings. Plays are a valuable instructional tool for any subject material and can also be used with background music to enhance the emotional impact of the information. Students may even participate in writing their own plays and selecting the music to accompany the script.

Accelerated learning methods recommend the use of Classical and Romantic styles of music for active concert readings. The following Baroque, Classical, Romantic, and ambient music selections can be used successfully in active sessions. Each piece of music has its own feeling and flow. Teachers will want to explore these and other selections to find the most appropriate music for each active learning session.

—Selections for Active Styles

Beethoven, Ludwig van. *Piano Concerto No. 5 in E Flat Major, Opus 73*
Handel, George Frederick. *Royal Fireworks Suite*
Haydn, Franz Joseph. *Symphony No. 94 in G Major*
Mozart, W. A. *Eine Kleine Nachtmusik*
Mozart, W. A. *Mozart Piano Concerto Nos. 17 and 18*
Mozart, W. A. *Symphony in D Major, Haffner*
Mozart, W. A. *Violin Concerto No. 5 in A Major*
Tchaikovsky, Peter Ilyich. *Piano Concerto No. 1 in B minor*
Vivaldi, Antonio. *The Four Seasons*

Soundbreaks

Short active phases of music can be used to stimulate awareness, create greater focus, and synchronize brain waves. A two- or three-minute soundbreak can be of great benefit to learners of all ages. This use of sound can shift the whole mood, intention, and rhythm of the classroom. When learners are tired or have scattered energy, music that stimulates and activates kinesthetic imagination creates a unified field of attention. During the after-lunch energy slump, when there is subject material to be covered, highly charged music with imagery of dancing, moving, running, or clapping can rejuvenate students. At other times, soundbreaks can be used as cues to gain student attention, as noted in the activity "How to Have Quiet without Really Asking" on page 122. Students can bring in their favorite three-minute selections of active sound and help teachers to build a good soundbreak library. You may find many soundbreak selections in your personal collection of popular, classical, jazz, or other music styles.

"Music is one of the things, like the ability to laugh, that has kept mankind going for all of these thousands of years."
—Charles M. Schulz

The following list provides musical suggestions for a variety of activation techniques. Some selections will be appropriate for kinesthetic release, others as stimulating background sounds, and some for gaining student attention.

—Selections That Help Activate

Bach, J. S. *Well-Tempered Klavier*
Campbell, Don. *The Mozart Effect. Music for Children*, Vol. III, Mozart in Motion
Campbell, Don. *Music for The Mozart Effect*. Vol. I, Strengthen the Mind
Chappelle, Eric. *Music for Creative Dance, Vol. I*
Deep Forest. *Deep Forest* (African music)
Jensen, Eric. *Music Magic* (a collection of sound cues)
Lewis, Brent. *Earth Tribe Rhythms* (Drums)
Lewis, Brent. *A Tisket, A Tasket, A Rhythm Basket* (Drums)
LIND Institute. *Relax with the Classics* (Classical Rhythms)
Louis Clark. *Hooked on Classics Collection*
Lynch, Ray. *Deep Breakfast*
Mannheim Steamroller. *Saving the Wildlife*
Sousa, John Phillip. *Marches*
Winter, Paul. *Earthbeat*
Yanni. *Keys to Imagination*

Vocal Patterning

There is a rhythm and tone in everything we say. As we begin to pay attention to the vibrancy and flow of our words, we realize the effects that the pattern and tone of our words have not only on ourselves but on those around us. As teachers develop a sensitivity to the rhythmic patterning and tonal potential that lie within the voice, they will find powerful abilities to entrain students and move the classroom tempo with their voice alone.

Speaking in different rhythms and rhymes with a variety of tonal and melodic variants has created remarkable success in clinical settings. In many instances, older people who have had strokes remember childhood rhymes, songs, and poems quite well even though speech skills are impaired. Skills developed in childhood have been observed to assist in the rehabilitation of stroke patients. Those patients who had a high degree of sensory integration in childhood seem to have more ease in relearning verbal and physical skills.

The use of some of these same rhythmic speaking techniques are of great value in reading, writing, and learning. The systematic use of

the techniques in teaching has not yet been measured with the same degree of interest as it has in clinical or therapeutic settings. Yet the results have been recorded significantly through teachers, parents, and the students themselves.

Speaking techniques that use the tool of vocal patterning, with or without music, provide students and teachers with fun and easy methods of learning. "Rap" or rhythmic rhyme is much easier for the brain to organize than long, sophisticated sentences. Attention can be heightened by merely changing the texture of the voice. Accelerated learning methods involve changing the vocal tonality to perk interest. In passive concerts in which lists of word definitions are to be memorized, accelerated learning teachers are instructed to rotate between two or three different vocal textures to reduce the possibility of habituation to the voice and music. Active concert sessions depend as much on the dramatic power of the voice as on the excitement of the music.

The transfer of information from voice to ear, from mind to paper, and from self to another involves many of the elements found in music. The rhythm of the consonants, the flow of the vowel sounds, the melodic freedom or constraint of each sentence can be measured and, in a sense, notated as musical form. These elements can effectively blend music with spoken information for accelerated listening and learning.

The teacher's awareness of the skill in using the teaching voice and musical background in counterpoint is essential for obtaining effectiveness in active and passive learning sessions. The voice and music must work together to create a flow and pattern that will be easily accepted by the brain. Music with a slow, steady tempo slows down the voice in such a way that there is a subtle yet effective pacing that empowers the listening attention of the student. The movement of the dynamic styles of music can encourage the teacher to lend dramatic emphasis and interest to learning sessions. To create an educational harmony between music and voice, the teacher's voice need only emphasize pattern and meaning while following the flow of the musical sounds.

Teachers who are very comfortable with their voice and its potentially dramatic abilities are able to improvise concert sessions and guided imagery quite effectively. Others may need rehearsal to synchronize both the music and the voice. Activities in this chapter, as well as the gibberish and rap activities in other chapters, provide insights into vocal patterning for enhanced learning.

Building the Image

There is great power in the images that we see, create, and are given. The rhythms of our emotions, body, mind, and spirit can be nurtured and developed through imagery. Much recent research has focused on the success of imagery to cure disease. In learning, the image forms the basis of our thoughts and ideas. The ability to image may be one of the most important lifelong learning tools we can develop.

There is great
power in the
images that
we see, create,
and are given.

Learning Images

Win Wenger has investigated the development of the image in cognitive skills. He has looked carefully at the learning methods employed by Socrates to develop the observational skills of students. Socratic method nurtures heightened awareness and perception, the first step in creative intelligence. The term education itself was named after the Socratic concept of observation: "drawing forth" from internal observations.

The ability to observe patterns and rhythms in both the inner and outer worlds gives the individual a wealth of information from which to create intelligent thoughts and actions. Many of the great breakthrough discoveries in science have been made by individuals who continuously made detailed recordings of their personal observations. The importance of astute observational skills to perception and intelligence can be seen through the examples of the great thinkers and scientists.

"The soul never thinks without a picture."
—Aristotle

Wenger discovered that a crucial aspect in the process followed by Socratic thinkers and learners involved telling others about their observations. They continually asked questions and explored new dimensions about the object of attention. The process of "search and describe" is a pole-bridging, brain-integrating technique that provides the important key of motivation. The questions, and often the answers, all evolve from the inner world of the student, stimulating the learner's curiosity. There is great success in learning when the student is enthused and involved in the process of discovery. Even when the answers a student intuits are not correct, the depth of understanding obtained when one realizes what is not right as well as what is right may be greater than a superficial memorization of only right answers.

Wenger developed an observational technique called image streaming, "the practice of allowing undirected, spontaneous images to come into one's mind's eye, while at the same time describing those images aloud to an external focus." This type of visual thinking draws subtle perceptions into the focus of full consciousness. These perceptions can be more readily examined for content and meaning through descriptions. The verbal expression of free-formed, even unconscious, perceptions and impressions into concrete descriptive words is believed to be critical in obtaining substantial gains in intelligence. Research by Professor Charles Reinert with students at Southwest State University in Minnesota on I.Q. gains from the development of the image-streaming technique has revealed a .9 increase in I.Q. gain on standardized tests for every hour of image-streaming practice.

The expression of observations is a key element in the process of observational learning. How many of us as teachers know the value of explaining what something means to someone else? Often, the best way to learn is to teach: our observational abilities heighten, and the concept is solidified in our mind as we explain it. We remember better when we have expressed something ourselves, than when we have only heard someone else express it. Students, too, can benefit when given the same opportunity to express themselves.

Wenger has investigated other methods of increasing intelligence and contends that the pole-bridging effect of creating communication pathways between brain regions occurs during activities that demand concurrent processing within the brain. The expressive activities such as those involved in music, art, movement, drama, and oratory can each result in positive effects on the intelligences because they rely on an expression of inner images in the outer world.

Building the ability to work with images internally develops our powers of creative thinking in many aspects of living. As we develop observational abilities, awareness of our surroundings increases. The ability to articulate our observations is an important tool in communication and career skills. Lifelong learning skills rely on the integration of concepts and images internally and the outward articulation of our beliefs and perceptions.

Guided Images

Guided imagery can teach awareness skills through example. When we provide images for students, we are giving them a model for their development of undirected imagery. Used as a teaching technique while students are in a passive learning state, guided imagery can be a relaxing, brain-integrating method of obtaining information.

Guided imagery often uses music to create a state of relaxed alertness. The music enhances the flow of words and images by creating the mood and emotional context for the imagery. An important aspect of effective guided imagery is the use of verbal images that bring to mind various sensory stimuli: smell, touch, taste, sound, color, emotion, and texture. The use of metaphors will anchor images within the right brain and enhance memory retention.

Passive learning concerts can be developed in the format of a guided imagery journey. For example, teachers can lead students in a guided imagery of the flow of blood through the body, the growth of a plant, the historical struggle of people from bondage, or the life of an important composer. Guided imagery can be used for short reviews of material immediately following presentation of the information, or at periodic review points. The benefits of incorporating the senses and emotions make this a successful, memory-enhancing review method.

The Image of Self

The Latin word *persona*, for person or personality, translates as "through sound." Through our sounds, we express our personality and who we are. Our communication depends not only on what we say but on how we say it. Listening to the sounds people express will tell us much about their personality and who they are. When we consciously attune to the subtle messages within the vocal expression of others, we can determine much about their present state.

Through sound we are able to receive communication and contact from the outer world. Our own sound allows us to move from the inner world to the outer world, to express what impresses us. Because of this, our own sound is a particularly vulnerable part of us. When we are empowered, it is reflected in our voice. When we are not empowered, this, too, is reflected by the inflection in our sounds.

Teachers recognize the need within the classroom to build students' self-image. Only through the comfort of a positive personal view can students comfortably move from the inner world to the outer world and be receptive to learning. Listening to students' expression of sound can provide great insights into their persona, their person, or personality. In this same way, providing students with the opportunity to express sound in new ways can open the door to the expression of new aspects of their personality.

Sound expression can alter the physical, emotional, mental, and spiritual state. The extended sounding of vowels with full frequency range can actually electrically charge the brain and change the brain-wave sequence by synchronizing brain waves into a state of unified consciousness. The use of sound for release of tension can assist the student in making room for new learning experiences. Release of emotion through vowel sounds frees the limbic brain to focus on the task at hand and allows the student to enter the learning process with greater attention.

Accelerated learning techniques and many other teaching methods recognize motivation as the first step in learning. Positive imagery is used to build the image of the self. Guided imagery techniques can be used to lead the student into memories of positive aspects about themselves and their learning. These short imagery activities can be used to begin a learning session and empower students to know that they learn quickly and easily.

Studies have shown that when people hear reinforcement about their abilities, they have a greater tendency to believe in themselves and manifest positive results. Conversely, students who often hear that they lack abilities are just as likely to believe that those statements are true. When students hear their own voices speak in positive ways about themselves and their learning abilities, even more benefit can be gained. When we truly believe in our learning potential, we are able to develop learning as a lifelong goal and desire.

Composing the Classroom

In Phase Forward Education, music and other instruments of learning can be used to empower the teacher, the student, and the method. But it is not the music or method itself that unifies as much as the ability to creatively observe what is actually happening in the classroom. The harmony between the learner, the subject matter, and the teacher creates the optimal engagement for learning.

Achieving the lifelong ability to recall and understand information is paramount. In childhood the acute ability to associate taste, texture, touch, sounds, and smells in the form of dance, music, games, sports, and art creates integrated sensory experiences. These experiences are successfully patterned when the rhythm of the inner and outer worlds harmonize. It is through the use of these tools that the harmonization of long- and short-range memory are made apparent.

As we move into more research on the brain, learning, and retention, we realize that the child's play, rest, and involvement with creative and cognitive activities all determine learning desires and ability. When learning time is enhanced through concentration, joy, and interest, we can easily reap the lifelong benefits of learning. Simply, we are allowing the rhythmic orchestrating of what the mind-body does naturally: learn, heal, rest, and create.

Activities for Teachers
Tuning Up Our Teaching

As we now begin to blend our knowledge and sensitivity to inner and outer rhythms into a rhythmic pattern of teaching, we can compose a stimulating and comfortable classroom environment with the use of music, accelerated learning methods, and image-building techniques. With these tools and the discovery process, the journey of lifelong learning becomes a stress-free, exciting, and important focus of living. In our role as teacher, we become an orchestrator of lifelong learning.

CHOOSING MUSIC FOR THE LEARNING ENVIRONMENT

✧ Listen to one or two selections from each of the following music categories:

—Selections That Help Concentration

Barzak Educational Institute. *Music for Optimal Performance*
Bear, Keith. *Echoes of the Upper Missouri* (Native Flute)
Campbell, Don. *Essence*
Campbell, Don. Music for *The Mozart Effect*. Vol. I, Strengthen the Mind
Campbell, Don. *The Mozart Effect. Music for Children*, Vol. I, Tune Up Your Mind
Daub, Eric. *Pianaforte*
Gregorian chant*
LIND Institute. *Relax with the Classics* (Adagio)
Peacock, Christopher. *Oceans*
Serles, Richard. *Dance of the Renaissance*
Winston, George. *December*

OBJECTIVE
To develop the use of music as a classroom learning tool

DESCRIPTION
The teacher will explore the use of different kinds of music for various activities.

MATERIALS
Cassette tapes from the suggested lists and the teacher's personal library, and a cassette player

SCHEDULING
Time to become familiar with a few suggested cassette tapes and review personal libraries for appropriate music

* indicates use for imagery activities

253

—Selections for Passive Styles

Selections with consistent slow tempos:

Bach, J. S. "Jesu Joy of Man's Desiring"
Campbell, Don. *Music for The Mozart Effect(*, Vol. II, Heal the Body
Daub, Eric. *Pianoforte*
Halpern, Steven. *Spectrum Suite*
Kobialka, Daniel. *Velvet Dreams*
LIND Institute. *Relax with the Classics* (Adagio)
LIND Institute. *Relax with the Classics* (Largo)
Pachelbel, Johann. *Canon in D*
Satie, Erik. *Gymnopedies**
Speero, Patricia. *Classical Harp*

Selections with a variety of tempos:

Bach, J. S. *Brandenburg Concertos*, especially No. 2
Barzak Educational Institute. *Baroque Music No. 1 or 2*
Barzak Educational Institute. *Baroque Music to Empower Learning and Relaxation*
Barzak Educational Institute. *Mozart and Baroque Music*
Handel, George Frederick. *Water Music Suite**
Kobialka, Daniel. *Celtic Quilt*
Vivaldi, Antonio. *The Four Seasons*

Selections of ambient music:

Bearns and Dexter. *Golden Voyage Nos. 1-4*
Campbell, Don. *Essence*
Crutcher, Rusty. *Macchu Piccu Impressions*

—Selections for Relaxation

Campbell, Don. *Essence*
Chapman, Phillip, Anthony Miles and Steven Rhodes. *Music for Relaxation*
Daub, Eric. *Pianoforte*
Debussy, Claude. *Afternoon of a Fawn*
Gardner, Kay. *Rainbow Path**
Goldman, Jonathan. *Dolphin Dreams** (deep relaxation)
Goodall, Medwyn. *Medicine Woman*
Halpern, Steven. *Comfort Zone*
Kobialka, Daniel. *Celtic Fantasy*
Kobialka, Daniel. *Path of Joy**
Kobialka, Daniel. *When You Wish Upon a Star*
LIND Institute. *Relax with the Classics* (Adagio)
LIND Institute. *Relax with the Classics* (Classical Impressions)
LIND Institute. *Relax with the Classics* (Largo)
Locke, Kevin. *Dream Catcher* (Native Flute)
Narada Collection. *African Voices*
Robertson, Kim. *Wind Shadows* (Celtic harp)

—Selections for Active Styles

Beethoven, Ludwig van. *Piano Concerto No. 5 in E Flat Major, Opus 73*
Handel, George Frederick. *Royal Fireworks Suite*
Haydn, Franz Joseph. *Symphony No. 94 in G Major*
Mozart, W. A. *Eine Kleine Nachtmusik*
Mozart, W. A. *Mozart Piano Concerto Nos. 17 and 18*
Mozart, W. A. *Symphony in D Major, Haffner*
Mozart, W. A. *Violin Concerto No. 5 in A Major**
Tchaikovsky, Peter Ilyich. *Piano Concerto No. 1 in B minor**
Vivaldi, Antonio. *The Four Seasons*

—Selections That Help Activate

Bach, J. S. *Well-Tempered Klavier*
Campbell, Don. *The Mozart Effect*. Music for Children, Vol. III, Mozart in Motion
Campbell, Don. Music for *The Mozart Effect*. Vol. I, Strengthen the Mind
Chappelle, Eric. *Music for Creative Dance, Vol. I*   (cont.)

Deep Forest. *Deep Forest* (African Music)
Jensen, Eric. *Music Magic* (a collection of sound cues)
Lewis, Brent. *Earth Tribe Rhythms* (Drums)
Lewis, Brent. *A Tisket, A Tasket, A Rhythm Basket* (Drums)
LIND Institute. *Relax with the Classics* (Classical Rhythms)
Louis Clark. *Hooked on Classics Collection*
Lynch, Ray. *Deep Breakfast*
Mannheim Steamroller. *Saving the Wildlife**
Sousa, John Phillip. *Marches*
Winter, Paul. *Earthbeat**
Yanni. *Keys to Imagination*

✧ Go through your personal library of cassettes. Find selections that are similar to each of the music categories. Instrumental selections are preferred. Vocal music generally distracts listeners, although foreign language vocal music can be usable in guided imagery exercises and in some advanced exercises. Music that keeps a consistent pulse or mood for over ten minutes is preferred. Short pieces do not provide enough time for the tonal and rhythmic patterns of the music to successfully integrate, except for short activation pieces used to quickly change the learning pace.

✧ Add the appropriate selections from your personal library to your classroom sound library. Become very familiar with three or four selections in each category. Ten to fifteen cassette selections can create a full and powerful library.

✧ After you have become familiar with the selections, experiment in the classroom with a selection to help concentration in the following ways:

> play the music as students enter the classroom
> play the music during a study period
> play the music very softly while students are reading aloud
> play the music during classroom activities

✧ Experiment with a selection for relaxation in the same way. Note any differences in student response. Which activities worked best with the concentration music, and which were aided by relaxation music? What were the student rhythms before you played the music? How did the music change their rhythms? How did the music affect your rhythms? Which selections improved your teaching abilities and student learning abilities?

❖ Keep a record of the effects and positive uses for each selection.

As you discover the effects of each style of music and become sensitive to student rhythms, you will develop a sense for the effect of the music in the classroom. Be very conscious of the mood you wish to create when you use music intentionally. Knowing the learning state you wish to develop is essential to effectively selecting music that will create the appropriate rhythm. When you have developed a feel for the daily flow of energy in the classroom, you will be able to use music to direct the energy toward an optimal learning environment.

PASSIVE CONCERT READINGS

Passive concert readings are designed to provide students with information while they are in a state of relaxed alertness. Your voice and the music in a passive concert will be most effective if you allow the sounds to flow smoothly together. There is no need in a passive concert reading to pattern your voice with the rhythm of the music.

❖ Play a selection of music from the selections with consistent tempos in the passive styles list.

❖ Read the following passage aloud. Notice how the music changes your pace, depth of voice, and phrasing.

> *"Music is the archetypal ordering of sound. It patterns and enforces the powers of listening, attention, and memory for people in every culture. Music is not only art and a refined form of beauty's expression. Music is a subtle and dynamic power that unifies breath, tone, and rhythm within the human instrument for better memory and communication. Every sentence and every thought has musical qualities.*

OBJECTIVES
To develop the passive concert reading technique; to find effective music for use during passive concert readings; to experiment with the effect of musical pulse and flow during passive concert readings

DESCRIPTION
The teacher will read aloud to different styles of music and experiment with passive concert readings.

MATERIALS
Cassette tapes from the selections for passive styles list on page 254, a cassette player

SCHEDULING
15 to 30 minutes

When music is used in a meaningful way in a classroom, it trains listening. The pulsing and patterning of high frequencies demand attention on the part of both teacher and student. As the teacher's speech and the student's attention are harmonized in rhythmic and melodic phrases, optimal opportunities are created for ease in memory, learning, and formal thinking.

Studying the ear, the brain, and the manner in which patterns of sound assist in improving student attention, the teacher and parent can understand the vital significance of music in accelerated memory and learning."

—Don Campbell

✧ Experiment with volume and placement of sound. Never feel that the music is in competition with your voice. Instead, the music and your voice will enhance each other. Keep the music light and transparent, yet full. Optimally, use a stereo cassette playback unit with separated speakers, so the sound does not come from just one location. The position of the stereo sound is best when the teacher's voice is dominant on the right side of the listener, and the music, slightly softer, is on the left.

✧ Now change the music to a selection from the list of ambient music and reread the same passage. Notice the differences in your voice. Begin to see which music slows your voice the most. Which music gives you the most support?

✧ Experiment in the same way with selections with a variety of tempos.

✧ Find music from your own library and practice reading aloud with it.

✧ Choose three or four selections of music that allow you to be the most comfortable.

✧ Now find important passages from your curriculum guides or textbooks and practice reading these with your passive music selections.

✦ When you feel comfortable with the technique, begin to use it in the classroom to read lesson material in passive concert reading style for memory enhancement. You may also write your own text in the manner described in the activity "Learning Imagery" on page 263. Use the following procedure:

>Ask students to close their eyes and become as comfortable as possible.

>Play the passive music for two or three minutes before you begin speaking to allow students to entrain to the slower pace. You may wish to do a guided relaxation imagery before as well.

>Read the lesson material with the music.

>When you have finished reading, experiment with playing a slightly faster selection to assist students in moving to a more active state. A faster movement from the selection with a variety of tempos will be appropriate.

You may wish to use the technique for word definitions or spellings. In the accelerated learning format, before a passive concert of this type begins, the teacher reads through the word list once varying vocal intonation but using no music. The students follow along, reading silently from a worksheet. The teacher continues with the following procedure:

✦ Ask students to find a comfortable position and close their eyes. Then play the passive music for one or two minutes, and if desired, use guided imagery to bring students into a state of relaxed alertness.

✦ Read the first word, pause for 3 or 4 seconds, and then read the spelling or definition. Pause again before reading the next word. With each word, change your intonation slightly to avoid habituation to the sound. Speaking in almost a whisper, in a strong, full voice, and in a normal speaking voice are good variations of sound. In this style of passive concert reading you may use the pulse of the music to assist in developing a rhythmic flow in your reading.

259

❖ When the word list is complete, bring students slowly back to full alertness with the use of more active music.

In your uses of the passive concert reading technique, notice student response to the music. Which selections create a state of relaxed alertness for the students? How does the use of the technique aid student learning? How do students respond to the technique? Can you see differences in the students' daily rhythm patterns when they have an opportunity to vary their learning tempo? Does the music help students to refocus? How do you feel when you have an opportunity to vary your teaching style and rhythms?

As you experiment with passive concert readings, you will find optimal times to use the technique in your lesson plans. You may wish to investigate the accelerated learning format further to discover a way to blend passive concert readings with active concerts and activation exercises in this highly effective learning cycle.

RHYTHMS OF YOUR VOICE

OBJECTIVES
To assist in developing a rhythm and flow within the voice; to gain confidence in using the voice in different ways

DESCRIPTION
The teacher will read a sentence with various rhythmic patterns.

SCHEDULING
10 minutes

—ALL LIFE IS MOLECULAR

❖ Repeat "All life is molecular" to each of the rhythms below. Keep the eighth note as a steady pulse. Pay close attention to the accents within each phrase. Notice how the accents change the phrasing, meaning, and engagement of your voice.

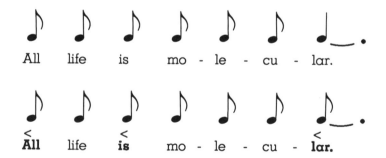

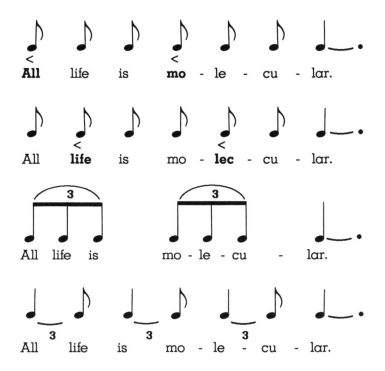

All life is **mo**-le-cu-lar.

All **life** is mo-**lec**-cu-lar.

All life is mo-le-cu-lar.

All life is mo-le-cu-lar.

FINDING YOUR OWN TEMPO

✦ Select three or four very short stories and read them aloud to a selection of music from one of the categories. Be conscious of your vocal inflection and the sense of flow, engagement, and patterning. Pause briefly between each sentence. Be dramatic with your voice, then be very quieting, as if reading to a small child falling asleep. The best results occur when your voice blends with the power of music.

✦ Choose another musical selection, and read the stories again. Notice which tempo and flow accentuates the story line. You may wish to experiment with a variety of selections.

OBJECTIVES
To be aware of the flow and power of your voice; to explore different textures, tempos, and inflections within the voice

DESCRIPTION
The teacher will experiment with dramatic reading to background music.

MATERIALS
Reading material, cassette tapes of selections from the categories listed on pages 253-256, and a cassette player

SCHEDULE
15 to 30 minutes

ACTIVE CONCERTS

OBJECTIVE
To develop active concert reading as a teaching tool

DESCRIPTION
The teacher will practice active concert reading.

MATERIALS
A cassette tape of selections from the active styles list (page 255), reading material, and a cassette player

SCHEDULING
30 minutes

✧ After you make a selection from the active styles list, find a short story or poem that has some dramatic energy in it. A parable, fable, or short fairy tale are good selections for reading in the active concert style.

✧ Listen to the musical selection a number of times. Be aware of dramatic highpoints in the music. Does it have an introduction that invites listening? Listen for two or three sections in the music where mood, pace, or energy change.

✧ Notice points of change within the story you have selected. Where does the action intensify? When does the mood change?

✧ Begin to experiment with the music and the text to discover if they can be paced accordingly. In active concert readings, the emotional flow of the information is developed to enhance memory through emotional association. Use the dramatic power of your voice to create an emotional rhythm. Experiment with changing the texture of your voice to enhance the presentation. Don't be inhibited. There is no one right way to create an active concert. The refinement comes with courage and practice.

✧ When you feel comfortable with your active concert style, begin to use the technique within your classroom to enhance lessons.

✧ Notice student response to the reading. Does the technique enhance learning and memory? How are student rhythms affected? What is their rhythm following the active concert reading? How do you feel? Is there a positive effect in the flow of the daily learning rhythm when you use this technique?

✧ You may find students who are interested in presenting their own active concert reading to the class. You might make this a special student project in place of a report or paper.

LEARNING IMAGERY

A guided imagery session can be an important technique for learning new material or reviewing information. The use of music and the relaxed presentation allow the information to be anchored in the memory system effectively. Nearly any material can be used in this form. Here is an example:

—THE WATER CYCLE

❖ Have students lie on the floor or sit comfortably in their chairs. Ask them to close their eyes, breathe deeply, and relax.

❖ Play the music for two minutes before beginning the imagery.

❖ With the music still playing, begin the imagery:

> *"Imagine that you are a molecule of water in the ocean. You are warmed by the sun and its energy changes your form. The sun evaporates you into the sky where you are suspended in the atmosphere. Eventually, you are joined by other particles of moisture in the sky and you bond together, condensing. As more and more particles join together you form a cloud. The wind blows you apart, but you bond together again. Finally, there are so many particles together that you fall as rain to the earth, wetting everything below. Some of the drops of water are absorbed into the soil, taken up by the roots of plants, and used to sustain their life. Other drops absorbed by the soil find their way to underground rivers and become a part of the water table. As you hit the ground, many other droplets fall by you, and you run together in a little rivulet of water. Others fall onto rocks and objects where they sit until the sun comes out later and evaporates them again.*
>
> *You have become a part of a rivulet that finds its way into a small creek. You join the moving waters and float in the creek for a long way. The creek joins with another creek, and the two blend and flow into a large lake. Many of the water molecules in the lake stay in its depths. Those on the surface are evaporated by*

OBJECTIVES
To develop a technique for review of learning material that enhances sensory integration; to relax students

DESCRIPTION
The teacher will present or review subject material in the form of guided imagery with music.

GRADE LEVEL
4 through adult

MATERIALS
A cassette tape from the relaxation list on page 255 or a selection marked for imagery, and a cassette player

SCHEDULING
10 minutes

the sun and wind. You, however, move slowly across the lake and flow out of the lake into a river. You move with the river many miles.

Your journey slows as the river comes to flatter ground, and you meander slowly through plains and fields. The river widens and is joined by many smaller creeks along the way. Ultimately your journey moves you into the ocean once again. The sun warms the surface of the ocean, and you find yourself heating and changing form to become a particle of moisture in the air. Your journey has come full cycle: through evaporation, condensation, rain, travel through creeks to the rivers and lakes, and ultimately to the ocean once again.

Now you may come back to our classroom."

✧ Play the music for a minute or two as students are returning to more active consciousness. Now play a slightly more active selection as students share their experience with a partner.

✧ Many different subjects can be used for guided imagery reviews. Here are a few suggestions:

> explore the stars and planets
> become a blood cell traveling through the heart and body
> be a seed of a beautiful flower that grows, buds, and unfolds
> become a bug living on a world traveler dog or cat and travel to foreign countries
> go back in time and become an important person in history
> become a famous composer and explore his or her life
> become a comma in Punctuationville
> develop a metaphorical story that assists in providing insight into a particular subject

✧ Learning imagery can be used to introduce a new lesson or to review previously learned material. As a quick break after a strenuous learning session or an opening activity in the morning, this imagery technique enhances the learning process.

264

Activities for Students

Tuning Up with Students

The tools we have used to explore our own personal patterns of thinking, feeling, and creating empower us to nurture this same awareness within our students. As students become aware of personal rhythms of learning, they can develop learning techniques that enhance their own discovery process and increase their ability to perceive and create. The gift of personal responsibility and desire for learning provides the strength through which a new creative intelligence can emerge. Blended with the desire and curiosity to seek new understanding, a foundation of personal learning and thinking skills leads the student along the discovery journey to lifelong learning.

TEXTURES OF READING

Reading material that is not interesting can often be made more exciting by reading it in different styles.

✦ Select a short story or poem for reading material.

✦ Use two or three of the following suggestions as you read the selection to students. Read the selection as if:

    making a speech to Congress
    it were being spoken to a kitten
    it were a very important secret
    it were being silently shouted across a football field
    one were skipping rope
    it were very, very rough
    it were very, very smooth
    one had a very British accent
    one were a cowboy from Texas
    it were a voice in a dream

✦ Have students read in some of the suggested ways or make up their own textures of reading.

OBJECTIVES
To explore the range of potential vocal intonations; to create interest in reading; to develop rhythm and vocal color in reading

DESCRIPTION
The teacher and students will read in a variety of intonations.

MATERIALS
A short passage, story, or poem

GRADE LEVEL
1 through 6

SCHEDULING
15 to 20 minutes

INSIDE, OUTSIDE, IN-BETWEEN

OBJECTIVES
To enhance memory;
to allow time and
space for connections
to be made between
new knowledge and
previously stored
information; to
develop the ability to
create an internal
image

DESCRIPTION
Students will hear
or read a sentence
or fact and then
close their eyes and
hear or visualize it
internally.

MATERIALS
For the student and
teacher: literature or
study materials.
For the teacher: a
cassette tape from the
concentration or
passive list on pages
253 and 254, and a
cassette player

GRADE LEVEL
4 though adult

SCHEDULING
10 to 20 minutes
during regularly
scheduled classroom
times

Use the following methods for enhancing reading sessions and developing comprehension:

❖ Play passive or concentration music softly.

❖ Read aloud to the students while the music plays. Pause after every sentence. Ask students to repeat the sentence with their inner voice during the pause.

❖ Then ask students to read to themselves. While students are reading silently, ask them to take a moment between each sentence or each paragraph and close their eyes while they visualize and think about what they have read.

❖ In foreign language instruction ask students to close their eyes. Say a phrase and ask the students to echo the phrase silently, then say it out loud together.

❖ For difficult material, change the rhythm of the wording, the pace of the music, or the tone of voice, and use the previous suggestions.

MAKING CLASSROOM TAPES

Often students feel that their music is not represented in the classroom music. After a few weeks of experimentation with background music in the class, have students bring in their own musical selections for the activation music, passive and active concerts, and background music.

✦ Discuss the important properties of sound and music in learning. You may want to have students do the Rhythms in Studying activity again (page 126).

✦ Each day, ask a different student to bring in a musical selection. Play students' selections for the class daily or set aside a half hour a week to work with music as a learning tool.

✦ Let students choose their three favorite selections in each musical use category.

✦ Begin a library from which the teacher can borrow students' music. Students may wish to start their own library. They will be enthused to have these tapes used in classroom learning sessions.

OBJECTIVES
To provide an opportunity for students to help select classroom music; to have students develop an understanding of how to select music to enhance learning

DESCRIPTION
Students will explore their personal music libraries and find selections for background music, passive and active concerts, and activation.

MATERIALS
Cassette tapes of various selections, and a cassette player.

GRADE LEVEL
4 through adult

SCHEDULING
Over a period of time; partly during regular school hours

RHYTHMSCAPE STUDY GUIDES

OBJECTIVES
To develop the skill of interpreting information in an expression of visual images; to allow the expressions of the right hemisphere and limbic brain centers to be seen; to provide a stimulus for students to share as a study tool

DESCRIPTION
Students will create a series of rhythmscapes for a particular subject and use them as a study guide.

MATERIALS
For each student: 8 1/2" x 11" sheets of unlined paper and a folder or a notebook of unlined paper, colored markers, and a paper cup to trace around

GRADE LEVEL
4 through adult

SCHEDULING
5 minutes for each rhythmscape during study time

Learning facts and concepts becomes easier when multiple senses are used. This activity incorporates kinesthetic, visual, and auditory learning modes as the students create a study guide. For example, have them create a rhythmscape history study guide:

✧ Read a history lesson.

✧ Give the students the materials listed.

✧ Ask students to make four circles on separate papers by tracing around the paper cup. Have students draw a rhythmscape to answer each of the following questions about the history lesson:

> What were the typical feelings of the place where the historical incident occurred?
> What were the feelings involved in the event which created history?
> What were the feelings like after the event?
> What was the most important feeling involved in this incident?

✧ Label each rhythmscape and write a paragraph by it describing the significance in this historical incident. Include names, dates, and other specific facts in the description.

✧ Use the notebooks or folders as study notes. Have students review their rhythmscapes periodically. Students can work in pairs, describing and sharing their rhythmscape interpretations.

Rhythmscape study guides also work well for social studies, language arts, science, music, and other subject areas.

IMAGE STREAMING

The ability to describe and observe builds strong language skills and develops the process of scientific inquiry. Everyone images all of the time, but we are generally not consciously aware of our images. The following activity is called image streaming and was developed by Win Wenger of the Institute for Visual Thinking. This technique will assist students in learning to observe and describe the images they see in their mind. For best results, have students do 10 to 15 minutes of image streaming each day for two weeks before moving on to the next activity.

The bell, chime, or glass of water and spoon provides a cue for students to listen for directions. Explain to your students that when you play one chime, they have 30 seconds to finish their imaging. Two or more chimes mean to stop speaking immediately.

✧ Have students find a partner and sit close together so they can hear one another's voice. One student will be the "imager," and the other will be the "spotter." Ask students to select their roles.

✧ Have the imagers close their eyes. Spotters will keep their eyes open. Imagers should make a point of breathing slowly, deeply, and smoothly.

✧ Tell your students:

"When we begin, imagers please close their eyes and describe any and every image they have, even if it seems unimportant. Describe the image to your spotter so that it is as real as possible to the spotter. Don't stop talking about your image; just continue to observe everything you can about it. Provide as much detail as you can and tell the spotter how your image looks, smells, feels, tastes, and sounds, the emotional aspects, and everything you are aware of in your imagery."

OBJECTIVES
To build language skills; to explore the scientific process of observation and inquiry; to develop the powers of observation and expand levels of awareness; to encourage the ability to produce imagery

DESCRIPTION
The teacher will provide students with opportunities to develop their abilities to make observations from their personal imagery.

ENVIRONMENT
A quiet room

GRADE LEVEL
3 through adult

MATERIALS
A bell, chime, or glass of water and a spoon

SCHEDULING
10 to 30 uninterrupted minutes for each session

✧ Allow three to five minutes for the imagers to describe their images. Ring the bell once and say:

> *"Be ready to stop speaking in a half minute, and I will give you further instructions."*

✧ At the end of 30 seconds, sound the chime two or more times and ask students to switch roles so the spotters are now imagers, and the imagers become spotters. Allow three to five minutes for the new imagers to share their images with their spotters.

✧ Next, have students find new partners and tell your students:

> *"When astronauts return from a mission, they tell the scientists at Mission Control every impression they can possibly remember from their experience. This debriefing process helps the scientists record important details that may lead to further discoveries. In this session, you are like the astronaut, and your new partner is in the same role as the Mission Control scientist. When you debrief your image streaming experience to your new partner, you will have two minutes to tell him or her everything you observed in your imagery. Tell it in the present tense as if it were just happening. For instance, you might say: 'I am seeing a picture of a small, worn, brown teddy bear lying on a large bed with a bright blue bedspread.' Your eyes are to remain open in this experience. Decide who will share their experience first and then begin."*

✧ After two minutes, chime the half-minute notice, wait 30 seconds, and chime two or more times for students to stop.

The images we perceive have more meaning when we describe them and interpret them for content and relevance. The students will gain greater benefits from the experience if you provide time to synthesize the experience and review the images for overall meaning. As a final step in this process, allow each student two or three minutes to interpret their images to their partners. For more information on the interpretation process, you may contact Win Wenger at the address listed in the Resource Guide appendix.

IMAGE BOOSTERS

The following techniques can be used as entertaining activities to encourage students to expand their ability to image. Some people have a difficult time in seeing their internal images. Win Wenger has found the following techniques to be successful as "triggers" to help students with their imaging ability. If imagers begin to see different images, instruct them to let their new images flow and describe these in detail. The important point is to get the imager to begin to see his or her own inner images.

The spotter can act as an assistant to help the imager develop imaging abilities. Tell the spotters:

> "You can help your partners recognize and describe their images. When imagers are breathing slowly and deeply, they will occasionally catch their breath for a moment. When they do this, they are probably seeing an image. Then you can ask them, 'What are you seeing now?' The movement of your imager's eyes under closed lids also tells you that an image is appearing. When you see movement under the imager's eyelids, ask, 'What are you seeing now?'"

✦ Memory Streaming—
   Have imagers close their eyes and remember a real experience, one with especially vivid colors and sensations. Ask imagers to describe this experience in great detail.

✦ Feeling Images—
   Tell spotters to lead their imagers around the room blindfolded and have them feel different objects. Then ask imagers to describe in detail the appearance of each item they feel.

OBJECTIVE
To provide students with additional techniques to develop the ability to image

DESCRIPTION
Students will use a variety of methods to help stimulate their own inner images.

GRADE LEVEL
1 through adult

MATERIALS
For each student: a few drops of vanilla on a cotton ball, and other aromatic foods. For the teacher: a short story

SCHEDULING
10 to 20 minutes

✦ Hearing Images—
Play music from the selections for active styles list on page 255. Have the imager notice images that the music triggers and describe these images fully to the spotter.

✦ Smelling Images—
Have imagers close their eyes and give them a smell of a strong, aromatic food. Ask them to describe the appearance of the food in detail while their eyes remain closed.

✦ Word Painting—
Read an interesting story, and ask imagers to paint word pictures of scenes from the story. See if the imagers can create images of scenes related but not described in the story.

✦ Setting the Scene—
Provide some guided imagery to set the scene for the imager. Begin the imagery with a multisensory description of the scene and then ask the imagers to explore the scene on their own. They may want to change their point of view and image the scene from above, from a different time period, as if they were a giant, or as if they were very small. Some suggestions for scenes:

Imagine:

walking in a meadow
drifting down a river
being a windblown leaf
floating on a cloud in the sky
looking through the bottom of a boat
climbing a mountain

IMAGE STREAMING THROUGH THE CURRICULUM

There are many useful applications for image streaming that relate to curriculum material. When image streaming is used as a process in the context of a lesson plan, student knowledge of the subject material will be greatly improved. Learning from any experience, event, or concept will be enhanced by the student's careful observation and detailed description. The added benefit is the development of language abilities.

Ask your students to image stream freely when you use the technique in a lesson plan. Remember to suggest to your students that they let their image stream go beyond the information that was in the book, the lecture, or demonstration as this assists students in drawing on their own thinking skills and makes connections with existing information.

The following list provides image-streaming examples that would be appropriate while studying these topics. The use of image streaming can become a natural part of any course of study. You and your students will find many topics for image streaming as you develop this technique.

Examples:

✦ Science
Image stream following a demonstration or experiment.
Image stream about a scientific process such as the life of a cell, the flow of blood through the body, the process of uplifting mountains

✦ History
Set the scene of a historical moment and image stream on the event
Become a historical character and image stream about his or her role in history (especially how the character feels about that role)

OBJECTIVES
To use the image-streaming technique as a tool to increase comprehension of cognitive information; to enhance perceptual abilities in understanding learning materials; to develop the image-streaming technique as a tool in creative intelligence; to increase memory retention; to provide an effective learning tool that reduces the time and stress involved in learning

DESCRIPTION
Students will use the image-streaming technique to describe their observations of classroom subject material.

ENVIRONMENT
A quiet room

GRADE LEVEL
3 through adult

MATERIALS
Classroom subject material

SCHEDULING
5 to 20 minutes, uninterrupted

❖ Social Studies
   Image stream life in another country

❖ Music and Art
   Image stream about compositions or art work
   Image stream about the composer's or artist's life

❖ Mathematics
   Image stream everything in students' awareness as they
   move step-by-step through a problem to a solution

Another interesting application is to pre-question subject material.
Ask students to image stream an object or idea before you explain it.

   For example:

   Give students a sedimentary rock and have them image
      stream about it.
   Show students a violin and have them image stream about
      how it is played and what it sounds like.
   Show students a picture of a foreign country you will be
      studying and ask them to image stream about the scene.
   Pass a starfish around the room and have students image
      stream about its life in the ocean.

This type of image streaming helps develop curiosity and motivation
in learning more, which also stimulates students to remember lessons
better.

CHAPTER VII

ORCHESTRATING INTELLIGENCE

Creating Form

Phase Forward Education develops a conscious intent to harmonize creative awareness with cognitive skills. The culmination of this focus is a unified intelligence. Through music, movement, rhythmic speech, the creative arts, and imagery, the stages of learning are integrated and provide a pathway to creative intelligence. The various parts of the brain (left and right neocortex, frontal, limbic, and reptilian) attain greater access to one another and enhance the facility of thought. The harmony and patterns of knowledge, creativity, common sense, foresight, and freedom to think in both logic and abstraction activate a unified intelligence.

Within life there is rhythm, pattern, flow, and form. Through the empowerment of teacher, students, and methods in Phase Forward Education, personal rhythms, patterns, and flow are explored. The blending of these elements creates the form of our life. Our intelligence, the ability to learn and create throughout life, is manifested through this form. We are each responsible for the development of the form of our personal lives, which shapes our local, national, and worldwide community. The future of our planet is shaped by the forms of living we choose together.

As teachers, we become a part of each child's learning experience and can have a great effect upon the form a student's life will take. Our success in the classrooms is greatly dependent upon the form and structure of our teaching. The model of the musical sonata-allegro form can provide insights into the development of form and lifelong goals.

The sonata-allegro form is a three-part form of music that became popular in the Classical and early Romantic periods of European music. Most of the little piano sonatinas learned by beginning piano students were built on this poetic form of sonic architecture:

> I. Exposition
> II. Development
> III. Recapitulation

"If the people lived their lives, as if it were a song, for singing out of light - it would provide the music for stars to be dancing circles in the night."
—from a Russian folk song

This structure involves the repetition and contrast that has been observed as the ideal way to teach by such diverse educational theorists as Plato, Piaget, Howard Gardner, and Dewey.

The sonata begins with the *exposition of a theme*, a fairly simple melody with harmonies that accompany it in a rhythmic sequence. In symphonies and sonatas the theme is the recognizable melody. In the exposition, the theme is presented a few times and repeats very clearly the statement of the music. After the theme is firmly established in the exposition, the music changes to a key that is relative (different but with similar aspects), and the theme develops.

The *development* may have a different background, slight variations in the melody, new sound colors, and a change in mood. The development section of the sonata empowers the theme with flexibility, vocabulary, and the freedom to explore and expand.

Lastly, the sonata comes home by *recapitulating*. The materials and the possibilities that have been presented are reviewed. The theme that began as a simple statement becomes ornate and full of variations. The theme's statement has been strengthened by going to new tonal centers, perhaps over new rhythms and harmonies. The journey is completed as the theme returns.

Learning also is a series of developments and recapitulations on many themes. Each step along the journey explores and expands our knowledge base. The more we allow ourselves to be creative and explore new variations, uses, and expressions of a theme of knowledge, the greater becomes our understanding and ability to purposefully use the knowledge. When our theme returns home and recapitulates, our lives hold greater interest as our development has provided more ideas to draw upon.

The sonata-allegro form is a metaphor for life's journey. The music has made a statement, developed the thought, and come home. Each piece of music has had its own theme and zeal for expression. We each create our own form and style for the journey of life. We may develop and model our journey upon the themes of parents, teachers, or environments. The life themes we choose give us a sense of purpose that encourages creative intelligence and lifelong learning.

The choices that make the greatest changes in the direction of our journey are often the most dangerous, the most enchanting, and the most rewarding. The challenges we conquer and transform may be the ones that provide us with our most important life theme. Our role as teachers is to orchestrate the themes and variations: to assist students in discovering their own unique form of unified intelligence.

Finding the Theme

The ideas and viewpoints of this book are based on thirty-five years of combined teaching experience in creative arts, language, science, and music with children from around the world. We have taught and consulted in inner-city schools where there was little enthusiasm and much anger; in the rich, yet poorly integrated school districts of the South; and in a variety of public and private schools in Japan, Montana, Haiti, Texas, Africa, and India. Classrooms still blend late-nineteenth-century discipline with the computer sciences. Some school districts in America have the highest SAT and ACT scores but also have the highest suicide rates, similar to Japan and Scandinavia. We have seen motivated teachers with few tools or little psychological support from administrators create the miracle of joy and learning in very dry soil. We've seen teachers who are certified in a variety of methods, working in good facilities, but who are still unable to motivate students.

In this wide range of experiences, we have been startled to see the similarities in what encourages children to learn. Once enthusiasm, desire, and empowerment is given to the student, motivation for learning follows. The most important role of the teacher, whether it be a parent, teacher, friend, or the imagination of the child, may be that of unlocking the desire for knowledge, expression, and joy.

The simple fact is that each teacher influences tens of thousands of others in a career. Some interesting figures imply that every high school teacher may reach nearly 10,000 people in his or her career of teaching. Part of our enthusiasm, boredom, and positive or negative attitudes about learning is carried to our students in the methods, style, and personality of our teaching along with the information we share.

The teacher's job has become increasingly complex. This age of information, educational methods, artificial intelligence, and aware-ness of learning styles has provided so much information that the volume of information is out of proportion to what we can realistically expect any teacher to observe or understand. The social, biological, neurological, and psychological data we've acquired in the past two decades is more than any of us can assimilate. Truly, to be con-sciously aware of all the emotional, physiological, and neurological

Finding the theme . . . has a deep sense for the longing and fulfillment of greater meaning along life's journey.

principles that are essential for optimal learning is to be stuck in an endless kaleidoscope of concern for knowing and doing what is right.

Is there such a thing as "accelerated" learning? Is there any unique method that will give us optimal results for our students? Is there a core to perception that does not depend completely on the social, political, or pedagogical methods of the time? Is the accumulation of information the goal of our schools? Or is the goal the ability to reach our full human potential and co-create a society that can adapt to the changing physical and psychological environments?

The Spanish word *carrera* curiously means both racing and career. Does our career take us through the race of life, or do we race through life with our career? A person's career or course through life is highly altered and enhanced when the principle urge of vocation is harmonized with it. Vocation means calling or summons and has a deep sense for the longing and fulfillment of greater meaning along life's journey. There is a spirited sense of dedication for wholeness and oneness in vocation. Most artists, musicians, dancers, and athletes have a powerful sense of dedication to a calling from an early age. Young students who personally choose to spend hours each day after school practicing an art or a sport have this calling.

"To find out what one is fitted to do and to secure an opportunity to do it is the key to happiness."
—John Dewey

As teachers we can honor the wide differences of those callings within each student. To impassion a student with the delight of living to such an extent that a vocation emerges is one of the most important aspects of education. The linking of one subject to another with the flame of quiet enthusiasm could be the greatest gift any teacher can give.

When vocation is blended with career, we find a different quality in our life's rhythm. The many situations that divert us from a constant focus in career can be brought back to focus by re-empowering our vocation. Unified intelligence calls us to be aware that the occupation and preoccupation to which we voluntarily devote most of the hours of our life is our true vocation. We can be constantly uplifted when we are able to find an occupation that gives us daily happiness, new enthusiasm for more thought, and greater presence for ourselves and each other. This is the great vocation.

> *"No man is an island entire of itself; every man is a piece of the continent. "*
> —John Donne

A Unified Field

Our life begins in complete dependence on and connection with our mother. We emerge from within the safety of her body to be cradled in the safety of her arms and home. As we move from the delicate inner world to the complexity of the outer world, we become woven in an ever-growing web of interdependence. Our perception of ourselves as individuals evolves to the recognition that we are members of a community. Today, with the realization of the innumerable ways we are bonded to one another globally, the local community has expanded to encompass the world. While we each stand alone, we also stand together.

One of the original goals of public education in the United States was to create literate citizens with the necessary capabilities to make decisions for government by the people. This goal still stands today as one of the most important aspects of our educational paradigm. Our focus during the last century on logic, competition, and economic gain has diverted us from acknowledging the unique potential of each individual and from developing creative, flexible thinkers. Education needs to not just honor one way of thinking and knowing, but to nurture the skills to perceive, communicate, and create intelligently for life, liberty, and the pursuit of happiness.

The classroom can provide a blending of mental, physical, and emotional rhythms through the integration of knowledge, experience, and creative expression. From this process there emerges a common thread between our home life, entertainment, school, occupation, and community. When our beliefs and actions are congruent in all areas of our life, a sense of integrated purpose unifies us. Lifelong learning becomes an important tool that supports our goals and provides a form for life's journey.

As teachers, our sense of purpose in our vocation and career creates a motivation that we will pass on to our students. We have the opportunity to share in the joy and discovery that leads to lifelong learning. We have accepted the challenge to contribute to the personal growth of another person. Creative, unified intelligence is empowered by each individual's conscious awareness of the rhythms of learning. The journey begins as we reach from the inner world to the outer world to listen with mind, body, emotions, and spirit.

Music has the unique ability to bond across cultures, to be a message from the people that goes beyond words. Sound speaks our desires and expresses the depths of our soul. Even when we cannot understand the language of others, we can honor and appreciate the sound that speaks from their heart. The sounds and music we create together will be the bridge between us. Our harmonies will blend our differences, and our rhythms will add strength and unity.

"I am certain that after the dust of centuries has passed over our cities, we too will be remembered not for our victories and defeats in battle or politics, but for our contribution to the human spirit."
—John F. Kennedy

As we move to a new paradigm of learning and teaching, rhythms will show us the way, and sound will allow us to listen and be heard. Our rhythms of learning and living unite to create the patterns, flow, and form of a unified intelligence not only for us as individuals, but as community members and world citizens. Each journey becomes a song with its own themes: listen and you will hear the rhythms of the symphony!

APPENDIX 1
The Tomatis Method and Empowering Learners
Billie M. Thompson, Ph. D.

> Night, day . . .
> Winter, spring, summer, fall . . .
> Inhale, exhale . . .
> Wake, sleep . . .
> Listen, speak . . .
> Accept, resist . . .
> Live, die . . . .

That we have rhythms of living and learning is easily observable to us, moment to moment, day to day, year to year. These rhythms are imbedded within our mind, body, and spirit and known automatically. We can use this spontaneous knowledge, or not, to understand what is involved in learning and to improve the future of education.

Connecting with our rhythms and those of others and our universe depends greatly on how well our auditory system functions, on how well we listen. No one knows that better than Dr. Alfred Tomatis, French ear, nose, and throat specialist and psychologist, who has researched this vital rhythm between listening and learning throughout his lifetime. He has created a program for people of all ages so that they may improve their auditory functioning and be better able and motivated to learn and develop their potential. The Tomatis Method is an innovative program of sound stimulation, audio-vocal activities, and counseling that promises to change the future of education - if we listen!

Early in his career, Dr. Tomatis discovered that the voice can produce only what the ear can hear. This principle is called the Tomatis Effect. It was proved independently at the Sorbonne in 1957 in the Academics of Science and Medicine and is the basis for the Tomatis Method. The method involves both a hard and a soft technology and has resulted in the development of a new science, that of audio-psychophonology, to explain the relationship of the ear, voice, and psychology.

Dr. Tomatis was trained medically to help people with voice problems. According to his original training and the established procedures of medicine at the time, to improve one's voice, one had to work with the instrument of voice - the larynx. Yet when this procedure was used, the desired results were not achieved. Out of curiosity, Tomatis gave the singers a hearing test. It was then that he noticed similarities between this test and a spectrographic analysis of their voice. He also noticed similarities between the tests of the singers and tests of factory workers with whom he was also working who had lost their ability to hear certain sounds. He observed that we speak and sing with our ears.

By working with these famous opera singers whose voices could no longer produce sounds that they once had produced, Dr. Tomatis developed a technique to improve their voices by re-educating their ears. The singers were pleased by the improvements in their singing voices but noted additional changes as well. They began to tell Dr. Tomatis about many other positive changes they were experiencing: improved reading and writing, improved concentration and memory, improved balance and motor coordination, and more desirable sleeping and eating habits.

After a while the singers brought their children to him, not because the children had singing problems, but because they had learning problems. The singers wondered if his method would help their children. It did, though there was a difference between the problems of the singers and those of their children. With the singers, the problem was one of re-educating the ear. With the children, the problem was one of educating the ear.

Through his work with the children, and even earlier work with the factory workers with hearing problems, Tomatis discovered that motivation plays a key role in determining what we hear. He began to distinguish between hearing and listening. Hearing is the passive reception of sound. Listening is the active motivated focusing on sounds we want to hear and the tuning out of those we do not.

The Tomatis Method improves learning comprehension, musical ability, language, speech, auditory focusing, attention, memory, concentration, and motor coordination. His method improves learning and education by changing the *functioning* of our ears, our *emotional response*, and our *relationship* to ourselves, others, and our world. It stimulates the brain by creating greater cortical charge with improved reception of high-frequency sounds. The high-frequency Corti cells in the cochlea account for thousands of nerve connections to the brain, whereas the low-frequency nerve connections number only in the hundreds.

Following the development of his method, Dr. Tomatis researched how the auditory system evolved through the different species and in the development of the human fetus. He found that human listening begins in the womb at about four and one-half months. He also found that the child experiences a "sonic birth" when air conduction occurs following the drainage of the middle-ear fluid after birth, and that listening development continues with prelanguage, language, and reading.

The Tomatis Method is based on a number of understandings, including the Tomatis Effect and the following assumptions:

- ✧ The motivational and emotional needs for communication begin with listening.
- ✧ Listening plays the fundamental role in processing all language information and hence all information learned through language.
- ✧ One role of the auditory system is to relate self to self, others, and the universe.
- ✧ The brain needs sound energy to enable the thinking processes and the development of intelligences.

The Tomatis Method is provided mainly in private centers to individuals, schools, and businesses. It consists of two parts: a passive phase followed by an active phase. A break of four to eight weeks is given between the two phases for integration of the changes. The passive phase usually begins with an intensive training of two hours a day over fifteen days. The length of the second (and any other additional intensives) varies according to individual needs; a typical program length is thirty days.

During the passive phase, the person listens to sounds of music and voice filtered through the patented Electronic Ear. Developed by Tomatis, this device helps the ear develop better focusing ability. During an early phase of a child's individual program, the child hears a filtered recording of his or her mother's voice, which simulates the sound of intrauterine hearing (prenatal stage of listening development) and increases the desire to communicate.

The active phase is an integral part of the Tomatis Method. Here the listener establishes an effective ear-voice relationship. Now that the ear is functioning better, the listener hears his or her own voice filtered through the Electronic Ear with good quality and tone so that he or she might produce it independently.

In the true sense of education, that of leading out, the Tomatis Method empowers students to be more connected to themselves, others, and the universe. Learning becomes more naturally easy, as it is meant to be. According to Dr. Tomatis, the ear is what connects us with the cosmos, what allows us to receive the rhythms of life and learning. Dr. Tomatis views the auditory system as one organ with one function, that of analysis of movement. The vestibule analyzes muscle movement in our body, while the cochlea analyzes air movements picked up as sound and charges the brain with this sound.

Besides empowering students, the Tomatis Method also empowers parents and teachers by helping them to create an environment that supports and develops independent learning, the ability to observe, and the energy to think. The method presents schools with a comprehensive group program for having more attentive, articulate, motivated students in the regular classroom. And it offers to special education students a method to develop better language patterning, motivation, motor coordination, and attention.

A number of schools in Canada have used the method for as many as ten years. Now, a progressive Colorado school district has a pilot study to research the effectiveness of the group Tomatis School Program to help poor learners, and a private school in Arizona has begun to offer the program. Other school districts are inquiring about funding to do research and to provide the program.

Following a screening by teachers and a meeting with parents to explain the program and ask for their child's participation, a trained Tomatis consultant completes an initial listening assessment for each child and recommends those appropriate for the school group program. Those for whom an individual program is more appropriate are referred to the Tomatis Center.

The students participate for two and one-half hours on the days the active and passive sessions take place (for a typical length of thirty to forty days plus breaks for integration). Eight children at a time gather in a classroom where they listen to sounds of filtered music and voice through special headsets with bone and air conduction. While they listen, the students can paint, draw, play games, or even sleep. In the active phase of the program, they become familiar with their own voices filtered with good quality and tone as they repeat humming, songs, words, and phrases. If they can read, they will also read aloud, becoming more upright, focused, and confident as they use language.

Changes are frequently seen in drawings and paintings done by students during the course of the program. For example, two family pictures done just eight weeks apart by the same child showed a dramatic difference. In one, the family members were all drawn in a small portion of a sheet of paper. Little detail was shown about clothing or body parts. No names were on the paper to identify the people. In the later drawing, the picture covered almost an entire page and included details of hair, clothing, and dress. The family name as well as individual names were clearly noted. These gains were achieved in weeks instead of years and reflect a change in the perception, language ability, self-esteem, and motivation of the child.

Parents and teachers of the participating children attend workshops every few weeks to learn how to improve listening and learning environments so that when the children change, the adults will know how to best support those changes. The school district provides this group program, thereby allowing many children to benefit and also acknowledging that before students can "read, write, and compute," they must first listen well.

Listening is a skill that can be both lost and recovered. Students in the Listening Training program often have a history of ear infections, accidents, a difficult fetal development or birth, traumatic or disrupted home lives, difficulties with school work, and/or problems with motor control. Poor listening can begin at any age. Symptoms of poor listening include problems with attention span and memory, concentration, language, voice, auditory discrimination, sequencing, speech fluency and articulation, reading, writing, dyslexia, posture and motor skills, and diminished energy levels.

Just as the solution to the singers' voice problems was the ear, not the obvious one of the larynx, so the solution to improving learning may first depend on improving the desire to learn, having the energy to learn, possessing the functional abilities to process sound so learning is possible, and having the advantage of a discriminating ear in all activities, in science, math, music, art, reading, writing, or sports. Listening is an important component of learning and more than just a cognitive ability. It is more basic than reading, writing, and arithmetic. When we are able to listen well, we have the ability to learn well. Good listening enables us to express our potential intelligences.

Most of the ways in which adults try to assist students to achieve and participate in their learning activities do not address readiness for learning within the context of the Tomatis Method. In this context, the ability to listen underlies the complete ability to learn. If Tomatis is right, and good listening is part of the future of education, then, as in the Tomatis Method, we must do the following:

Acknowledge the inherent importance of listening to learning.

Make the ability to listen the first and constant focus of educators, parents, policymakers, and funding sources.

Find a way to incorporate the listening theories of Tomatis in public schools and with the student at risk.

Identify, develop, and use listening curricula and diagnostic procedures in school settings to prevent and overcome listening-related learning problems.

Provide early screening for poor listening.

Involve and educate parents in how to provide a supportive listening environment at home and to recognize listening-based problems.

Acknowledge the role of parents as the child's first teachers and source of motivation and language, and use this insight when planning the education of the child.

Prepare and train teachers to use techniques that develop and encourage good listening skills.

Place listening as a major focus for educational change.

Begin to look at prevention of learning problems as much or more than correction. We must look at long-term monetary and personal savings versus short-term cost to see the real value.

Teach students about their ears, how they function, how to take care of them, how to tell if a problem with listening is occuring.

The Tomatis Method works at three levels: functional, emotional, and relational. It accomplishes specific tasks with remarkable effectiveness: it evaluates the ability to listen, stimulates the auditory system, provides motivation to listen, develops right audio-vocal control, develops a supportive listening environment, and develops the ear-voice relationship essential to receive and self-monitor speech. The components of the Tomatis Method are many and integrated, and they differ slightly for individual and group programs. The method is not the Tomatis Method unless all components are included.

We learn. We learn through rhythms. We learn through rhythms of ourselves, others, and our world. Our ear connects us to these rhythms. Our rhythms of learning form our foundation for learning.

We must turn students on to learning. We need more than a short-term solution or superficial techniques. Our students' rhythms of learning are changing. Their future and the future of education are changing, too. We can use the Tomatis Method as a practical approach that empowers learners by connecting them to their natural rhythms of learning.

References

Campbell, Don. *The Mozart Effect*. Avon, 1997.

Gilmor, T. M., Paul Madaule, and Billie M. Thompson, eds. *About the Tomatis Method*. Toronto: Listening Centre Press, 1989.

Madaule, Paul. *When Listening Comes Alive*. Ontario: Moulin, 1993.

Tomatis, A.A. *The Conscious Ear*. Station Hill Press, 1991.

___. *The Ear and Language*. Ontario: Moulin, 1996.

APPENDIX 2
Suggestology and Suggestopedy*
Georgi Lozanov

Suggestology is the comprehensive science of suggestion in all its aspects, but for the time being it deals mainly with the possibilities of suggestion to tap man's reserve capacities in the spheres of both mind and body. Consequently it is the science of the accelerated harmonious development and self-control of man and his manifold talents.

SUGGESTION

The word *suggestion* derives from the Latin word *suggero, suggessi, suggestum*, to place, to prompt, to hint. This word has acquired a more or less negative meaning in many languages, but in English a shade of meaning has been given to the word which is close to our understanding of it: to offer, to propose. Thus, according to our understanding of the word, suggestion is a communicative factor which is expressed in "proposing" that the personality should make its choice, should choose both rationally and intuitively and according to its structure and disposition from among a wide range of possibilities among complex stimuli which are being intricately associated, condensed, coded, symbolized, and amplified. The choice is founded upon the external orchestration of the stimuli which come from outside of or arise within the personality itself, not only within the limited sphere of consciousness but also, simultaneously and to a fuller extent, in the various and numerous levels of *paraconsciousness*. In fact the utilization of the conscious-paraconscious stimuli, well organized, psychologically orchestrated, and harmonized with the personality, is suggestion in its most manifest and positive form. Such utilization can reveal the personality's universal reserve capacity and stimulate its creativity. A visual representation of suggestion is art. For is art not the greatest form of suggestion?

Reserve Capacities

Suggestion in its most positive manifestation and when well organized can uncover the personality's reserve capacities. By reserve capacities we understand the unmanifested but genetically predetermined capacities operating mainly in the paraconscious and surpassing the normal ones several times over. The laws governing these capacities are to a certain extent different from the ordinary psychophysiological laws.

---

* Abridged from "The Lozanov Report to UNESCO." Full text can be ordered from Lozanov Learning Institute, 6325 Woodside Court, Suite 220, Columbia, MD 21046.

Among the many examples of suggestively tapped reserve capacities we can mention the following: (1) *Hypermnesia* or supermemory (in long-term memory). This supermemory surpasses the possibilities of ordinary memory several times over. Sometimes it occurs in psychotherapy, in hypnosis, and when applying methods of catharsis. Mass hypermnesia can be brought about under the conditions of suggestopedic instruction with both healthy and sick people, when the educational-curative process is carried out properly. Hypermnesia as an important reserve capacity is characterized by the following specific psychophysiological laws: (a) manifestation either after a latent period and without any conscious effort, or suddenly and spontaneously; (b) increasing recollection without reinforcement (reminiscent curve); (c) amnestic covering and sinking of the basic sense-bearing nucleus of the complex stimulus into paraconsciousness until it is "raised" out of paraconsciousness into consciousness; (d) making the first recollection easy under the conditions of emotional impetus, of the associative connections of the peripheral perceptions and of concentrative psychorelaxation; (e) great durability of the reproduced memory traces; (f) decreased susceptibility to fatigue; and (g) a considerable psychotherapeutic, psychohygienic, and psychoprophylactic effect. (2) *Provoked hypercreativity* or suggested or autosuggested creative superproductivity. Intuition is activated and states similar to inspiration arise. These are outwardly expressed in a decidedly greater creative manifestation of personality. A number of experiments have shown that the manifestation of artistic, musical, and even mathematical abilities (in accordance with any given person's manifested and potential abilities) increases considerably both quantitatively and qualitatively. Suggestological experiments have shown the possibility of accelerated creative self-development. Here again we find the same psychophysiological laws as are characteristic of hypermnesia. (3) *Suggestive control and self-control of pain, bleeding, the functions of the sympathetic nervous system, metabolism,* etc.

The tapping of man's reserve capacities can be achieved only under the conditions of excellent suggestive organization, orchestration, and utilization of the conscious-paraconscious functions. Though inseparably connected with consciousness, yet the basic "store" of the reserve capacities is paraconsciousness.

Paraconsciousness

By paraconsciousness we understand more or less unconscious mental activity. Here we include everything that, for the given moment, is outside the scope of consciousness. When we operate with various concepts, when we read or solve problems and are, on the whole, consciously concentrating our attention on some activity, we are not aware of the many unconscious components which constitute these activities, for example, the ideas which build up notions; the letters and even the words of sentences which we happen to be reading; the unconscious judgments and premises hidden in the shortened formulas of thinking; the codes and symbols. The concept of paraconsciousness comprises also the numerous unconscious forms of associating, coding, and symbolizing which have an informational, algorithmical and reprogramming effect on personality. Paraconsciousness embraces the unconscious sides of creativity as well as intuition and inspiration.

All these sides of paraconsciousness penetrate each other and take part in the desuggestive-suggestive process.

Antisuggestive Barriers

There is no suggestion without desuggestion, without freeing paraconsciousness from inertia of something old. The means of suggestion are usually referred mechanically only to subliminal stimuli or only to emotional involvement. One often loses sight of the fact that the whole personality takes part in every reaction. Then this means that no effect can be expected if the subliminal perceptions, the peripheral perceptions, and the emotional stimuli are not in accord with the manifold and often conflicting dispositions of the personality, both inborn and acquired. It is difficult to realize a suggestive situation if it is not in accord at the moment with the particular needs of the instincts and with the motivation, attitude, mind set, expectancy (with the placebo effect), interests, and in general, all the factors of the personality which take an unconscious part in building up the *antisuggestive barriers.*

As a manifestation of conscious-paraconscious unity, the antisuggestive barriers are a peculiar characteristic of personality. They are, in fact, overcome through harmonization with them. The three antisuggestive barriers, *critical-logical, intuitive-affective,* and *ethical,* are inseparably connected and are subject to continual dynamic changes.

Social Suggestive Norm

Overcoming the antisuggestive barriers means also overcoming the social suggestive form of one or another of the limitations set to what we can do. Caught in the net of the numerous social suggestive norms in most cases, we do not even attempt to do anything that is at variance with them. We do not believe that it is possible to increase our memorization in volume and soundness, to accelerate our creative development, to have more self-control over both our mental and our physiological functions. The social suggestive norm teaches us that it is impossible, and contains a note of warning not to attempt it. And if it really happens somewhere it is considered a miracle, an exception, or a falsification. That is why suggestology in its development as a science for liberating the personality's reserve capacities (and hence for displacing the social suggestive norm and for freeing the larger fields of personality) encounters great opposition.

THE MEANS OF SUGGESTION

The means by which suggestion overcomes the antisuggestive barriers and tops the personality's reserve capacities are complex. It is very difficult to separate them and show them mechanically, all the more so because their realization is a question of both the personality's abilities and its qualities. If we do, however, try to separate them in order to study them, infantilization and pseudopassivity belong to one group of controlled states of personality which can be provoked from the outside suggestively or which arise by themselves autosuggestively.

Infantilization is a controlled state of intuitive activity, emotional plasticity, increased perceptiveness, and confidence in the possibility of freeing one or another of the reserve capacities in a given situation. Infantilization arises when a highly harmonized contact is established with a person possessing authority (prestige), but it can come about unaided.

Pseudopassivity (concert pseudopassiveness) is a controlled state, resembling the state in which we find ourselves when listening to classical music. It is a state of concentrative psychorelaxation. We are speaking neither of hypnoidal relaxation nor of muscle relaxation that is an end in itself, but of a calm mental state, lacking any stress, free of needless thoughts and action, with lowered ideomotor activity. On the background of this calm mental state a pleasant, untiring concentration is realized similar to our concentration at a concert.

The part played by authority in creating confidence and emotional stimulus and the part played by harmonious intonation and rhythm do not call for any explanation here.

Peripheral Perceptions and Emotional Stimulus
(Double-planeness and Psychological Orchestration)

If we try to simplify our understanding of the means of suggestion, we can reduce them, somewhat schematically, to two basic physiological mechanisms: peripheral perceptions and emotional stimulus. The peripheral perceptions are caused by stimuli that are in strength—supraliminal stimuli which at the moment of perceiving have got into the periphery of attention and consciousness. They do not fall in the focus of consciousness because of its limited volume. The receptive fields of the sense organs and the brain are, however, much wider than the scope of conscious perceptions. Consequently the peripheral perceptions fall into the sphere of paraconsciousness. They are characterized by considerable dynamism. At any moment they can enter again into the realm of conscious perception. The peripheral perceptions are realized not only outside the receptive field focused by the consciousness, but also in the field itself. Having reached the brain, this information emerges in the consciousness with some delay, or it influences the motives and decisions and is operative in tapping the reserve capacities. This peripheral information included in the paraconsciousness underlies long-term memory.

The peripheral perceptions suggest and control unconsciously but reliably, while the emotional stimulus impregnates all the activities of the personality as a whole. Complex desuggestive-suggestive situations can be controlled and self-controlled through the unity of the two basic psychophysiological mechanisms: the peripheral perceptions and the emotional stimulus.

The Basic Principles (Foundations) of Suggestology

Suggestology has developed as an attempt to translate the ancient and perennial searching to tap reserve capacities genetically predetermined in man into a modern reality. It combines desuggestive-suggestive communicative psychotherapy with the liberating and stimulating aspects of art and some modifications of the old schools of concentrative psychorelaxation. The experimental research and the new theoretical meaning given to the phenomena researched have led to definite psychophysiological conceptions. In close connection with this research, the following three *inseparable* psychophysiological fundamental principles of suggestology have been formulated: (1) *Interpersonal communication and mental activity are always conscious and paraconscious at the same time.* (2) *Every stimulus is associated, coded, symbolized, and generalized.* (3) *Every perception is complex.*

We dealt with the first principle in discussing the problem of paraconsciousness, its unity with consciousness, and the role it plays in harmonizing the entire personality for the purpose of stimulating its harmonious and creative development.

The second fundamental principle shows that with the continually increasing abstraction a number of the original levels of perceptions, the original ideas and notional generalizations of a lower level, are being constantly pushed into paraconsciousness in order to make room for the following higher codes and symbols.

The three basic principles of suggestology, no matter how schematically given, are indicative of the possibilities of the two basic psychophysiological mechanisms, the peripheral perceptions, and the emotional stimulus.

SUGGESTOPEDY

On the basis of this general theory of suggestion which we have outlined we have worked out an educational and curative desuggestive-suggestive pedagogical system—suggestopedagogy or suggestopedy (suggestopedia).

The socially and historically built-up norm concerning above all the level of man's memory and the speed of skill mastery as well as the idea of the "throes" of creative work have brought into being a suggestive mind set which in fact slows down the development of man's genetically conditioned mental powers. That is why one of the most important aims of suggestology is to liberate to a considerable extent, to desuggest all students from the social suggestive norm, desuggesting the accumulated inadequate ideas about man's limited capacities.

Instead of creating conditions for the joyous satisfaction of the personality's basic need—the thirst for information, and instead of bearing in mind the way the brain functions, teachers often seem to want to "teach the brain how to function."

The following are some of the things in ordinary education which are inconsistent with the physiological, psychological functions of personality:

1. It is well known that in no case does the brain function only with its cortex structures, or only with the subcortex, or with only the right or the left hemisphere. The functional unity of the brain is unbreakable no matter that in some cases one activity or another comes to the fore. Therefore, the emotional and motivational complex, the image thinking and logical abstraction, must be activated simultaneously. But most often there are the following two kinds of deviation from this natural fact:

a. The teaching is addressed only to the cortical structures and the left hemisphere of the learner, as if he were an emotionless and motivationless cybernetic machine.

b. Although the learner may be taken as a psychophysiological entity, the educational process is not directed globally to all parts of the brain simultaneously.

2. It is well known that analytical-synthetical activity under normal conditions is accomplished simultaneously—there is no such thing as a stage of pure analysis or of pure synthesis. This simultaneous and indivisible connectedness of the physiological process has its own psychological expression. It also underlies cognition—from the general to the particular and back to the general. But these natural laws often undergo "correction" in pedagogical practice in one of the following ways:

a. Elements are studied separately, in isolation from the sense-bearing whole; they are automated through tiring exercises, and only then are they connected one after the other and systematically to form the whole.

b. The whole is studied without paying attention to its component parts and to the mistakes arising in this way. In both cases attempts are made to break up the natural simultaneity of the processes of analysis and synthesis.

3. Man's personality takes part in every communicative process simultaneously at numerous conscious and paraconscious levels. This nature granted fact is "utilized" in pedagogical practice most often in the following two ways:

a. The principle of conscious participation in the educational processes is formalized and turned into a fetish. According to it the learners must learn and automate each element of the material in a strictly conscious and rational manner in spite of the fact that it can be learned to a certain degree spontaneously and intuitively at the first perception of the globally given lesson.

b. Weight is laid only on the paraconscious and intuitive powers of the learner, and the necessity for a conscious finalizing and creative reassessment of the material is overlooked.

In contrast to the above inconsistencies which violate the physiological and psychological functions of personality, the three basic principles of suggestopedia take into account psychophysiological laws: (1) the global participation of the brain, (2) the simultaneous processes of analysis and synthesis, and (3) the simultaneous and indivisible participation of the conscious and paraconscious processes. If we do not abide by these unchangeable psychological laws and by the basic principles of suggestology, the education process becomes an inhibiting factor and one causing illness. Any educational process of that kind precludes any tapping of the reserve capacities. What is more, some sociopsychological factors are added to the psychophysiological ones, and this increases the difficulties. For example:

1. The mind set of fear of learning. Many nations have some kind of proverb that means "learning is torture." Making the process of teaching and learning more intensive often intensifies this fear and also the inner counteraction, in both learners and teachers.

2. The social suggestive norm of the personality's capacities being limited. According to this norm, man can supposedly assimilate new material only to a definite, fairly low level.

The combination of a fearful mind set and the social suggestive norm of man's limited capacities under the conditions of a nonmedical pedagogical approach results in mass "covert didactogeny": Pupils suffer to a greater or lesser degree from "school neurosis." They have no confidence in their powers; they do not trust their own inner reserves. For them education has been turned from the natural process of satisfying the personality's essential need—the thirst for knowledge—into a psychotrauma.

It is only too natural that with this mind set the nonmedical attempts to intensify the educational process may lead to reinforcing inner mental conflicts, to the fixation of neurotic states, and instead of the results of the educational process getting better they get worse.

The mind set of fear of learning and the social suggestive norm of man's limited capacities make the erroneous approaches and methods worse. The following are some examples of how far some of these erroneous approaches go:

1. The material to be studied is broken up into smaller and smaller elements. These elements must be grasped, memorized, and automated and then are gradually united into larger entities. In this way are formed some useless primitive habits on the lowest level, which have to be given up in order to build up habits on a higher level, and then the latter have also to be got rid of. And thus it goes on until at last we acquire habits and skills on the necessary highest operating and creative level. This building up and fixing of elementary habits which have to be given up afterward in order to acquire fresh higher-level habits is due to the mind set of fear of our limited learning capacities. But creating a "hierarchy of habits" worsens this mind set and lowers motivation. The hierarchy of habits in any nonmedically organized pedagogy is dangerous for the health. Consequently dry recapitulation results in demotivation and delaying the effect of the instruction instead of accelerating it.

2. Often teachers, aware of the harmful effect which the negative mind set of students toward instruction and learning brings with it, deliberately introduce intervals for relaxation and joking. But by introducing these intervals they in fact suggest that the learners need some relaxation and distraction. They suggest to him that his inner mind set of fear of learning and his fatigue and displeasure with it are justified. Gaiety that is an end in itself when introduced in lessons, no matter how refreshing it may be, brings a risk of still more deeply inculcating the conviction that their basic negative mind set toward instruction is justified.

3. Attempts to accelerate the process of instruction are being made through mechanizing and programming it. The learner communicates with the machines and obtains feedback through the programmed materials. But in this the learner is isolated from the social environment and the wealth of emotion provided by the group. Regardless of the favorable aspects of

mechanizing and programming instruction, the feedback information which the learner obtains about how well he has assimilated the assigned material, because of its lack of warmth, not only does not stimulate him but even reinforces his negative mind set toward learning.

This cursory analysis of some of the methods aimed at bettering the efficiency of the process of teaching and learning shows that in pedagogical practice in fact pressure is often exerted on the learner's personality. He reacts against this pressure. The motivation for learning is lowered. Pupils begin to learn only when they are pressed by the necessity to obtain some kind of qualification for the sake of the practical requirements of their plans in life. Thus the satisfaction of their basic need, the thirst for information, is accompanied with displeasure instead of pleasure.

Becoming aware of these negative sides of the process of instruction, teachers in some countries have switched to the other extremes: advocating full freedom for the learner. The learner should be free to choose what and how he is going to learn. However, this search, in its essence justifiable, leads in practice to the absence of any sound form of education. Why should the learner be given freedom in the process of instruction and not be freed from his inner fear of his own limited powers of assimilating new information? Freedom accompanied with fear of learning is equal to giving up learning.

The Psychotherapeutic, Psychohygienic, Physiological, and Sociopsychological Aspects of Suggestology

The most important thing in our opinion is to do away with mass didactogeny and bring the process of instruction into line with the laws governing the functioning of the brain. If an educational system succeeds in liberating the learner from fear and from the social suggestive norm of his limited powers, and is brought into line with psychophysiology, it will easily achieve its other pedagogical aims; But the difficulty arises not so much from considering how to bring about the initial liberation, as from how to create a system of sustained, continuous inner liberation. The learner's confidence in his own capacities for learning should grow constantly, and in this way instruction gradually develops into self-instruction. It will gradually go beyond the limitations of the social suggestive norm and penetrate into the sphere of human reserve capacities.

It is this trend toward inner liberation and self-discipline that suggestopedic education develops. It creates conditions for developing skills and habits of inner concentration on the background of optimal psychorelaxation. Man's global capacities are utilized. The emotional stimulus is enhanced; motivation, interests, and mind sets are taken into consideration and activated; the purposeful participation is organized of as many conscious and paraconscious functions of the personality as possible. For example, in regard to attention as an integral element of the learner's activity the process of instruction is organized in such a way that not only the close active attention of the learners is made use of, but also their incidental passive attention, and particularly the peripheral perceptions which take an unconscious part in both active and passive attention.

Suggestopedy looks for ways to overcome the social suggestive norm. It taps reserves also through organizing the paraconscious elements in the conscious-paraconscious complex. In this respect it leans on the suggestological theory of the paraconscious basis of long-term memory and also on the part played by paraconsciousness in motivating intellectual activation, creativity, and global stimulation of personality. In this way it tries to respond better to the globality characteristic of the natural psychophysiological laws and above all the three basic principles of suggestology.

Suggestopedic Reserve Complex

All the factors mentioned above make it possible for the suggestopedic educational system to release a *reserve complex* with the following obligatory characteristics:

1. Memory reserves, intellectual activity reserves, creativity reserves, and the reserves of the whole personality are tapped. If we do not release many-sided reserve capacities we cannot speak of suggestopedy.

2. Instruction is always accompanied with an effect of relaxation or at least one without a feeling of fatigue. If learners get tired in lessons, we cannot speak of suggestopedy.

3. Suggestopedic teaching and learning is always a pleasant experience.

4. It always has a favorable educational effect, softening aggressive tendencies in pupils and helping them to adapt themselves to society.

Principles and Means of Suggestopedy

The principles and means of suggestopedy take into account the age characteristics and the pedagogical aims of students. The principles are: (1) joy, absence of tension, and concentrative psychorelaxation; (2) unity of the conscious-paraconscious and integral brain activation; and (3) suggestive relationship on the level of the reserve complex.

The principle of joy, absence of tension, and concentrative psychorelaxation presupposes joy with learning, mental relaxation, and "nonstrain concentration." The emotional release creates conditions for undisturbed intellectual and creative activity without causing the fatigue and the consumption of energy that accompanies strained attention.

The observance of these principles means that the teacher should teach his pupils how to learn.

We must emphasize that this principle means neither passiveness in the sense of lack of will, lack of discrimination and subordination, nor gaiety per se. It calls for calmness, steadiness, inner confidence, and trust.

The principle of unity of the conscious-paraconscious and integral brain activation is in fact a principle of globality. Not only are the learner's conscious reactions and functions utilized but also his paraconscious activity. This principle recognizes the simultaneous global participation of the two brain hemispheres and the cortical and subcortical structures, and also the simultaneously occurring analysis and synthesis. When this principle is observed, the process of instruction comes nearer to the natural psychological and physiological regularities in personality. The consciousness, in the sense of attitude and motivation, is lifted to a still higher level. Under the conditions of the suggestopedic educational system the process of instruction is not set against the natural inseparability of the conscious and paraconscious functions.

The principle of suggestive relationship on the reserve complex calls for a reorganization of the educational process which will make it similar to group psychotherapy with the particular relationship established in it. The level of suggestive relationship is measured by the degree of the tapped reserves in a learner. The qualitatively different characters of these reserves (a new type of assimilation of material, considerably great volume and retention of what is assimilated, positive psychohygienic effect, useful educative influence, etc.) make them reliable criteria for the realization of this principle.

This principle makes it imperative that the process of instruction should always run at the level of the personality's unused reserves. This cannot, however, be achieved if the principles are applied separately (if each principle is observed in isolation from the others). Many good teachers create a pleasant atmosphere in the classroom. It would seem that they are following the first principle of suggestopedy. But assimilation of the material in this atmosphere does not reach the level of the suggestopedic assimilation with its new objective laws governing the processes and with its psychohygienic effect from the process of instruction. In these circumstances one gives one's smiling confirmation to the validity of the brain's limited capacities and backs up the accepted ideas that studying can only be made more pleasant. Such confirmation of the old norms, in spite of the gentle approach, can be of little advantage. Under suggestopedic conditions joy springs not so much from the pleasant outward organization of the educational process, but rather from the easy assimilation of the material and the easy way it can be used in practice. The observance of the three principles simultaneously in every moment of the educational process makes learning joyful and easy, and leads to the tapping of complex reserves.

There is another important and characteristic feature of suggestology involved here: while attention is drawn to the consciously understandable, generalized unity and the sense of it, the processes of paraconscious perception and thinking process the implied elements included in the general code: for instance, in teaching foreign language the learners' attention is directed to the whole sentence, to its meaningful communicative aspect, to its place and role in the given life situation. At the same time pronunciation, vocabulary, and grammar remain to a great extent on a second plane. They are also assimilated, but the well-trained teacher draws the students' attention to them only for a short time and then goes back quickly to the sense of the whole sentence and situation. A considerable part of these elements is learned along with the whole structure without any specific attention being paid to them.

When children are taught to read, they do not learn the separate letters first in order to be able later to join them to form syllables, words, and sentences. But neither are they taught by the so-called "whole-word" method where no interest is shown in the letters that form the words. The children learn meaningful units—words and short sentences—and they discover the letters on the second plane, in the form of finding the answer to the picture puzzle which illustrates the material. Thus they stimulate the whole in its elements simultaneously, their attention being directed in most cases to the meaningful whole.

When the educational process is of a linear nature, which suggestopedy rejects, it consists of dry logicalized teaching that is separated from the essentially inseparable "emotional presence." An educational process of a linear nature has an especially harmful effect in regard to the misunderstood "principle of consciousness," having led to an unsuccessful attempt to break the inherent unity of the conscious and the paraconscious processes. At the same time it has resulted in demotivating and unpleasant conscious learning of isolated, senseless elements before the learners have grasped the idea of the meaningful whole, of the pleasant and motivating global unit which is eventually formed out of these meaningless elements.

Suggestopedic Foreign Language Systems for Adults

In every suggestologically well-organized communicative process there is a leading procedure with a ritual of "placebo" meaning. The other stages are more or less subordinate to this focus.

The conviction that the new material which is to be learned will be assimilated and become automatic and creatively processed without strain and fatigue is suggested by the weight and solemnity given to the carrying out of this session. This session must, above all, facilitate the memorizing and psychohygienic sides of teaching and learning, although these are of necessity bound up with the whole personality. The suggestopedic session is adapted to the subject taught and to the age of the learners. Such a session for little children is quite different from the one for grown-ups. (For children this session is most often a didactic opera performance.) One of the most important of the peculiar characteristics of the suggestopedic session is that it is a source of aesthetic pleasure for the learners.

The recital-like characteristic of the session has advantages over all other types of "special" procedured sessions.

1. The session is acceptable from the point of view of the ordinary level of culture and of practical experience, in this respect resembling certain forms of art.

2. There are no hypnotizing procedures, nor does the student feel any undesirable suggestive pressures on his personality.

3. The liberating-stimulating, desuggestive-suggestive influence of specific selected music and specific histrionic mastery, adapted to the requirements of suggestopedic teaching and learning, are used.

4. Ritualization of the musical-theatrical performance, with its rich possibilities of additional positive associating and revised according to the requirements of the educational process, is made use of.

5. At the some time students are learning, their aesthetic interests are aroused and their ethical development is improved.

6. Instruction is made pleasant, is never tiring, and has favorable motivation strength.

The suggestopedic session in the regular foreign language courses for adults comprises two parts. In the first part the students listen to classical and early Romantic music of an emotional nature, while in the second part they listen to preclassical music, of a more profound and more philosophical nature.

The new material that is to be learned is read or recited by a well-trained teacher, once during the first part of the concert and once during the second part of it. At the same time the teacher must, while taking into account the features of the music when reading the material with intonation and with behavior, convey a feeling of conviction to the students that the material will be mastered very easily.

There are three principal phases of the suggestopedic lesson in a foreign language: the presession phase, the session phase, and the postsession phase.

The presession phase takes about 15-20 minutes. In this phase the students are made familiar with the key topics of the new material for the first time. The organization of this "first encounter" is of particular importance in creating a positive mind set for reserve capacities. A great part of the material is memorized during this phase. (The anticipation of the next phase, the one consisting of the real "first encounter," arouses pleasant emotions.) The teacher explains the new material very briefly, i. e., deciphers the thematic dialogue in a few supporting points. In doing this, he must suggest through his behavior that the assimilation has already begun and all is pleasant and easy. Already during the deciphering, which is a stage of giving the primary information, the following stages should be noted: fixation, reproduction, and new creative production.

The session phase comprises the session itself, which has already been described above. It lasts for 45 minutes, and with it the day's lessons always come to an end.

The postsession phase is devoted to various elaborations of the material to activate its assimilation.

The elaborations comprise reading and translation of the text, songs, games, an extra text (a monologue), retelling, and conversation on given themes. All this merges into role-playing, but the role-playing should take place only when the students themselves express the wish to do it. The activation must be spontaneous. Thus the teaching and learning acquires sense and meaning.

The suggestopedic system for teaching foreign languages to adults is subject to a number of psychological principles which should be observed, for example, good, authoritative organization; purposeful, double-plane behavior of the teacher; motivating initial instructions which are read to the students; directing of the students' attention to sense-bearing wholes; no obligatory homework, though permission can be given to the students to go through the new lesson for about 15 or 20 minutes in the morning and in the evening, but only informatively, the way one skims through a newspaper.

The textbook is also of importance. Its contents and layout should contribute to the success of the suggestopedic process of teaching and learning. A lighthearted story with a pleasant, emotional plot should run through the textbook. The greater part of the new material is given in the very first lesson—600 to 850 unfamiliar words and the greater part of the essential grammar. In this way, at the very beginning the students have a wide choice of language possibilities at their disposal, to cope with the communicative elaboration. Thus they do not feel themselves "conditioned" to speak within the limits of a few words and patterns. Each line of the textbook contains parts that can be substituted by others. Thus hundreds of patterns are assimilated at once and under natural conditions. The pictures used as visual aids are connected with the subjects of the lesson and not with elements of it.

The translation of the lesson in the mother tongue is given to the students at the beginning of the lesson to look through cursorily and is then taken away. In this way the instruction is modeled on what is natural for adults—to have a translation of the text in the foreign language. But we do not stay long at this stage; we quickly pass on to the stage in which there is no translation at all.

There can be different variants of the suggestopedic foreign language system, from courses with several lessons a week to courses of whole days' "immersion" in the suggestopedic foreign language atmosphere. The leading factor is not the number of lessons but the psychological organization of the process of instruction.

If we take as a basic pattern the 24 days' foreign language course with four academic hours a day, either no homework or only some informative reading allowed for 15 minutes in the evening and in the morning, the following results can be expected: (1) The students assimilate on the average more than 90 percent of the vocabulary, which comprises 2,000 lexical units per course. (2) More than 60 percent of the new vocabulary is used actively and fluently in everyday conversation and the rest of the vocabulary is known at translation level. (3) The students speak within the framework of the whole essential grammar. (4) Previously unseen texts can be read. (5) The students make some mistakes in speaking, but these mistakes do not hinder the communication. (6) Pronunciation is satisfactory. (7) The students are not afraid of talking to foreigners who speak the same language. (8) The students are eager to continue studying the same foreign language.

APPENDIX 3
Resource Guide

Don Campbell
The Mozart Effect Resource Center
P.O. Box 4179
Boulder, Colorado 80306

Chris Brewer
P.O. Box 227
Kalispell, Montana 59903

Lifesounds
160 Seashore Drive
Jupiter, Florida 33477

Barzak Educational Institute International
885 Olive Avenue, Suite A
Novato, California 94945

Carla Crutsinger, Director
Brainworks
1918 Walnut Hill
Carrollton, Texas 75006

Dee Coulter
Coulter Publications
4850 Niwot Road
Longmont, Colorado 80501

Dee Dickinson
New Horizons for Learning
4649 Sunnyside North
Seattle, Washington 98103

Edu-Kinesthetics
P.O. Box 5002
Glendale, California 91201

Educational Kinesiology Foundation
161 Viewpoint Circle
Ventura, California 93003

Simon Guggenheim School
7141 South Morgan
Chicago, Illinois   60621

Jean Houston
Foundation for Mind Research
P. O. Box 3300
Pomona, New York   10970

Eric Jensen
Turning Point for Teachers
P. O. Box 2551
Del Mar, California   92014

LIND Institute
P.O. Box 14487
San Francisco, California   94114

Barry Louis Polisar
Rainbow Morning Music
2121 Fairland Road
Silver Spring, Maryland   20904

Polyform Products Company
9420 Byron Street
Schiller Park, Illinois   60176

Colin Rose, Director
Accelerated Learning Systems
50 Aylesbury Road, Aston Clinton
Aylesbury, Bucks HP22 5AH England

Richards Institute of Music Education and Research
(Education Through Music)
149 Corte Madera Road
Portola Valley, California   94025

International Alliance for Learning
1040 South Coast Highway
Encinitas, California   92024

Judith Belk, Director
Sound Listening Center
14674 Rainbow Drive
Lake Oswego, Oregon   97035

Dr. Billie Thompson, Director
Sound Listening and Learning Center—Tomatis Center
The Quadrangle, Suite 205
2701 East Camelback Road
Phoenix, Arizona   85016

Tomatis Listening Centre
599 Markham Street
Toronto, Ontario   M6G 2L7   Canada

Win Wenger, Director
Institute for Visual Thinking
Box 332
Gaithersburg, Maryland   20887

BIBLIOGRAPHY

Allen, T. Harrel. "How Good a Listener Are You?" *Management Review* (February 1977): 37-39.

Arlin, Patricia Kennedy. "Cognitive Development in Adulthood: A Fifth Stage?" *Developmental Psychology* II, no. 5 (1977): 602-606.

Asher, James J. *Learning Another Language Through Actions: The Complete Teacher Guidebook.* Los Gatos, California: Sky Oaks Production, Inc., 1985.

Ayensu, E., and P. Whitfield. *The Rhythms of Life.* New York: Crown Publishing, 1982.

Bagley, Michael T., and Karin K. Hess. *200 Ways of Using Imagery in the Classroom.* Monroe, New York: Trillium Press, 1984.

___. *Using Imagery to Develop Memory.* Monroe, New York: Trillium Press, 1987.

Benzwie, Teresa. *A Moving Experience.* Tucson, Arizona: Zephyr Press, 1987.

Biggers, Julian L. "Body Rhythms and Student Teacher Performance." 1985. Unpublished manuscript.

___. "Body Rhythms, the School Day and Academic Achievement." *Journal of Experimental Education* 49 (1980): 45-47.

Bonny, Helen, and Louis Savary. *Music and Your Mind.* New York: Harper and Row, 1990.

Botkin, James, Mahdi Elmandjra, and Malitza Mircea. *No Limits to Learning.* New York: Permagon Press, 1987.

Briggs, Dorothy Corkille. *Your Child's Self-Esteem.* Garden City, New York: Doubleday, 1970.

Briggs, John. *Fire in the Crucible: The Alchemy of Creative Genius.* New York: St. Martin's Press, 1988.

Brooks, Richard. "Hemispheric Differences in Memory: Implications for Education." *The Clearing House* 53 (1980): 248-250.

Brown, Frederick M., and R. Curtis Graeber, eds. *Rhythmic Aspects of Behavior.* Hillsdale, New Jersey: Lawrence Erlbaum Associates, 1982.

Campbell, Don G. *Introduction to the Musical Brain.* St. Louis: Magnamusic Baton, 1983.

___. *The Mozart Effect.* New York, New York: AVON Books, 1997.

___. *The Roar of Silence.* Wheaton, Illinois: Quest Books, 1989.

___. comp. *Music: A Physician for Times to Come.* Wheaton, Illinois: Quest Books, 1991.

Canfield, Jack, and H. Wellis. *100 Ways to Enhance Self-Concept in the Classroom.* Englewood Cliffs, New Jersey: Prentice Hall, 1976.

Caskey, Owen L. *Suggestive-Accelerative Learning and Teaching.* Englewood Cliffs, New Jersey: Educational Technology Publications, 1980.

Cherry, Clare, Douglas Goodwin, and Jesse Staples. *Is the Left Brain Always Right?* Belmont, California: David Lake Publishers, 1989.

Clark, Aminah, Harris Clemes, and Reynold Bean. *Raising Teenager's Self-Esteem.* Capitola, California: APOD Publishers, 1987.

Clark, Barbara. *Optimalizing Learning.* Columbus, Ohio: Charles Merrill, 1986.

___. *Growing Up Gifted.* 3rd ed. Columbus, Ohio: Charles Merril, 1988.

Clark, Faith, and Cecil Clark. *Hassle-Free Homework.* New York: Doubleday, 1989.

Clemes, Harris, and Reynold Bean. *Self-Esteem: The Key to Your Child's Well-Being.* New York: Putnam, 1981.

Colquhoun, W. P., ed. *Biological Rhythms and Human Performance.* New York: Academic Press, 1976.

Condon, William S. "Communication: Rhythm and Structure." In *Rhythm in Psychological, Linguistic and Musical Processes,* edited by Manfred D. Clynes and James R. Evans, 55-57. Springfield, Illinois: Charles C. Thomas, 1986.

Coulter, Dee Joy. *Children at Risk: The Development of Drop-outs.* Longmont, Colorado: Coulter Publications, 1986. Sound cassette.

___. *Classroom Clues to Thinking Problems*. Longmont, Colorado: Coulter Publications, 1986. Sound cassette.

___. *Enter the Child's World*. Longmont, Colorado: Coulter Publications, 1986. Sound cassette.

___. *In Defense of Music: A New Vision for Education*. Longmont, Colorado: Coulter Publications, 1986. Sound cassettes.

___. *Mind and Music*. Longmont, Colorado: Coulter Publications, 1986. Sound cassettes. Includes booklet entitled "The Brain's Timetable for Developing Musical Skills."

___. *Our Triune Brain*. Coulter Publications, Longmont, Colorado, 1986. Sound cassettes.

Dasen, Pierre R. "Cross-Cultural Piagetian Research: A Summary." *Journal of Cross-Cultural Psychology* 3, no. 1 (March 1972): 23-29.

Davalos, Diane. *Activities to Expand Learning: A Manual to Help General Ideas for Games and Skits for Instructors and Students of Accelerative Learning*. Denver, Colorado: Davalos, 1982.

Dawson, Jim, and Susan Perry. *The Secrets Our Body Clocks Reveal*. New York: Macmillan, 1988.

Dennison, Paul, and Gail Dennison. *Brain Gym: Simple Activities for Whole Brain Learning*. Glendale, California: Edu-Kinesthetics, Inc., 1986.

___. *Brain Gym: Teacher's Edition*. Glendale, California: Edu-Kinesthetics, Inc., 1989.

Dhority, Lynn. *Acquisition Through Creative Teaching, ACT: The Artful Use of Suggestion in Foreign Language Instruction*. Sharon, Massachussetts: Center for Continuing Development, 1984.

Diamond, Marian. *Enriching Heredity*. New York: The Free Press, Macmillan, 1988.

Eagle, Charles T., Jr., and Mark S. Rider. "Rhythmic Entrainment as a Mechanism for Learning in Music Therapy." In *Rhythm in Psychological, Linguistic and Musical Processes*, edited by Manfred D. Clynes and James R. Evans, 225-245. Springfield, Illinois: Charles C. Thomas, 1986.

Elkins, Dov Peretez. *Teaching People to Love Themselves: A Leader's Handbook of Theory and Techniques for Self-Esteem and Affirmation Training*. Rochester, New York: Growth Associates, 1979.

Elliot, Charles A. "Rhythmic Phenomena - Why the Fascination?" In *Rhythm in Psychological, Linguistic and Musical Processes*, edited by Manfred D. Clynes and James R. Evans, 3-12. Springfield, Illinois: Charles C. Thomas, 1986.

Epstein, Herman T. "Phrenoblysis: Special Brain and Mind Growth Spurt Periods: I, Human Brain and Skull Development: II, Human Mental Skill Development." *Developmental Psychobiology* 7, no. 3 (1974): 207-216.

___. "Growth Spurts during Brain Development: Implications for Educational Policy and Practice." In *Education and the Brain*, edited by J. S. Chall and A. F. Mirsky, 343-370. Chicago, Illinois: University of Chicago Press, 1979.

Epstein, Herman T., and C. F. Toepfer. "A Neuroscience Basis for Reorganizing Middle School Education." *Educational Leadership* 36, no. 8 (1978): 656-660.

Evans, James R. "Dysrhythmia and Disorders of Learning and Behavior." In *Rhythm in Psychological, Linguistic and Musical Processes*, edited by Manfred D. Clynes and James R. Evans, 249-274. Springfield, Illinois: Charles C. Thomas, 1986.

Felker, Donald W. *Helping Children to Like Themselves*. Minneapolis, Minnesota: Burgess Publishing Co., 1973.

Flugelman, Andrew. *The New Games Book*. New York: Doubleday/Dolphin, 1976.

Folkard, Simon. "Circadian Rhythms and Human Memory." In *Rhythmic Aspects of Behavior*, edited by Frederick Brown and R. Curtis Graeber, 241-272. Hillsdale, New Jersey: Lawrence Erlbaum Associates, 1982.

Gardner, Howard. *Frames of Mind: The Theory of Multiple Intelligences*. New York: Basic Books, 1983.

Gawain, S. *Creative Visualization*. Mill Valley, California: Whatever Publishing, 1978.

Gibbon, U., and Allan L., eds. *Timing and Time Perception*. New York: Academy of Sciences, 1984.

Gilbert, Anne Green. *Teaching the Three R's Through Movement Experiences: A Handbook for Teachers*. New York: Macmillan Publishing Company, 1977.

Gilmor, Timothy M., Paul Maudale, and Billie Thompson, eds. *About the Tomatis Method*. Toronto, Ontario: Listening Centre Press, 1988.

Gordon, Edwin, and Lili Muhler Levinowitz. "Preschool Music Curricula: Children's Music Development Program." Princeton, New Jersey: Birch Tree Group Ltd., 1988. Typescript.

Graeber, R. Curtis. "Helping Teachers Teach." *Today's Education.* Annual publication (1982-83): 35-37.

Hand, James D., and Barbara L. Steing. "The Brain and Accelerative Learning, Part II: The Brain and Its Functions." *Journal of Accelerative Learning and Teaching* 11, no. 3 (1986): 113-121.

Harman, Willis, and Howard Rheingold. *Higher Creativity: Liberating the Unconscious for Breakthrough Insights.* Los Angeles, California: Jeremy P. Tarcher, Inc., 1984.

Hart, L. A. *How the Brain Works: A New Understanding of Human Learning, Emotion, and Thinking.* New York: Basic Books, Inc.,1975.

___. *Human Brain and Human Learning.* New York: Longman, 1983.

Hemming, Roy. *Discovering Great Music.* New York: Newmarket Press, 1988.

Hendricks, Gay, and Thomas B. Roberts. *The Centering Book.* Englewood Cliffs, New Jersey: Prentice Hall, 1975.

Holzman, Thomas G., and M. Carr Payne, Jr., "Rhythm as a Factor in Memory." In *Rhythm in Psychological, Linguistic and Musical Processes,* edited by Manfred D. Clynes and James R. Evan, 41-54. Chicago, Illinois: Charles C. Thomas, 1986.

Houston, Jean. *The Possible Human: A Course in Enhancing Your Physical, Mental and Creative Abilities.* Los Angeles, California: Jeremy P. Tarcher, 1982.

Jensen, Eric P. *Super-Teaching.* Del Mar, California: Turning Point for Teachers, 1988.

Johnson, Virginia R. "Myelin and Maturation: A Fresh Look at Piaget." *The Science Teacher* (March 1982): 41-49.

Jones M. R., G. Kidd, and R. Wetzel. "Evidence for Rhythmic Attention." *Journal of Experimental Psychology: Human Perception and Performance* 7, no.5 (1981): 1059-1073.

Laborde, Genie Z. *Influencing with Integrity.* Palo Alto, California: Syntony Publishing, 1984.

Levinowitz, Lili, and Kenneth Guilmartin. "Music and Your Child: A Guide for Parents and Caregivers." Princeton, New Jersey: Birch Tree Group Ltd., 1988. Typescript.

Loviglio, Lorraine. "Teaching by the Body's Clock." *The Massachusetts Teacher* (November 1980): 8-15.

Lozanov, Georgi. *Suggestology and Outlines of Suggestopedy.* Translated by Marjori Hall-Posharlieva and Krassimira Pashmakova. New York: Gordon and Breach, 1978.

Luce, Gay G. *Biological Rhythms in Human and Animal Physiology.* New York: Dover Publications, 1971.

Luria, A. R. *The Working Brain.* New York: Basic Books,1974.

Machado de Andreade, Luiz. "Intelligence's Secret: The Limbic System and How to Mobilize It Through Suggestopedy." *Journal of Accelerative Learning and Teaching* 11, no. 2 (1986): 102-107.

Machlis, Joseph. *The Enjoyment of Music: An Introduction to Perceptive Listening.* New York: W.W. Norton and Company, Inc. 1983.

MacLean, Paul. "A Mind of Three Minds: Educating the Triune Brain." *Seventy-seventh Yearbook of the National Society for the Study of Education, Part II.* Chicago, Illinois: National Society for the Study of Education, 1978.

Master, Robert, and Jean Houston. *Listening to the Body: The Psychophysical Way to Health and Awareness.* New York: Delacorte, 1978.

Minors, D. S., and J. M. Waterhouse. *Circadian Rhythms and the Human.* Boston: John Wright and Sons, 1981.

Monk, Timothy, Victoria Lenge, Simon Folkard, and Elliot Weitzman. "Circadian Rhythms in Subjective Alertness and Core Body Temperature." *Chronobiologia* 10 (1983): 46-55.

Monk, Timothy, Elliot Weitzman, Jeffrey Fookson, and Margaret Moline. "Circadian Rhythms in Human Performance Efficiency under Free-Running Conditions." *Chronobiologia* 11 (1984): 343-354.

Murdock, Maureen. *Spinning Inward.* Long Beach, California: Kenzel Publications, 1982.

Novak, Joseph, and Bob D. Gowin. *Learning How to Learn.* Cambridge, Massachussetts: Cambridge University Press, 1984.

Nummela, Renate M., and Tennes M. Rosengren. "What's Happening in Students' Brains May Redefine Teaching." *Educational Leadership* (May 1986): 49-53.

O'Connor, Joseph. *Not Pulling Strings, NLP and Music.* Portland, Oregon: Metamorphous Press, 1979.

Orff, Carl. *The Schulwerk, Vol. 3 of Documentation: His Life and Work.* Translated by Margaret Murray. New York: Schott Music Corporation, 1976.

Palmer, John D. *An Introduction to Biological Rhythms.* New York: Academic Press, 1976.

Pearce, Joseph Chilton. *The Magical Child.* New York: E.P. Dutton, 1977.

___. *The Magical Child Matures.* New York: E.P. Dutton, 1985.

Perkins, David. *The Mind's Best Work: A New Psychology of Creative Thinking.* Cambridge, Massachussetts: Harvard University Press, 1983.

Phillips, John L., Jr. *The Origins of Intellect: Piaget's Theory.* San Francisco, California: W. H. Freeman, 1969.

Prichard, Allyn, and Jean Taylor. *Accelerating Learning: The Use of Suggestion in the Classroom.* Novato, California: Academic Therapy Press, 1980.

Prince, Lucya. *Movement, Sound, and Reading Readiness.* River Forest, Illinois: Prince Publications, 1975.

___. *Movement and Sound Supplement for Exceptional, for Young Children.* River Forest, Illinois: Prince Publications, 1976.

Rankin, Paul T. "The Importance of Listening Ability." *English Journal* (College Edition) II (November 1981): 623-630.

Rappaport, D. A. *Emotions and Memory.* 5th ed. New York: International Universities Press, 1971.

Reinert, Charles. "A Preliminary Comparison Between Two Methods of Intellectual Skill Development." Presented to the annual Conference of the Society for Accelerative Learning and Teaching, San Diego, California, 1989.

Richards, Mary Helen. *Aesthetic Foundations for Thinking: Rethought, Part 1: Experience.* Portola Valley, California: Richards Institute, 1984.

Rider, Mark S., "The Relationship between Auditory and Visual Perception on Tasks Employing Piaget's Concept of Conservation." *Journal of Music Therapy* 14, no. 3 (1977): 126-138.

___. "The Assessment of Cognitive Functioning Level Through Musical Perception." *Journal of Music Therapy* 18, no. 3 (1981): 110-119.

Ristad, Eloise. *A Soprano on Her Head.* Moab, Utah: Real People Press, 1982.

Robert Muller School. "New Beginnings." A learning program. Arlington, Texas, 1987.

Rose, Colin. *Accelerated Learning.* London: Accelerated Learning Systems, 1985.

Russell, Richie. *Explaining the Brain.* Oxford: Oxford University Press, 1977.

Safranek, Monica. "Effect of Auditory Rhythm on Muscle Activity." *Physical Therapy* (Winter 1973).

Samples, Bob. *Openmind Wholemind.* Rolling Hills Estates, California: Jalmar Press, 1987.

Samuels, Mike, and Nancy Samuels. *Seeing with the Mind's Eye.* New York: Random House, 1975.

Schuster, Donald H., and Charles A. Gritton. *Suggestive Accelerative Learning Techniques, Research into Mind: A Manual of Classroom Procedures Based on the Lozanov Method.* Ames, Iowa: S.A.L.T., 1985.

Shaeffer, L. H. "Rhythm and Timing in Skill." *Psychological Review* 89 (1982): 109-123.

Shiekh, A. A., ed. *Imagery: Current Theory, Research and Application.* New York: John Wiley and Sons, 1983.

___. *Anthology of Imagery Techniques.* Milwaukee, Wisconsin: American Imagery Institute, 1986.

Sinatra, Richard. "Everything You Always Wanted to Know but Were Afraid to Ask . . . about Sensorimotor Experience and Brain Growth." *Early Years* (March 1983): 22-43.

Sund, Robert B. *Piaget for Educators.* Columbus, Ohio: Charles E. Merrill Publishing Company, 1976.

Toepfer, Conrad F., Jr. "Brain Growth Periodization—A New Dogma for Education." *The Middle School Journal* 10, no. 3 (1979): 3, 18-20.

___. "Brain Growth Periodization Data: Some Suggestions for Re-Thinking Middle Grades Education." *High School Journal* (March 1980): 222-227.

Tomatis, A. A. *Education and Dyslexia*. Montreal, Quebec: AIAPP, 1972.

___. *La Nuit Uterine*. Paris, France: Editions Stock, 1981.

Verny, Thomas. *The Secret Life of the Unborn Child*. New York: Dell, 1981.

Viscott, David. *The Language of Feelings*. New York: Arbor House Publishing Company, 1976.

Vygotsky, L. S. *Thought and Language*. Cambridge, Massachussetts: MIT Press, 1962.

___. *The Psychology of Art*. Cambridge, Massachussetts: MIT Press, 1971.

Wagner, Michael J., "Effects of Music and Biofeedback on Alpha Brain Wave Rhythms and Attentiveness." *Journal of Research in Music Education* 23, no.1 (Spring 1975): 3-13.

Webb, Roger A. "Concrete and Formal Operations in Very Bright Six- to Eleven-Year-Olds." *Human Development* 17 (1974).

Weinstein, Matt, and Joel Goodman. *Playfair: Everybody's Guide to Noncompetitive Games*. San Louis Obispo, California: Impact Publishers, 1980.

Wenger, Win. "Great Way to Increase Your Intelligence: How to Image Stream." Gaithersburg, Maryland: Project Renaissance, 1990. Typescript.

___. "A Method for Personal Growth and Development." Gaithersburg, Maryland: Project Renaissance, 1987. Typescript.

Werner, Elyse K. "A Study in Communication Time." Master's thesis, University of Maryland, College Park, 1975.

Wilkinson, Robert T. "The Relationship Between Body Temperature and Performance Across Circadian Phase Shifts." In *Rhythmic Aspects of Behavior*, edited by Frederick Brown and R. Curtis Graeber, 213-240. Hillsdale, New Jersey: Lawrence Erlbaum Associates, 1982.

Wilson, Tim. "Chant: The Healing Power of Voice and Ear. Research of A. A. Tomatis." Documentary. Boulder, Colorado: Sound of Light, 1984. Sound cassette.

Wingfield, A., and D. L. Byrnes. *The Psychology of Human Memory*. New York: Academic Press, 1981.

Zender, Mary A., and B. F. Zender. "Vygotsky's View about the Age Periodization of Child Development." *Human Development* 17 (1974): 24-40.

Increase Student Learning by Understanding the Effects of Your Voice and Music

You've discovered the joy of learning through music and sound with *Rhythms of Learning* . . .

Today we are discovering facets of ourselves which will be accepted as fact tomorrow. Rhythms of Learning points to new realms and opens the way to their exploration. New experiences leading to a richer self-awareness await us and Rhythms of Learning is an invitation to seek this adventure.

—Paul Messier, U.S. Department of Education

. . . Now, continue the journey with this key resource from Don Campbell!

100 WAYS TO IMPROVE TEACHING USING YOUR VOICE & MUSIC
Pathways to Accelerate Learning

By Don G. Campbell

Grades K–12+

Make your classroom presentations more interesting and increase your students' learning. Enhance your students'—and your own—memory through voice and music. Through the multisensorial activities of this professional resource, you can—

- Make lessons more engaging simply by learning to listen to your voice
- Select music for optimal learning
- Improve the enthusiasm and variation in your voice

112-page book and 60-minute audiotape

1906-W . . . $27

Buy it on the web: http://zephyrpress.com/cgi-bin/zephyrcat/1906.html

Campbell is a true genius. This book is chock-full of specific practical ways to boost learning—a great resource.

—Eric Jensen
author of *Super Teaching and Student Success Secrets*

Add time-tested techniques to your math and science curriculum with stories, raps, and songs!

SING A SONG OF SCIENCE

by Kathleen Carroll, M.Ed.

Grades K–6

featuring Gwendolyn Jenifer and the students of the Duke Ellington School of the Arts

Explore these new dimensions in learning—

- Stories—the George Washington Carver story
- Raps—tropical rain forest rap, energy rap
- Songs—matter song, classifying song
- Resources—brain-based teaching overview, annotated references, web connections, and musical scores

35-minute audiotape and 64-page activity manual

1094-W . . . $27

Buy it on the web: http://zephyrpress.com/cgi-bin/zephyrcat/1094.html

ELLA VANILLA'S MULTIPLICATION SECRETS

Building Math Memory with Rhythm and Rhyme

by Rosella R. Wallace, Ph.D.

Grades K–8

This complete program gives you 13 delightful stories about Ella Vanilla's adventures. Your students will—

- Learn raps and rhymes about the multiplication tables
- Find out about math facts
- Explore choices, teamwork, and responsibility

120 pages in a 3-ring binder and a 30-minute audiotape

1085-W . . . $39

Buy it on the web: http://zephyrpress.com/cgi-bin/zephyrcat/1085.html

Order Form

Qty.	Item #	Title	Unit Price	Total
	1906-W	100 Ways to Improve Teaching	$27	
	1094-W	Sing a Song of Science	$27	
	1085-W	Ella Vanilla's Multiplication Secrets	$39	

Subtotal	
Sales Tax (AZ residents, 5%)	
S & H (10% of Subtotal, min. $4.00)	
Total (U.S. Funds only)	

CANADA: add 22% for S& H and G.S.T.

Name _____

Address _____

City _____

State _____ Zip _____

Phone (_____) _____

E-mail _____

Method of payment (check one):

❑ Check or Money Order   ❑ Visa

❑ MasterCard   ❑ Purchase Order Attached

Credit Card No. _____

Expires _____

Signature _____

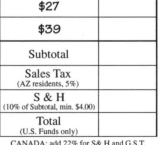

Zephyr Press, Inc.®

REACHING THEIR HIGHEST POTENTIAL

To order write or call:

P.O. Box 66006-W

Tucson, AZ 85728-6006

1-800-232-2187

FAX 520-323-9402

http://www.zephyrpress.com